Old Nantucket

The Faraway Island

Old Nantucket

The Faraway Island

William Oliver Stevens

Illustrated by the Author

DODD, MEAD & COMPANY • New York

Copyright, 1936 by Dodd, Mead & Company, Inc.

All rights reserved

No part of this book may be reproduced in any
form without permission in writing from the
publisher

Printed in the United States of America

2 3 4 5 6 7 8 9 10

Library of Congress Cataloging in Publication Data

Stevens, William Oliver, 1878-1955.
  Old Nantucket, the faraway island.

  Reprint. Originally published: Nantucket, the
faraway island. New York: Dodd, Mead, 1936.
  Includes index.
  1. Nantucket (Mass.)—History. 2. Nantucket (Mass.)
—Description and travel. I. Title.
F72.N2S77   1981   974.4'97   81-3297
ISBN 0-396-07947-4   AACR2

ACKNOWLEDGMENTS

To the many friends who, in one way or another, have helped me in gathering material for this book, I wish to express my appreciation. Naming them all would make a list much too long for a word of thanks like this. Therefore, I must express my sense of obligation to them collectively, but I do so none the less gratefully.

WILLIAM O. STEVENS

INTRODUCTION

"In America," announced a British lecturer after his recent trip to this country, "there are no villages." Perhaps he was using the word in an esoteric sense of his own, or perhaps he did not venture away from the lecturer's beaten (railroad) track of New York, Boston, Chicago, and saw no villages from the windows of his Pullman.

On the contrary, there *are* villages in America—at least in the East and South. At random there is Fredericksburg, Virginia, in one direction, and Wiscasset, Maine, in the other, with a galaxy of lovely ones in between, especially in Connecticut and Vermont. The typical American village is very different from the typical English one, but it is none the less beautiful for that, and redolent of history, too. In the American scene the streets are broad, shadowed by tall, graceful, "wine glass" elms, the like of which exist nowhere else in the world. The houses are, for the most part, old, of the gracious and dignified styles of the late Georgian and neo-classic periods. And there is at least one ghostly white church built in the same tradition. It happened that these farming hamlets were passed over by the Industrial Revolution; Progress, like the priest and Levite, "passed by on the other side." Thus their beauties were spared to charm a generation that had almost forgotten that leisure and simplicity ever existed.

Of these villages, Nantucket is the queen. To a greater degree than any other, Nantucket possesses the special virtues of the American village. And the purpose of this book is to catch as far as possible the particular charm of this little island town, its rich history, with its traditions, its characters, its streets and wharves and houses, and its surrounding moors.

To the whalemen returning from a four-year cruise the home port was affectionately called "The Little Grey Lady of the Sea." She still wears her burden of the years gracefully with a sort of lavender and old lace dignity. She sits on her low hills, still looking out upon the sea from which her ships have long since vanished. Once the mistress of a great and heroic industry, the sperm whale fishery, which reached the uttermost corners of the seven seas, she is now in "reduced circumstances." Like many another lady of the old régime, she is now obliged to take in "paying guests" for a living. But she has not forgotten her past, and she has actually gained in beauty. Indeed, she is very well worth knowing. May I introduce you? Little Grey Lady of the Sea, allow me to present the Gentle Reader.

CONTENTS

Old Nantucket

The Faraway Island

CHAPTER I

THE FIRST GLIMPSE

THE name Nantucket covers a county, an island, and a town in Massachusetts. It is supposed to mean, in the Indian tongue, "far-away island," or "land far out at sea." Certainly the island must have seemed remote in the days of the birch-bark canoes which had to make the choppy crossing from Cape Cod, twenty miles to the north, or the thirty-mile stretch from the mouth of Buzzards Bay. Probably the Indian route was by the shorter stages of island to island, via Martha's Vineyard.

To the modern traveler, even the trip from New Bedford by the steamer makes the Indian name seem appropriate. If he is accustomed to bowl along some four-lane cement highway at sixty miles an hour, the plodding gait of the steamer dogtrotting its daily route to Woods Hole, Martha's Vineyard, and thence to Nantucket, at the rate of five hours for thirty-odd miles, does make the journey surprisingly long. "Far-away island," in sooth!

But that journey isn't without its leisurely charm, and is a fitting preparation for the leisurely pace of life at Nantucket. The traveler may take his comfort in a stateroom on the steamer, with easy chair, couch and card table at his command, or he may stay on deck so as not to miss anything on the water, the buoys, fishing boats, schooners, freighters, rocky islets, queerly garbed summer tourists, and the lightship. After leaving

Martha's Vineyard, the steamer comes close aboard the Cross Rips lightship. Sometimes it is the gay relief ship on duty, which is painted a dazzling vermilion like a Five-and-Ten-cent store. The lightship here is indispensable to the tall four-masted schooners or low, black freight steamers that navigate the Sound, for there are deadly shoals about. Indeed, not even Cape Hatteras itself can rival the waters around Nantucket as a graveyard of ships. The steamer used to slip close alongside the lightship so that members of the crew could toss bundles of papers and magazines on board. Usually this reading matter fell short and had to be fished out with nets. But after the *Olympic* ran down the South Shoals lightship the order went forth for steamers to keep at a safe distance, and this little routine excitement of the trip to Nantucket is no longer enjoyed.

Before long you see a thin, violet haze on the eastern horizon, which is the first sign of Nantucket. This gradually rises from the sea. Anon the steamer shoots between long stone breakwaters that guard the channel, the whistle gives a glad whoop (and so do you if it has been a rough crossing), the boat rounds close to the stubby little white lighthouse at Brant Point— "within biscuit toss"—and turns into the inner harbor, gliding up to the wharf.

Before you rises a low, grey and green pyramid of houses and old trees. At the apex of the pyramid stands the tower of the "Old South" or Unitarian Church with its little gilded dome flashing in the sun. If the hour is right, and the wind, too, you may hear the sweetly resonant dong-dong-dong of the famous old Portuguese bell in the clock tower. Many a proud city church would be glad to possess that bell. Anyhow, you don't need to be told that this is Nantucket Town.

THE FIRST GLIMPSE

A hundred years ago—even two hundred—this peaceful little harbor was forested with the masts of whalers. Sometimes along these wharves were packed as many as one hundred ships at a time. And those same wharves were covered with endless rows of barrels containing sperm oil. Even before the Revolu-

tionary War this little town furnished illumination for half the capitals of the civilized world. Her candles were sold from Lisbon to Singapore. Fine ladies of many lands laced themselves into corsets of Nantucket whalebone, or scented their handkerchiefs with perfumes made from Nantucket ambergris. You would not suspect it now. Here and there on the blue surface of the harbor are the gay sails of the little "rainbow fleet," fussy motor boats are chugging about, and stately yachts lie at anchor. But these are pleasure craft. Along the wharves are only a few small fishing vessels, all that is left to remind one of Nantucket's maritime glory.

By this time the steamer is securely lashed alongside the pier, the gangplank is run out, and we go ashore. Having disembarked, the visitor may take one of the many taxis at the wharf, or perhaps drive his own car if he brought it on the boat, and bowl off to his place of lodging. There are all kinds of accommodations to be had, from elegant hotels all the way down the scale of rates through "houses" and "inns" to unpretentious "boarding establishments" and "rooms to let." Supposing the formalities of registering and unpacking are over, we may take a preliminary ramble about the town.

The center of Nantucket is the Square. At the upper end stands the brick structure of the Pacific Bank; "Pacific," because the wealth of the whaling industry of Nantucket was made on the Pacific Ocean. This building dates from 1818, and in recent years has been cleansed of an ugly coat of grey paint so that it now looks as it did a century ago when whaling shipmasters walked up its steps to deposit their profits after a "greasy voyage." It is a dignified but plain little building. In the great crash of 1933, when huge city banks, gorgeous with marble and gold, fell in ruin, be it noted that this Pacific National Bank of Nantucket came out of the crisis unscathed.

And the lower end of the Square is a still older brick building, the Rotch (pronounced "Roach") Market. This, too, bears the date of its erection, 1772. In the period of the American Revolution, the Quaker shipowner, Rotch, was the leading citizen of the island. He built this market and warehouse near the wharves

PACIFIC NATIONAL BANK

for his shipping business. Over the doors are painted the names of three famous vessels of his firm—the *Beaver,* the *Eleanor,* and the *Dartmouth.* Between these two red brick buildings stretches the Square, paved with cobblestones and shadowed with overhanging elms. On either hand are the familiar shops found in any New England village.

Before going farther, the stranger should find his way to the office of the *Inquirer and Mirror,* just off the Square on Orange Street, and get for the asking the most convenient and readable pocket guide to Nantucket. This is full of photographs, and the text was written by Mr. Edouard Stackpole, the author of several stirring novels of Nantucket's whaling days.

To get an introduction to the unique character of the old town, the visitor should stroll away from this business section. He may go in any direction, it really doesn't matter where, but perhaps the best route is to start up Main Street past the Pacific Bank and follow the cobbled thoroughfare as it winds between the old mansions of the whaling captains. From Main Street one may readily branch out into the lanes on either hand. If the spell of the place does not fall upon the stranger at once, he may as well turn back to the wharf and catch the next boat home to what the islanders would call "the Continent." To be sure, there are motor cars bouncing over the cobbles, and very modern young ladies in shorts on the sidewalk, if the season is midsummer, but nothing can dim the loveliness of that street of an ancient day.

The fact is that Nantucket is more beautiful now than it ever was in its history, although it has shrunk to about one-third its size of a hundred years ago. One outstanding reason for this increased beauty is the presence of these towering elms that soften the outlines of the houses and throw their blue shadows over the cobbles, the red brick, the grey shingles, and the white doorways. Photographs taken in the forties, fifties, and sixties, show a bare, treeless town that must have been rather forbidding. These elms on Main Street were planted

in 1851-52 by the brothers Charles and Henry Coffin, two public-spirited citizens who labored not only to beautify their native town, but also to establish forests on the island and introduce new kinds of shrubs and plants.

Indeed it was only as the orthodox Quaker tradition waned that the Nantucketers busied themselves to make their homes and streets agreeable to the eye and to fill their gardens with gay flowers. Thus it is that the Little Grey Lady became handsomer in her later years than she ever was in her girlhood. Her lace cap and Paisley shawl are more becoming than the old gingham apron!

But the unique glory of Nantucket in this twentieth century is that, more than any other American village, it is "all of a piece." It is true that Mr. Rockefeller's money is restoring Williamsburg, Virginia, to what it looked like in 1770, but the visitor there is conscious of such a garish newness of brick and stone that he gets no more feeling of antiquity than he would from one of the new Harkness buildings in Harvard or Yale. In contrast, Nantucket's air of an ancient day is genuine. The reason is that when its great industry was done for, the factory did not come in to take its place. Salem and New Bedford, for example, when their shipping days were over, fell victims to mills and slums and immigrants. But this did not happen to Nantucket. There were some feeble efforts to start industries, but they all failed because the island situation was unfavorable. One was the movement to start a factory for "dusters," another was a scheme for raising silkworms. A few mulberry trees here and there in the town are the last relics of that effort.

Nothing succeeded. Instead, people picked up their belongings and left the island. Some even pulled down their houses and moved them to the mainland. Several of these were actually carried in the holds of ships all the way to California—the land of the rainbow in those days—and put together again on an alien shore. But in all this era of change to industrialism which went on in America, the old town, while it lost its fortune, preserved its character. By and by, some artists happened along who rediscovered it; then others came to see for themselves, and Nantucket became famous as a sort of museum piece among American towns. That hard period of depression after the death of the whaling industry saved Nantucket from both the horrors of the boom years of the factory age and the slump that followed. So the old town was preserved, and that antiquity is its greatest asset today.

Nowhere in America can one wander among so many lanes and streets composed entirely of dwellings that were built in the eighteenth and early nineteenth century. Still you can see the wide chimneys, the "walks" atop the roofs, the grey shingled houses, the graceful doorways and white fences of a bygone era. And as a background for these whites and greys of the buildings there are quantities of flowers—syringa, lilacs, honeysuckle, roses, hollyhocks, hydrangeas. Whatever the season, from April to November, there is a profusion of bloom in the dooryards and gardens. No wonder that artists come to Nantucket!

The antiquity of the town, which has just been referred to as its greatest asset, is not merely a matter of long life but it is age steeped in historical tradition. Two great factors were at work in Nantucket. One had to do with the means of making a living; this was whaling. The second had to do with the art of living; this was the Quaker religion. In both these matters Nantucket was preëminent. For many years she was the whaling capital of the world. In that same epoch she was the Quaker capital also, in the sense that in no other community was there so large a proportion of Quaker citizens. In order, therefore, to read the significance of what one sees in present-day Nantucket, we shall have to step back into the story of its past.

CHAPTER II

THE BACKGROUND OF HISTORY

THE earliest historians of Nantucket, the Indians, had a picturesque story of the origin of the island. It seems that there was a mighty giant who used Cape Cod for his bed. Kicking about restlessly one night, he got his moccasins full of sand. In a fit of impatience he flung them off into the sea. One fell nearer, and became Martha's Vineyard; the other, that went farther out to sea, was Nantucket. The geologist's story is not so far different except that his giant is the glacier of the last ice age, and not only Martha's Vineyard and Nantucket, but also Long Island, Cape Cod and all the intervening miles of shoals are the dump heaps of this icy giant. But the peculiar history of Nantucket is largely due to the fact that it was the moccasin tossed farthest out to sea, thirty miles off the mainland. Hence the accepted meaning of the Indian name, "Far-Away Island," or "Land Far Out at Sea."

These thirty miles of tumbling water and deadly, ever-shifting shoals gave the people a particular island consciousness. All insular people have it to a degree. Not long ago, for example, the English Channel crossing was broken off by heavy gales, and the fact was announced by a headline in the London *Times* thus: "The Continent is isolated." That is quite in the Nantucket spirit. There the world was divided into two classes: "Islanders," and an inferior breed scattered over the rest of the earth, all lumped together as "Off-Islanders." Even the rest of

"UNDER THE BANK"

the nation to which the Nantucketer belonged was a kind of second cousin twice removed. Going to the mainland was going to "the Continent." Many an island shipmaster, who was at home in Rio, Shanghai, and the Galapagos Islands, never took the trouble to visit Boston. Indeed, during the two wars with Great Britain, Nantucket declared her neutrality between the government of His Britannic Majesty and that of the Congress. But this step, after all, was forced on the islanders by their exposed position and their helplessness to get the actual necessities of life without the consent of the commander of the British fleet.

The history of Nantucket has been written often. My own favorite account is the first, that written a hundred years ago by Obed Macy, a member of the very First Family of the island. He was proud of his heritage and wrote with a stately Quaker dignity. In his preface he introduces his subject thus: "There are few places of equal magnitude the annals of which would afford matters for a more valuable volume." When one stops to think that even in its palmiest days Nantucket never numbered above ten thousand inhabitants, one may admit that Obed Macy was right.

The annals really begin with his ancestor, Thomas Macy. A favorite story about him has been that on one occasion, while a citizen of the town of Salisbury, Massachusetts, he gave shelter to some Quakers during a storm, and for this affront to the prevailing laws against the Society of Friends he was fined and admonished. Hence, seeking religious liberty, he fled away with his family in a little boat and settled on Nantucket. Whittier, who seems to have had a gift for perpetuating misinformation, wrote up the story in his poem, "The Exiles." In this the hero,

"Goodman Macy," is chased down to the beach by his persecutors. He manages, somehow, to round up his wife and five small children, a miraculous feat under the conditions of the pursuit, and jumping into a "light wherry" he escapes to found what proved to be a happy hunting ground for Quakers in Nantucket. The late William F. Macy—another of the same family —who wrote a brief but very readable "Story of Old Nantucket," observes charitably of this yarn in verse that it is "good poetry but bad history."

The facts seem to be that Macy's being summoned for a Christian act of mercy to the despised Quakers happened some time after he had arranged for his share of the purchase of Nantucket. Further, five years after his first settlement in the island he was back in his old home town of Salisbury in residence for some time while settling his affairs, and nobody disturbed him then.

But it seems to be an accepted fact that Macy embarked from Salisbury with his wife and five children, accompanied by a fellow townsman and friend, Edward Starbuck, and a twelve-year-old boy, Isaac Coleman. Since Salisbury lies to the north of Newburyport, there was something of a rough and seasick cruise for the three adults and six children to round Cape Ann, then Cape Cod, and cross the Sound to the island in a small open boat. This was probably in the early fall of 1659. It is quite likely, too, that Macy had been on the ground to look the place over during the previous summer. At any rate, according to tradition, the little group camped down somewhere in the neighborhood of Madaket, at the westerly end of the island and spent the winter there.

In those days nobody wrote memoirs. One can only imagine,

therefore, what that winter meant to Mrs. Macy, in particular, with the problem of housekeeping in a rough cabin, the care of her own five youngsters and the Coleman boy besides, with no other white woman to talk to and only Indians for neighbors. It must have been a tremendous ordeal and she was not a young woman at the time. Her youngest boy, then four years old, was the only son who lived to maturity, and he is hailed as the ancestor of the whole clan of Macys, not only in Nantucket but all over the United States.

Thus Thomas Macy and his wife and children were the first white family to settle on the island, but the leader in the movement to make a white settlement on Nantucket was another citizen of Salisbury, Tristram Coffin. He had made a preliminary survey of the ground and opened negotiations with the owner, Thomas Mayhew, to whom the island had been sold by Lord Sterling in 1641. The result was that on July 2, 1659, a deed was drawn up between Mayhew and nine purchasers, selling to them the former's patent for "the sum of thirty pounds in good Marchantable Pay in ye Massachusetts under which government they now Inhabit, . . . and two Beaver Hatts one for myself and one for my wife. . ." By the agreement each of these purchasers was allowed to take on a partner, and later others were added on a half-share basis.

Altogether there were nineteen different names for the men owning the twenty-seven shares in this Nantucket project, and here they are: Mayhew, Coffin, Macy, Hussey, Swain, Barnard, Greenleaf, Starbuck, Smith, Coleman, Pike, Look, Stretor, Bishop, Worth, Wyer, Gardner, Folger, and Holland. On this list eight names soon disappeared: Mayhew, Greenleaf, Pike, Look, Bishop, Stretor, Smith and Holland. It is probable that several of the proprietors never went to Nantucket at all and disposed of their holdings. But the rest of them have multiplied to this day. Naturally they intermarried on the island until every Coffin, Macy, Hussey, Gardner, Starbuck and so on was a cousin to all the rest. And their descendants are to be found in distant corners of the world, as well as in the United States and the British dominions.

But to return to the first settlement in 1659. In the following spring Starbuck went back to Salisbury to report, and that summer about ten families arrived to settle. If it is true that Thomas Macy and his family spent the previous winter at Madaket, they had as bleak and unprotected a location as they could possibly have chosen on the wind-swept isle. And it is certain that when the lots were divided up among the settlers of 1660, the village was laid out in the neighborhood of Capaum pond, which was then a little harbor. The visitor today can see the stone post marking the site of Tristram Coffin's first homestead. This is in a sheltered little vale with easy access to the harbor of those days and probably to fresh water ponds and springs.

The next step of the colonists, after obtaining their "patent" from Mayhew, was to treat with the Indians for a second purchase of the land where they had settled. The unique feature about Nantucket's early history is the fact that it is the one ancient New England settlement that has no tradition of Indian fighting. Mark Twain's observation that when the Puritans came to New England "they fell first on their knees and then on the aborigines," does not apply to these settlers of Nantucket. From the first they tried to deal with the red men honorably. In that same year, 1660, they drew up a formal deed with the two principal chiefs of the two tribes that lived at opposite ends of the island.

Unfortunately, not much is known about these Indians. Nobody knows whether they were few or many. It is a credit to both races, however, that they got along together as good neighbors. When King Philip visited the island to incite the Indians to join his revolt against the whites, they refused. And the whites managed to save an Indian that Philip was determined to slay, one "John Gibbs," who later was sent to Harvard to be educated.

The most romantic of the Indian legends that have survived is the story of the young chief Autopscot, who ruled the tribe living at the western end of the island, and Wonoma, the daughter of Wauwinet, sachem of the Indians living at the eastern end. When the western tribe was afflicted with a pestilence, Autopscot sent for the girl, who had a reputation for skill in healing, and she came and ministered successfully to the stricken people. Of course, the young chief and Wonoma fell in love and exchanged their pledges of devotion. Some time later, war broke out between the two tribes because of a quarrel over the ownership of land. Wauwinet planned a surprise attack on Autopscot, but the daughter, overhearing the plan, made a trip by night to warn her lover. Consequently, when Wauwinet came with his men he found Autopscot ready for him, and abandoned the attack. Then the young chief sought an interview with Wauwinet, revealed the daughter's act of devotion, and asked her hand in marriage. After a brief moment of anger, Wauwinet consented, the land question was readily settled, and the two tribes lived happily ever after.

Although the Coffins and Macys and Starbucks and the rest

deserve all credit for trying to treat the aborigines honorably, the red man on Nantucket succumbed to the same fate as overtook his brethren elsewhere. One by one his lands went to the white man, firewater slew its usual share, and disease took the rest. For example, there was a mysterious epidemic in 1763 which smote the Indians but spared the whites. Before this pestilence came there had been three hundred and fifty-eight red men. Two hundred and twenty-two died, thirty-four recovered, thirty-six escaped it altogether, and eighteen were saved by being at sea.

The last man of Indian blood, a half-breed, died in 1854. There is a painting of this poor remnant of his race, Abram Quary, hanging on the wall of the Atheneum, the Nantucket public library. Obed Macy, in his history, sings this solemn requiem to the aborigines of Nantucket:

"Thus the existence of a tribe of natives terminated, and thus their land went to strangers. In the simple charity of nature they rescued our fathers. When fugitives from Christian persecution they opened to them their stores, bestowed on them their lands, treated them with unfailing kindness, acknowledged their superiority, tasted their poison and died. Their only misfortune was their connection with Christians, and their only crime, the imitation of their manners."

At any rate, it would have been a simple matter for the Indians to have exterminated the little settlement of some ten families at Capaum, or at least annoyed them so much that they would have fled. Instead, they evidently helped the colonists in every way they could. In particular, they started for the whites on the island what became their characteristic industry, the whale fishery. Not long after the original settlement in

1672, a small whale, called a "scragg," came into Wesco harbor, and, according to tradition, the Indians showed their white neighbors how to go after it with a harpoon. From that day the industry developed until it had made Nantucket the whaling capital of the world. This early form of whaling was by boats from shore, and the victim was the "right" whale.

In this year 1672, one James Loper was given a contract "to ingage to carry on a design of Whale Citching," for which he was offered ten acres of land at his own choice. It is not clear whether James ever accepted. In 1690, the islanders sent to Cape Cod to employ one Ichabod Paddock to instruct them in the art, for at that date the "Capies" were more skilled in the business, which by this time had become a thriving industry. The next important event in the Nantucket whale fishery was in 1712, when Christopher Hussey, blown out to sea, ran into a school of spermaceti whales and managed to kill one. Since sperm oil was much more valuable than the "right" whale oil, the hunt shifted to that type of beast.

Meanwhile, at the turn of the century, other things had happened, also of importance in the island history. In 1692, by act of Parliament, the settlement was turned over from New York to the Massachusetts colony, at the request of the owners. The little harbor of Capaum had its entrance blocked up by a storm about 1700, and became a pond, as it is today. The settlers gradually moved eastward to the site of the present town, where there was the Great Harbor vastly better suited to the growing whale fishery than the little cove at Capaum. It is hard to understand, in fact, why that site was not selected in the first place. As early as 1673, the village had been named "Sherburne" by Governor Lovelace of New York, and "Sherburne" it remained for a hundred years or more.

For a time the future of the settlement was seriously threatened by a feud between Tristram Coffin and John Gardner. The families lined up on one side or the other of this quarrel, with the usual unhappy results. It was concerned with the rebellion of the "half-share" men, and those who owned no land, against the high-handed way the island was governed by the proprietors. At first, Coffin, representing the proprietors, had the upper hand, and then Gardner, who led the revolt. The feud came to an end with Gardner's interceding for his old enemy before Governor Andros at a time when Coffin was in trouble over the salvage of a wreck. Then the two families were united by the marriage of Gardner's daughter Mary to the grandson of Tristram. The house, built in 1686 for the young couple still stands, known as the "Oldest House," the "Jethro Coffin House," or the "Horseshoe House" from the curious inverted horseshoe on its big chimney.

The most important event, next to the birth of the whaling industry, was the coming of Quakerism. Nantucket has been known for these two things, the pursuit of the sperm whale, and the devotion to the principles of the Quaker sect. These two characteristics seem absurdly incongruous. The dominant trait of the Quaker was his repugnance to fighting, and yet the pursuit of the whale in every corner of the watery world called for all the fighting qualities a man could possess.

The original settlers were not Quakers, but Baptists and Presbyterians. It is curious to observe that once they built their little village of Sherburne there seemed to be no hunger for the ministrations of a clergyman. Maybe it was one of the privileges of being island colonists that they did not have to go to church and listen to sermons two hours long, especially during a New England winter in an unheated meeting house. Possibly they had had enough of that at Salisbury. At any rate, these pious folk got along very comfortably without any organized worship for fifty years.

Then, at the close of the seventeenth century, came the Quaker missionaries. Some of them arrived from England, others from neighboring colonies. Their meetings attracted the curiosity and then the interest of the islanders. The most important event for the establishment of the new religion was the conversion of Mary Starbuck, an extraordinary woman. At this time she might have been described as the First Citizen of Sherburne, for her influence was very powerful over men and women alike. Her acceptance of the Quaker faith made many converts in itself. She also became one of the most famous Quaker preachers of her day. For some time meetings were held in her home, "Parliament House," which was then situated near the north end of Hummock Pond. In 1711, the Friends built their first meeting house, and twenty years later the adherents had increased to such a number that a second meeting house was erected. In fact, for nearly two hundred years after 1700, Quakerism was dominant in the life of Nantucket.

Meanwhile, the whaling business thrived. The earlier practice of going offshore to catch the whale and bring back the blubber to be "tried out" in furnaces on the beach, was gradually abandoned for ships that went on long cruises, equipped with try-pots or furnaces on board. In 1723, the first wharf was built, and by the middle of the eighteenth century ships were sailing with cargoes of sperm oil direct from Sherburne to London. In 1746, the first lighthouse on the island, and the second in the American colonies, was erected at Brant Point by private subscription. In 1772, the first candle factory was opened, thus inaugurating a very important business for the town. Two years later, a rich new whaling ground was discovered off the coast of Brazil. By the time Paul Revere was "riding to spread the alarm," this town of 4500 souls had 150 vessels in the whaling fleet. In short, the Nantucket whale fishery, with all its by-products, was booming, when suddenly the Revolutionary War broke out.

For this conflict with the Old Country the islanders had no stomach whatever. In the first place, the influential citizens were Quakers and therefore opposed to war on principle. Secondly, all their wealth lay on the sea, exposed to destruction by the nation that ruled the waves. Thirdly, the position far off the coast, beyond any hope of protection by the forces of the Continental Congress, made participation in war nothing short of suicide.

In 1773, three ships from Nantucket, whose names are now painted over the doors of the old Rotch Market on the Square, *Beaver, Eleanor,* and *Dartmouth,* sailed to London with a consignment of sperm oil. Coming back, they took cargoes of tea for Boston. Their arrival was the signal for the famous Boston Tea Party. From that time on, the trouble of the Nantucket shipmasters increased by leaps and bounds. No doubt, in addition to the Quaker attitude of nonresistance there were also a large proportion of the townspeople who were loyalist in sentiment. In trying to keep on friendly terms with both sides, a desperate and pathetic policy, the islanders became the enemies of both. Bands of Tories from the mainland ravished the fishing fleet and took possession of the town, and rebel forces also visited the place, breathing threatenings, if not slaughter.

To condense a long tale of misery, the war dragged on for eight years, during which the island folk were helpless, suffering from hunger and cold, seeing the complete destruction of all their business and enduring the death or imprisonment of a large number of their male population. "One hundred and thirty-four ships," writes a historian, "with their cargoes and crews, were captured by the British. The actual loss of life has never been accurately determined, but it has been estimated as high as sixteen hundred, or more than one-third the total population at the outbreak of hostilities. It is known that at least twelve hundred were killed or captured by the British. . . . So far as the property loss is concerned, the shipping destroyed, lost or captured probably represented a much larger investment of capital than all the buildings on the island, for one ship, even a small one, cost the price of many good houses, and Nantucket at that time owned a ship for every three or four houses." * This monetary loss amounted to a million dollars, and among the 800 families there were over 200 widows and 342 orphans. The worst year was 1780, when even the weather seemed to have joined the British; and the inhabitants were suffering acutely from actual hunger and cold.

Although the final treaty of peace was not formally ratified until 1784, the fighting had petered out early enough in favor of peace terms, so that Captain Mooers, whose name is perpetuated today by one of the streets in Nantucket, was able to take his ship to London with a cargo of oil as early as February, 1783. His ship, the *Bedford,* thus won the distinction of being the first to show the Stars and Stripes on the Thames.

* *The Story of Old Nantucket,* p. 81 ff.

But it must not be imagined that Nantucket was distinguished during the Revolution by nothing more than patient submission to suffering. A large number of young men, whether of Quaker origin or not, went into the fighting services of the Colonies. In her famous duel with the British vessel *Drake,* twenty-one of the *Ranger's* crew of 134 were from Nantucket, including the redoubtable Reuben Chase, of whom more anon. Apparently, most, if not all, of these men shipped later in the *Bonhomme Richard* under the same captain, John Paul Jones, and covered themselves with glory in the desperate action with the *Serapis* off Flamborough Head in September, 1779. The present Square in Nantucket has been named in honor of Thomas Turner, a Nantucket lad who was on the *Richard* and who was killed in the battle.

At all events, when the long deferred peace arrived it found the town utterly prostrate. Conditions looked so desperate that many moved away. Captain Rotch, for example, the most substantial shipmaster in Nantucket, had lost $60,000, a great sum in those days. After the war he moved to Dunkirk, France, and continued whaling with Nantucket captains and crews from that port. Later, as the French Revolution made things uncomfortable, he went to Milford Haven, England. Finally, as business began to look more promising in Nantucket, he returned, but the recovery had been very slow.

The next important date is 1791, the year in which the ship *Beaver* rounded the Horn and, with rich profit to her owners, opened for the first time the sperm hunting grounds of the Pacific. Thereafter, for at least two generations, Nantucket men lived on the Pacific Ocean, except for their brief vacations at home, and it was from that ocean that they brought back the wealth that distinguished the town in those palmy days.

It should also be noted that in 1795 the name "Sherburne" for the town was dropped in favor of the name of the island and the county, "Nantucket."

Although there was a technical peace at the close of the eighteenth century, the troubles of Nantucket shipmasters were not over. French privateers and British frigates harried American vessels in the long-drawn war that had begun between Great Britain and France. To the dismay of the island people they saw their country being steadily drawn into another conflict with England. This finally broke out in the summer of 1812. Again the Nantucketers pleaded with their government to avert war; again they were forced to a declaration of neutrality in order to get permission to fish and obtain firewood from the mainland. Again they went through all the miseries of lying helpless at the mercy of the British fleet. Their own country was unable to afford them the slightest help. In their extremity the citizens of Nantucket signed an agreement with the admiral in command of the squadron that controlled the waters not to pay any tax to the United States, as a pledge of neutrality, and as a necessary requisite to their being permitted to go offshore for cod and to the Cape for firewood. This humiliating agreement was made in September, 1814. A month later peace negotiations were under way, and this meant the practical end of war conditions.

The conflict had lasted only two years instead of eight; but when it dragged itself to the finish it left Nantucket about as badly off as it had been after the Revolutionary War. Out of her fine fleet she had only twenty-three vessels left. Again recovery was discouragingly slow, and many people thought there was no hope left for the place. But gradually, as new ships were fitted out and returned with full harvest of sperm oil, things began to look up. Abroad there was no real competitor in the business, for Europe had been embroiled in fighting for a score of years. A larger market for oil developed, and shortly after the war ended the Japan whaling grounds were discovered, and these were the richest yet. The recovery that began slowly in the first years after 1814 gained a quick momentum, and headed Nantucket toward its great era of prosperity.

CHAPTER III

THE GOLDEN AGE OF WHALING

"THAR she blows! And sparm at that!" shouted for two centuries from the crow's nest of many a whaling ship, was the battle cry of these fighting Quakers. This business of whaling called for all the courage a man could muster. It was also a highly technical trade. But as far as the science of it is concerned, it is enough to say that the world of whales may be conveniently divided into two classes, the right whale, and the sperm or "cachalot." Any lubber can distinguish these because the former has a mouth lined with whalebone, which serves as a strainer for its food. The sperm, in contrast, has a slender lower jaw lined with teeth. (It has no teeth in the upper jaw.) The head of the sperm is also more blunt and square than that of the right whale, and that is as scientific as I intend to be. The curious may look about the Whaling Museum and find in the reference books of the reading room all the information they desire concerning the sub-varieties of "Cetaceans"—that is the right word, I hope—such as Bowheads, Blues or Sulphur Bottoms, Finbacks, and what nots.

In the preceding chapter it was observed that the first whaling expeditions were in small boats that went offshore and brought back the blubber of the right whale to be boiled out in the furnaces on the beach. Perhaps the indescribable stench of these boat-loads of carrion, as they were unloaded beside the try-pots, and the subsequent more powerful fumes of the trying, kept

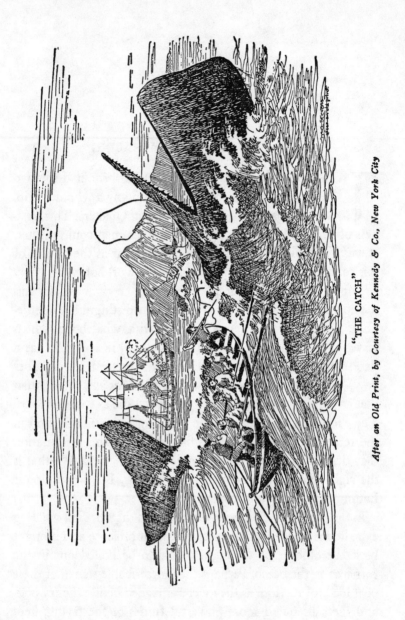

"THE CATCH"

After an Old Print, by Courtesy of Kennedy & Co., New York City

the people of Sherburne for some time living to the westward of the "Great Harbor." Even down to recent years the strip of beach between the present steamboat wharf and Brant Point was known as "Clean Shore" in distinction from the rest of it to the south, which was tacitly accepted as the dirty shore. In those days the east wind must have been particularly accursed, for, in addition to its penetrating qualities, it threw the fumes of the try-pots all over the town.

Hussey's first capture of the sperm whale drew attention to that species as the more profitable game for the Nantucketer, because it furnished oil of a much higher value in the market. But this meant going much farther at sea, specially to warmer waters. So the size of the boats and the radius of the cruises steadily increased together. The profits were extraordinary. Even a sloop, the *Tartar*, owned by the Folger family, made £4440 in a single voyage.

After the discovery of the "Brazeel" grounds, the Nantucketers braved the Horn and discovered a rich harvest of sperm in the Pacific. In 1818, the ship *Globe*, Captain George Gardner, found the famous "Offshore Ground" on the coasts of Chile and Peru. In a few months, the *Globe* had stowed away two thousand barrels of sperm; and, naturally, the news of that bonanza drew fifty more ships thither the following year. That same year, 1819, the whaling grounds off Japan were discovered, the richest yet. From this point on, the ruin of the War of 1812 was quickly left behind, and the island industry took a leap forward toward the greatest era of prosperity it had ever seen. It should be added that, although the sperm whale was the main interest, a Nantucket whaler took a right whale off the northwestern coast of the American continent, and thus opened up one of the most profitable whaling grounds in the world in the neighborhood of the Arctic Circle.

By 1820, the cargo-carrying ships of America were recovering from the paralysis of the Embargo and the war with England, and heading rapidly toward their climax in the clipper ship era. But there were differences between the whaler and the carrier. The most important one concerned the pay of the crew. In a merchantman a sailor was paid monthly wages. In a whaler he signed up for a "lay." This lay was a man's personal share of whatever profits the voyage might make. If the ship struck good luck with a "greasy voyage," all hands profited in proportion. If the luck was bad, the forecastle man shared the loss with the owner. Thus the whaling business, from first to last, was run on a coöperative basis, with the fascination of a gamble. This furnished much of the incentive to suffer the tedious voyages and to risk the perils of a hand-to-hand fight with the whale. For example, an apprentice or cabin boy might go aboard with a lay of 200 ($\frac{1}{200}$), which would mean that out of every 200 barrels of sperm oil his share would be one. From a trifling percentage like this the lays increased in proportion to a man's strength, skill, and experience. Then it was graded up through the ranks of boat steerers, harpooners, and mates, to the captain. The cooper was a very important member of the crew, and in the later days of whaling his lay was often as much as that of the mate.

As examples of the lays on a ship, the following is the list from the *Phebe* when she sailed from Nantucket on a whaling voyage in 1835. Captain George Allen received a lay of $\frac{1}{16}$; his first mate, $\frac{1}{25}$; the second mate, $\frac{1}{35}$; the third mate, $\frac{1}{55}$; boat steerers (harpooners) $\frac{1}{20}$; seamen, $\frac{1}{165}$; greenhorns, $\frac{1}{190}$; boys,

½00. It took one-third of the catch to cover the lays of the officers and crews. The captain, in addition to his regular lay, received a bonus of $300 or so for bringing home a cargo of 2400 barrels or more. In those days the cruises averaged 2000 barrels of sperm.

A curious fact about the whaler's crew is that they were seldom professional sailors. Life aboard a merchantman was no bed of roses in the first half of the nineteenth century, as anyone who reads *Two Years Before the Mast* can appreciate. Nor was the Navy a place for a pleasure cruise in those days, as Melville testifies in *White Jacket*. But apparently, in his time, life aboard a whaler was more filthy and more fraught with danger than that aboard the others, and the cruises were so indefinite in their dreary length that the deep-water sailor held off from the deck of a "spouter." In fact, he looked down upon the race of whale hunters as not really seamen. Melville, in *Typee,* says of the crew of the *Acushnet,* on which he shipped, that "with a very few exceptions our crew was composed of a parcel of dastardly and mean-spirited wretches, divided among themselves and only united in enduring without resistance the unmitigated tyranny of the captain." It will be remembered that he and a friend deserted the ship in the Marquesas Islands. At the beginning of the nineteenth century, however, these conditions were not true. Crews were composed of Nantucket boys starting to win their way in the whaling business, and ties of kinship and neighborliness made the rule of the captain and first mate far less brutal and tyrannical.

Dana, in his classic narrative of the sea, describes the general look of a whaler which he visited, this one also from New Bedford. "A spouter we knew her to be as soon as we saw her, by her cranes and boats, and by her stump topgallantmast, and a certain slovenly look to the sails, rigging, spars, and hull; and when we got aboard we found everything to correspond in spouter fashion, . . . her rigging was slack and turning white, paint worn off the spars and blocks, clumsy seizings, straps without courses, and 'homeward bound' splices in every direction. Her crew, too, were not in much better order. Her captain was a slabsided Quaker, in a suit of brown, in a broad-brimmed hat, bending his long legs as he moved about the decks, with his head down like a sheep, and the men looked more like fishermen and farmers than they did like sailors." Dana goes on to suggest that these whaling gentry had not yet got the "hayseed out of their hair," and observes that the whaler's crew of thirty men "were half an hour in doing" what the small crew of the *Alert,* Dana's ship, "would have polished off in fifteen or twenty minutes."

These remarks caused much indignation among the whalers of New Bedford, Martha's Vineyard, and Nantucket when the first edition of *Two Years Before the Mast* was issued. In subsequent editions, Dana added a footnote to the page, admitting regretfully that these uncomplimentary observations had not been popular among the spouter folk, but holding his ground with this final declaration that he had never seen a whale ship that showed "strictness of discipline and seamanlike neatness. Probably these things are impossibilities from the nature of the business." So much for the attitude of the regular deep-water sailor toward what he described scornfully as "blubber boilers."

And there is no doubt about it, "the nature of the business" was not tidy. Sailors used to say that a good nose could smell a spouter twenty miles to windward. Melville, in *Moby Dick,* admits the general reputation on land and sea that "the vocation of whaling is throughout a slatternly, untidy business." Of the smells of the boiling-out process he says, "the smoke is horrible to inhale,—an unspeakable, wild, Hindoo odor about it such as may lurk in the vicinity of funeral pyres. It smells like the left wing on the day of Judgment. . . ." All agree on the nastiness of being practically immersed in blubber grease during the process appropriately called "trying," but Melville, who had no love for his ship, insists that after the business was over everything was cleaned up so well that the deck was "immaculate."

The whale ship herself had peculiarities that made her distinguishable to the eye as well as to the nose. The following, from Raymond Weaver's biography of Melville, is an excellent summary of these characteristics: The spouters were "heavy, bluff-bowed and stubby crafts that were designed with fine contempt for speed, comfort, and appearance. . . . The bow was scarce distinguishable from the stern by its lines, and the masts stuck up straight, without that rake . . . of a clipper. . . ." There were three notable peculiarities: "1) At each masthead there was a crow's nest, in some a heavy barrel lashed to the mast, and in others merely a small platform laid on cross trees, with two hoops fixed to the mast within which the lookout could stand with safety. 2) On the deck amidships were the try works where the blubber was reduced to odorless oil. 3) Along each rail were heavy, clumsy, wooden cranes or davits from which hung the whaleboats . . . never less than five . . . while others were lashed to the deck." It might be added that the whaler's spars were shorter than those of other ships of corresponding size, in order that she could be handled by the three men left on her deck while the rest were out in the boats. These three were the cooper, the cook, and the cabin boy.

Of the whaleboat the same author says it had attained "prac·
tical perfection. Never has boat been built which for speed,
staunchness, seaworthiness, and hardness excels the whaleboat
of the Massachusetts whalemen. These were cockleshells, sharp
at both ends and clean-sided as a mackerel, were about twenty-
seven feet long by six feet beam, with a depth of twenty-two
inches amidships and thirty-seven at the bow and stern. These
tiny, clinker-built craft can ride the heaviest sea, withstand the
highest wind, and resist the heaviest gale. Incredible voyages
have been made in these whaling boats. . . ."

Another point noteworthy about the whalers of this period
was their surprising smallness. A ship of three hundred tons
was large for a whaler. Such a vessel might be about a hundred
and thirty feet long, thirty feet in beam, with a draft of fifteen.
But there were hosts of other vessels in this business that were
much smaller. These tubby little craft made voyages from two
to four years' duration and pried into every nook and cranny
of the world which might hide a whale. Many islands were put
on the map for the first time by the whaling captains, one God-
forsaken piece of rock having the homesick appellation of "New
Nantucket." Another, in pride of race, was named "Starbuck
Island." It was also a Nantucket captain, Mayhew Folger, of the
ship *Topaz*, who rediscovered Pitcairn Island in 1808, and, finding there one survivor of the nine mutineers of the *Bounty*,
solved for the first time the mystery of their fate. That part of
the log of the *Topaz* may be read in the Whaling Museum
today.

These roving, hunting expeditions in the Pacific must have
been deadly monotonous most of the time. Often there were

long, dreary stretches when few whales were sighted or none at all, as suggested by a brief but eloquent entry in a log, "Nine months out, and 23 Bbls of Sperm, Oh, dear." One never had the feeling of being each day nearer the port aimed for; or, better yet, nearer home. One never knew when the spars would be hauled about for the homeward run, because everything depended on the quantity of oil stowed in the hold.

Sometimes the dreariness of the long voyage was aggravated by bad health. The following, for example, are three entries made by Captain George Russell in the log of his ship, the *George Washington:*

Oct. 30, 1846.
Nothing in sight and My Self Sick and far from frinds and home and no tender wife to nurse me or Smooth my pillow. . . .
Oct. 31
Still nothing to be sean but hard times. Man that is born of a woman his days are few and full of trouble. . . .
Nov. 10
I am vary sick and bad off but small hopes of being any great better vary soon but shal trust in god for all things. . . .

There were not enough duties to keep the men busy during the times when there was no whale to pursue. Most of the sailors in the forecastle could not read, even if there had been ship's libraries. The books that were available to the rest were soon read to rags.

To relieve the tedium, whenever two whalers sighted each other, there was sure to be a "gam." This word meant a visit between ships. The vessels would lie to, and officers and men—also the captain's wife if she were aboard—would visit the other ship, exchange letters and news from home, spin long yarns, and swap books.

Another way of killing time was making "scrimshaw." This means carving all sorts of curious gadgets out of the teeth and bones of the whale. When the victim was hauled alongside for cutting up, the first gory morsel to be dragged on deck was the complete lower jaw. This, by an unwritten law of the sea, belonged to the crew. The most important part of this jaw for scrimshawing was the teeth. Although these are said to be of excellent ivory, they have never been utilized commercially. Hence, the men were free to use them as they pleased. These teeth were first put into brine to soften them for use. As they grew older they became harder and more difficult to work, but even at that, by use of hot water, the men managed to get a surface that would respond to their tools.

Working up these teeth into knicknacks to take home was no easy or rapid job. The surface of the sperm tooth is rough and ribbed in its natural state, and the entire area had to be carefully filed and polished down to the proper slickness. This was a process involving a series of different files of varying coarseness, and the final state was achieved by patient rubbing with the hand. It was a wonderful time killer, just that preparation process! Then, on the surface thus made smooth, the men of the ship, from captain to cabin boy, devoted weeks and months in loving work, usually with nothing but a jackknife. There was no end to their patience or ingenuity. Cane handles, handles to all sorts of kitchen equipment, "jagging wheels" for pie crust, and the like, were evolved in the sphere of the useful arts; but as often the masterpieces went the route of pure esthetics. Lovely ladies in the costume of the period, patriotic emblems, pious memorials, wreaths and leaves, and tangled flourishes in all directions, scenes among the cannibal islands, and, most attractive of all, little ship models made of bits of ivory and put together with infinite skill. The Whaling Museum at Nantucket has a typical collection of scrimshaw.

There were other devices also to kill boredom. In the reading room of the museum is a typed copy of the following letter from William Hussey Macy to his cousin Susan Burdick:

> On board ship *Alpha* at Sea
> Oct. 8, 1848
> (no matter what Lat. or Long.)
> 27 months out, 1150 sperm

Dear Coz;

Did you ever receive a letter from "round Cape Horn"? If not there must be a first time for everything, you know, so don't be alarmed. . . .

Twenty-seven months out and not a line from home. . . . I am in the enjoyment of perfect health, as usual, and well satisfied with my station, but the times are very dull with us now and we are obliged to resort to all sorts of shifts to drive away *ennui*. I will tell you some of the expedients we have resorted to, to vary the monotony of a dull cruise. There are only seven in the forecastle who can read and write the English language. . . .

First, then, (at the suggestion of your humble servant) we started a sort of Coterie or literary society, each member of which was to bring in and read, once a week, an original composition either in verse or prose. This we carried on for some time and many fine things were produced—some rare gems in the poetic line, for indeed we have three or four intelligent young fellows, and one young man from Philadelphia (James Stewart) is no indifferent poet. I have done more in that line than I have ever done before. My manuscript book is nearly full.

Well, in process of time, this grew stale, as everything will. Next we took to cotillions and contra dances, in which I filled the important position of dancing master and musician. This succeeded finely for a time. But when that grew flat, what do you think was our next speculation? Nay, don't laugh! A Theatre! A real, *bona fide* theatre. And this, I think, will last longer than the others. You would be surprised could you see the arrangement of the Alphean Marine Theatre, and read the play bills (issued in all due form) and see what a lovely heroine we make of Master Charles Bailey (of Buffalo, N. Y.) our favorite delineator of female characters. We commenced on a small scale with dialogues, single scenes from Shakespeare, etc., etc., and gradually mounted to greater efforts. We have produced Garrick's comedy of the "Guardian," with the most triumphant success. Our stage is on deck (as we perform only on fine evenings) with an immense drop curtain triced to the rigging. The costumes are very fantastical, and indeed 'tis astonishing what a display can be made with such limited materials.

The "Old Man" takes great delight in this, and is ever ready to accommodate with the loan of chairs from his cabin, signal lanterns, and so forth. But finding that Shakespeare was not properly appreciated by our audience, owing to their not understanding his language, well, what do you think we did next? Why, we even turned our hands to dramatic writing, and we now have some new pieces to bring on the stage.

I have just finished a new melodrama in five acts entitled "The Sailor's Wife," and my friend another in three acts called "The Cousins."—Both pieces are of thrilling interest, involving deep laid plots, counter plots, etc. These will soon be presented on our stage to our admiring public. Is it not a novelty? And the plays written by the actors themselves! We flatter ourselves 'tis quite an original idea and nothing short of an era in the history of the drama. . . .

Accept this humble scrawl for the sake of Auld Lang Syne, and when you read it over, bestow a passing thought on the absent

"Hussey."

It rather tickles the imagination to picture the "cotillions," the meetings of the "Coterie or literary society," and the dramatics among the bewhiskered spouter gentry of the forecastle, but it is clear that Hussey was not in the least miserable on his ship in spite of being twenty-seven months from home. There evidently were some whalemen who led happier lives than Herman Melville did on the *Acushnet.*

To us of today an outstanding drawback of the whaler's life was the fact that although the cruise might last as much as four or even five years there was apparently never a physician on board. In the novel *Miriam Coffin* the captain of a whaleship protests to a young doctor who wants to sign up that there is no need of a physician on board because "the work is so healthy." Of course, there was a medicine kit, which the captain administered according to his discretion, and he must have known how to set a broken leg or arm. But it does boggle the imagination to think what sort of medical or surgical practice that amounted to.

Battling the sperm whale in itself was a risky form of sport which must often have left a trail of serious injuries. A flip of the flukes could knock a boat to kindling, not to mention breaking the men's bones. As for dentistry, the daily practice of chewing on corned beef probably kept the teeth fairly healthy, though we know from Dana's narrative that even a sailor's jaws can develop a badly ulcerated tooth. The records of the ship's voyages show a fairly high mortality, and yet from what we know of medical practice in those years it may have been just as well that there were none of the profession on board. Anyhow, the men were not bled or stuffed with drugs!

In Macy's history of Nantucket appears this note from Captain Worth's autobiographical sketch. The last two lines or so suggest that one skipper at least had a remarkably good record in the matter of accidents at sea in a dangerous business:

I began to follow the sea in 1783, being then fifteen years of age, and continued until 1824. During this period of forty-one years I was shipmaster twenty-nine years. From the time I commenced going to sea until I quitted the business I was at home only seven years. At the rate of four miles an hour while at sea I have sailed more than 1,191,000 miles. . . . I have assisted in obtaining 20,000 barrels of oil. . . . While I commanded a vessel not one of my crew was killed or even had a limb broken by a whale.

In contrast with the foregoing is the dreadful story of the ship *Franklin* and what befell her in a single cruise in the year 1831. Soon after leaving Nantucket one of her crew fell from aloft and was laid up two months. Then another fell and broke both legs. Next a negro sailor was sent ashore dying of tuberculosis. During a whale hunt a boat fastened to a sperm was carried under and two men drowned. Then a Kanaka fell from aloft and was killed. A sailor taken on at Callao died of scurvy on board ship. The next casualty was a boat steerer snatched out of his boat by a foul line during a whale hunt. The mate "strained"—probably ruptured—himself and never recovered, dying finally on the homeward voyage. The captain himself died the same day; the reason is not stated. In the same week another sailor died from the effects of a fall from the rigging. Then scurvy attacked the crew and three died of that, with the survivors too weak to handle the ship, which finally ran aground on the coast of Brazil. So, despite the "healthy nature of the business," men could and did sicken and die in these long cruises.

Captain Worth's summary of his career is typical of the Nantucket citizen in those whaling days. His post office address was Nantucket, but his actual home was the Pacific. Not even the naval officers of the days of wooden ships and canvas ever knew such periods of separation from their families.

In 1849 Mrs. Charles Grant is said to have inaugurated the practice of going to sea with her husband. "Charles," she said, on the eve of a cruise, "you ship me too." And Charles obeyed the orders of his commanding officer like a good sailor. Probably however, it would not be hard to find other examples before Mrs. Grant. This intrepid woman went ashore at Pitcairn Island to take care of another sea captain's wife who was ill. She nursed her through a long illness until the latter died. Shortly after, Mrs. Grant gave birth to her first child there, with none but native women to help her. Some time afterwards Captain Grant returned with his ship and picked up his wife and babe. The second child was born in Upolo, Samoa. Apparently she thought nothing of having her babies on coral islands or in the captain's cabin. The only hardship she complained of while she was on Pitcairn Island was "the lack of good white bread."

Other women must have followed her example, for one comes across references to the visiting that took place in mid-Pacific between captains' wives of the different whalers. One Christmas there were nine of these seafaring ladies gathered in the cabin of Captain Grant's ship, having what was called a "simper," which seems to have been the feminine of "gam." One would think that raising a family in this seagoing fashion might have its drawbacks. Still, it gave the women, too, a chance to escape the meeting house, the Overseers, and their in-laws.

Captain Grant is still known in Nantucket as the "luckiest" of all her whaling captains. He seemed to have an unerring instinct for knowing where whales were to be found. On one occasion Mrs. Grant won the twenty-dollar gold piece which he had offered to the first one who sighted a whale. She was hanging out the family wash on deck one day when she sang out the welcome news, "Thar she blows!"

During these years of the first half of the nineteenth century, the value of the whaling business steadily increased. There were a number of important products besides oil. From tried out blubber came the "spermaceti" which was made into candles. The present Whaling Museum was formerly a candle factory, and at one time there were as many as thirty-five candle factories in Nantucket. Although the "right whale" was more or less an object of scorn among Nantucket whalemen, there was always a good market for whalebone. And every now and then a spouter would retrieve a barrel, sometimes several barrels, of the strange, waxy substance called ambergris, discharged from the bowels of a sick whale. Unpleasant as the stuff sounds, and doubtless was, it was worth its weight in gold for perfumers.

In 1835, the little town, which had never yet numbered ten thousand inhabitants, was rated as the third richest municipality in the state, being outranked only by Boston and Salem, the latter, at that time, the home of the clipper ships. But already

BRANT POINT LIGHT

influences were at work to undermine this prosperity. Across the northern shore of the island from Madaket to Great Point stretched a sand bar. Opposite the mouth of the inner harbor, this meant a depth of only six feet at low water. This caused no great worry when the Nantucket whaler was less than a hundred tons, as in the eighteenth century, but as the ships began to grow larger the problem of that bar became more and more acute.

It would not have been a great task to dredge a channel and protect it with breakwaters, as is the case now, but it was too much for the town to do by itself. Accordingly, an appeal was made to Congress as early as 1803 and again in 1806. But that body decided to do nothing because, apparently, there were not enough votes concerned in the project. Although the business of Nantucket still grew, the whalers had to come to anchor in what was called the "outer harbor," which is hardly more than an open roadstead, discharge their barrels of sperm into lighters, and thus get their cargoes up to the wharves. In bad weather they had to go to Martha's Vineyard or to a port on the mainland. This was both expensive and troublesome. The result was that the whaling town of New Bedford, which was really a daughter of Nantucket, began to grow at the expense of the mother town. It had the advantage of deep water, and it was nearer the large markets. By the eighteen-twenties, New Bedford had already outstripped Nantucket in the tonnage of its whaling fleet, and by 1846 there were only sixteen whaling ships registered in Nantucket to sixty-nine in New Bedford. In 1857, there were four from Nantucket and ninety-five from New Bedford. Nantucket shipmasters still owned vessels, but handled them from other ports.

To overcome this handicap of the bar, someone invented the

"camel," a sort of floating dry dock which would lift a vessel high enough to clear the bar. The ship would then be towed into the harbor, riding the back of the dromedary, so to speak, up to its berth. To be sure, the invention worked—you can see a large model of it in the whaling museum—but naturally it added considerably to the expense. In 1842 it was first tried and in 1849 it eased its last vessel over the bar.

This period of the early thirties and forties saw the building of the handsomest of the Nantucket homes as symbols of prosperity. But grim fate was hiding round the corner. Perhaps the avenging ghosts of the Quaker forbears determined to punish the town that had left the plain ways of an earlier day and dared to build elegant houses, dance, and wear fine clothes like the "world's people" on the mainland.

At any rate, the disasters came, four of them in close succession. Fires had been frequent in Nantucket. Lighthouses, for example, were always burning down, and there had been a particularly bad fire in 1838. But in 1846 occurred the worst conflagration in the history of the island. Starting in the business district, it spread with fearful speed among the shops, dwellings and especially the stored-up oil barrels, and before it was finally checked it had destroyed the very heart of the town, 360 buildings, covering 36 acres, with a loss of a million dollars, only one-third of it protected by insurance. Many business men never recovered from the losses of the fire. This was the first blow.

The second came in what seemed a friendly guise. It was the discovery, in 1849, of gold in California. Here, thought many, was a chance to recoup the losses of the fire. To young men, accustomed to long voyages on a small lay, that might or might not amount to something, the prospect of scooping nuggets of gold out of the hills of California sounded much more attractive. So off they went, deserting the ships that hunted whales for others that went to California. No town had a worse attack of the gold fever than Nantucket. This did not help business, pressed as far as it was then by rival whaling towns like New Bedford. That was blow number two.

Three years later, somebody puttering around a little shed in Waltham, Massachusetts, discovered a way of refining the "earth oil" of Pennsylvania into an illuminating oil that was both better and cheaper than sperm. How the whaler captains laughed when they heard that an earth oil had been discovered which might put whaling out of business! They did not laugh long. For a community that lived entirely upon the sperm oil market, this discovery was a mortal blow. Whale oil lamps and sperm candles were done for.

Then, on top of these three staggering disasters, came the fourth, the Civil War. This time there was no enemy fleet to blockade the port, but there were Confederate commerce-destroyers which made it their business to sink or burn all the Yankee ships on the seas. Whalers, not captured, for the most part went under British colors or stayed in port. The spouter fleet operating in the Arctic was destroyed wholesale by the Confederate cruiser *Shenandoah*. That was the fourth blow and the final one. The business of the old town was struck dead.

There is still in the possession of one of the descendants of Joseph Starbuck, a ledger account of Nantucket ships. This covers exactly the period of this chapter, beginning with the year 1815 and ending with the year 1863. In fact, the earliest entry was a notation of the ships of the island "taken by the English" during the War of 1812. These laconic entries are interesting for what they suggest, rather than for what they tell, of this whaling epoch. Some of the most terrible tragedies are dismissed with a brief sentence. For example, the dreadful story of the *Essex,* to be told in the next chapter, is thus put in a nutshell, "this ship was stove by a whale." And another tale of tragedy, the *Globe* mutiny, is disposed of in a single line. The following entry contains the material for a long adventure story: The ship *Hero* "was taken at island of St. Mary's by a pirate named Berevidis and carried to Auroco where Capt. Russell and a boy were taken out of prison in the night and shot. Obed Starbuck, the mate, with the assistance of some of the crew got on board and brought the ship home."

The fates of some of the other skippers read thus: "Capt. killed by natives," "Capt. Hussey killed by a native on board his brig," "Capt. Alex H. Coffin was killed by natives with his wife and child on going ashore after a shipwreck," "Capt. killed cutting last whale a blanket piece of blubber pinned him to the rail, going through his body, killing him instantly."

There is also this type of entry, "Second Mate of the *John Jay* who died of a wound was stabbed with a fork by Capt. D—— while at a meal in a fit of delirium tremens." The demon rum certainly took its toll in those days. Here is another victim: The *Phebe* "was the first ship from this port to sail without spirits as ships stores; the Captain took several barrels on board clandestinely and it killed him in 9m 1831 supposed to have died of consumption. The above remarks in relation to the Capt. of the *Phebe* are from his own confessions. When it was determined that he could not live he called his officers and crew into the cabin and informed them what the matter was with him. Gave them a lecture on temperance and advised them to avoid the Rock on which he had split." Picture, if you can, that edifying deathbed scene!

More and more the entries show the whalers leaving Nantucket without liquor on board as a consequence of the temperance movement of the eighteen-thirties. As Dana noted in his *Two Years Before the Mast,* the pious people blessed the Lord because shipowners fell into line so fast in regard to liquor, but nobody remarked the fact that, having taken the sailor's ration of grog away from him, these thrifty shipmasters put nothing else in its place to warm the poor men when they came down from the yards, drenched and chattering with cold. In this case the virtuous principle was accepted because it saved money.

The ledger shows that other captains misbehaved, too. "Capt. C—— did not conduct as he ought," "Capt. A—— did not conduct as he ought—died of bad habits." Capt. C—— "committed suicide at Sandwich Islands." Another skipper fell a victim to a black-eyed siren of the South. He "sold his vessel and cargo and shipped home some sugar, kept the balance and married a Portuguese wife, deserted his wife at Nantucket." It seems that this reprehensible conduct ran in the blood, for the next line adds "and so did his father . . . he died in 1862 leaving a wife and two children rich." Evidently the sinner never repented!

Speaking of scandal, the ledger reports the fact that in 1848 a girl shipped as a sailor on one of these whaling ships, and it was not until two years later that she was "discovered and sent home, she called her name Johnson, and belonged in Rochester, N. Y." The huzzy! But after all, she was only an off-islander.

The record of shipping diminishes rapidly as it nears the

sixties. In 1861, "no whale ship fitted from here . . . schooners put into cod fishing." In 1862, "nothing" in the way of a sperm, and the final entry of 1863 reads, "no ship fitted this year Whaling from here." In this last, disjointed sentence was written the epitaph of the Nantucket whaling industry.

The town was prostrate. Real estate values dropped to almost nothing. Building ceased. All who had any hope of employment elsewhere left the island. The population dropped from 9,700 in 1840 to 4,100 in 1870, and it kept dwindling steadily thereafter.

Douglas-Lithgow, in his history of Nantucket, sings this mournful requiem: "In this year, 1870, the town has reached the nadir of her misfortunes. Not a ship remains to the island; scarcely a sound is heard where erstwhile the busy hum of a mighty industry echoed and re-echoed among her glacial hills: all is silent save the lapping of waves on her sandy shores."

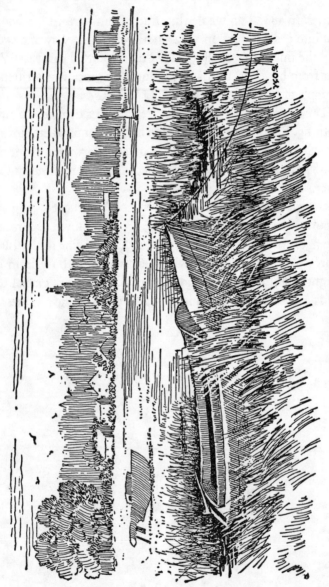

THE TOWN FROM THE CREEKS

CHAPTER IV

BATTLE, MUTINY, AND SHIPWRECK

WHEN a whaleman returned home from one of his long cruises and "First Day" arrived, of course his wife led him firmly to the Friends' Meeting House. At the time of its power, the Society of Friends had two of these tabernacles to accommodate the worshipers. It is quite possible that, during the long meetings, whether anyone was "moved" to speak or not, the minds of these seafaring men wandered. Their lives were packed with memories aplenty, far removed from the bare benches and blank walls. Perhaps the aforesaid wives, sitting primly with downcast eyes, might have been surprised if they had known what was going on in the minds of their husbands. There were strange and terrible adventures in the lives of these men, involving battle, murder, and sudden—or lingering—death, which were strangely out of place in the picture of these drab-coated, quiet-spoken Quakers, waiting there on the hard benches to be moved by the Spirit.

In the log books of the whalers, and even more in the memories of these men, there was many an unsung battle in which, despite their Quaker principles, they had to fight for their lives against cannibals or against equally bloodthirsty pirates, and many of these Nantucketers knew fighting in the two wars against Great Britain. Some met sudden death in battle, others a lingering one in prison. In the most famous ship action of the Revolutionary War Nantucket men played a valiant and important rôle.

NANTUCKET

THE BONHOMME RICHARD AND THE SERAPIS

In 1776, when John Paul Jones was given his first command, the little sloop *Providence* of 14 guns, he had in his crew devoted followers who managed for the most part to keep with him through the rest of the war, except where they fell in action. At the time when Jones mustered the crew of his next command, the *Ranger,* dispatched to France with the news of Burgoyne's surrender, the roll showed the names of twenty-one Nantucketers, eighteen seamen and three apprentices. The *Ranger* made an unusually speedy voyage and, after delivering the news, Jones set off on a cruise around the British Isles, which had as its climax the brilliant capture of the British sloop of war *Drake.*

When, after interminable delays, he was finally given another ship by the French government, which he named the *Bonhomme Richard,* in honor of Franklin's "Poor Richard," he collected as many of his old crew as possible. In particular, he picked up Henry Gardner of Nantucket, who had been with him on the *Providence,* and who had been stranded in the city of Nantes ever since the *Ranger* dropped him there. Gardner was appointed a warrant officer and gunner on the *Richard.*

In September, 1779, the *Richard* engaged the British ship *Serapis* off Flamborough Head, on the east coast of England, in what proved to be the most remarkable single ship action in American naval history. It is one of the few ship duels on record in which the ship that sank was the victor. Paul Jones, from the opening of the fight, was smitten by one disaster after another on his own ship, then by the treachery of a French captain of a vessel which was supposed to be his consort. Once, also, the whole mob of British prisoners in the hold were turned loose by the cowardice of one of his own men.

But the turning point of the action came with the exploit of three sailors and a midshipman. On orders from Jones, Henry Gardner, the Nantucketer, sent up to the main yard two buckets of hand grenades. Then he and two other sailors, led by the midshipman, went out on the yard. Gardner took care of the slow match, and the men behind him, one of whom also was a Nantucketer, Jerry Evans, carried the buckets of grenades. These men crawled to the very tip of the main yard. There the party lighted the hand grenades and tossed them down at the main hatch of the British ship. Soon one was landed that had been perfectly aimed and timed. It fell, bounced inboard, and exploded among some cartridges—loose bags of powder used in the guns—which lay scattered on the deck below. This explosion set off a pile of ammunition which went up with a roar. The blast killed twenty men and blew up the deck above. The action continued for some time afterward, but that was the point at which the day ceased to go against the American ship.

This Gardner was a very able man. The following year he was first lieutenant of a French privateer that brought home a million dollars worth of enemy cargoes and ships. When Jones was in Portsmouth, fitting out the ship *America,* at the close of the war, he says that Gardner arrived "in the nick of time" to superintend the mounting of the guns and the stowing of the ammunition.

In the desperate fight against the *Serapis,* two Nantucket warrant officers were killed, Henry Martin and Thomas Turner. The present square in front of the Pacific Bank in Nantucket has been called "Turner Square" in honor of the latter. The bronze plate in the lobby of the Historical Association rooms commemorates the services of all the Nantucketers who took part in that terrific sea fight.

PRINCE OF NEUFCHÂTEL AND THE ENDYMION

The next ship action, at first glance, has little to do with Nantucket except in its location, but for other reasons it became a tradition in the island history. This was the fight between the American privateer *Prince of Neufchâtel* and a boat party from the British frigate *Endymion*. Obed Macy, the historian of Nantucket, was a contemporary of this event, and we might look to his pages for some interesting details of this story; but he was a Quaker and this was a bloody affair. Accordingly, he dismisses the fight thus: "We forbear to state the particulars of this sanguinary engagement, believing that it would neither please nor edify a large part of our readers." It was indeed a "sanguinary engagement," being, in fact, one of the most desperately fought in the annals of the war. And it also has a droll sequel, which probably was not to the liking of Obed Macy either.

At any rate, here's the story. In October, 1814, the privateer *Prince of Neufchâtel,* Captain Ordronaux, returned from the other side of the Atlantic after a successful commerce-destroying cruise. Her last prize was the *Douglass,* an English ship bound for Liverpool with a rich cargo of rum, sugar, cotton, and coffee, and she accompanied her captor under a prize crew.

The privateer, with the *Douglass,* was in the neighborhood of Nantucket when she sighted the British frigate *Endymion* off Gay Head. The latter gave chase. At nightfall the wind had died down and both vessels were becalmed. At the time the privateer lay anchored off the south shore of Nantucket, "just abreast of Madequecham Pond," between Nobadeer and Tom Never's Head. Captain Ordronaux was short-handed and glad to accept the services of several Nantucketers who rowed out to offer their help. Among them was a pilot. It was clear before the night shut down that the Englishman was going to attack the little privateer by the usual means, when there was no breeze to bring an enemy within gunshot; namely, to send a boarding party in boats. Accordingly, Ordronaux made ready. He slushed the sides of his vessel with grease to make them slippery, spread boarding nettings along the bulwarks, double-shotted his guns with bags of musket balls, and filled lockers along the sides with cannon balls to be dropped through the bottoms of the boats. Then, having taken during his cruise a large quantity of fire-arms from his prizes, he stacked loaded muskets in piles on the deck at handy places, together with baskets filled with loaded pistols.

At eight o'clock the expedition came down, consisting of five barges filled with officers and men to the number of something between a hundred and a hundred and forty men. The crew of the privateer totaled about thirty-five, with thirty-seven prisoners below decks, who threatened to break loose any minute, and, as soon as the fighting began, howled encouragement to their friends. A savage combat began on all sides of the vessel at once. According to the log of the privateer, the struggle lasted just twenty minutes. A Nantucket account puts it at half an hour. Both may have been guess work. Certainly no one held a stop watch on that bout!

At any rate, at the end of approximately that time, the British survivors alongside cried for quarter. They had been unable, despite their numbers, to gain a foothold, although many times it was touch and go for the defenders. Boats drifted away on the tide filled with dead or desperately wounded men; the rest were in no condition even to row back to the *Endymion*. Thirty-three had been killed outright, thirty-seven were desperately wounded, and thirty others offered themselves as prisoners of war. On the deck of the privateer, six of her thirty-five men, had been killed, among them the Nantucket pilot, fifteen were badly wounded, six just plain "wounded," and eight reported themselves as "unhurt," that is, able to lend a hand for duty. The problem was to handle the situation of thirty-seven howling prisoners below, thirty able bodied prisoners in boats alongside, and a large number of wounded men, both American and British. Since the privateer's surgeon was among those badly wounded, the others had to bleed and groan without care from anyone all that night.

Ordronaux handled the situation with remarkable skill. All the rest of the night he and his first mate stood guard over the prisoners whom he had disarmed. As dawn came, he rigged a sail abaft the mainmast to conceal the quarter deck. There he kept two boys playing the drum and fife, and stamping back and forth to give the impression that there were many men in the after guard. The surviving Britishers alongside could still have taken the ship if they had had their arms. Having demanded their parole, for he suspected that the British controlled Nantucket, Ordronaux sent the boats ashore loaded with prisoners and wounded. They landed at Sesacacha, then a fishing village of about forty cottages north of Sankaty Head, of which scarcely a trace remains today. Two of the British wounded died in the boats. The rest were carried into the houses of the fishermen, who took care of them as well as they could. Those who were judged able to stand the journey were packed, together with the unhurt prisoners, and sent off to Nantucket in springless carts over the rutty and sandy roads, some eight miles of agony for many of the poor wretches. In the town they were taken to the tavern, which, in those days, stood on North Wharf. There the wounded were spread out on the floor and, amid the gaping multitude, the local physicians probed for the bullets after the cruel fashion of the day.

The townsfolk, as always, responded with a warm heart to the needs of both friend and foe, taking the wounded into their homes. The unwounded of the British ship were carried off by officers sent ashore by the captain of the *Endymion.* Two young midshipmen had such a pleasant time recovering from their wounds in the hospitable Defriez home on Fair Street that, according to tradition, they put off getting well and reporting for duty just as long as they could, and for many Christmas seasons thereafter they sent gifts to the daughters of that family in appreciation.

Captain Hope of the *Endymion,* in reporting this night action, took a very sporting attitude. He said that he had lost more men in that attack on the little privateer than he would expect to lose in a fight with a frigate of his own size. Later, he allowed the privateer to sail off in plain view to Boston, with no attempt to take her. He evidently thought she had earned her right to escape. Of this extraordinary fight against great odds it is only fair to add, for our own national conceit, that the stout-hearted captain was a Frenchman, his first mate was a Swede, and among the crew that night there were various languages spoken besides English.

The sequel is worth a few lines, even if it is not particularly heroic. Island folk all over the world have had a reputation for luring ships ashore. During the attack the *Douglass* had stood by, unable to fight because she was unarmed. Apparently, somebody who had suffered during the war conceived the notion of sending word to the prize master of the *Douglass* that the British were in sight around the corner, and no time must be lost in casting the vessel on the beach, where, at any rate, the cargo could be salvaged. So it was done forthwith on the shore off Sesacacha, and a pulley was rigged on the top on the low bluff, by means of which the contents of the *Douglass* were taken ashore. Then every islander who had a cart came to "help," but all night long there was a rifling of every thing on board the ship that could be of the slightest value. Some got deeply into the rum and became so confused that the next day they could not remember where they had hidden their loot. When the morning light shone upon the scene, there was nothing left for anybody to declare as "salvaged" cargo. But for the first time in two years there was sugar and coffee on Nantucket tables, not to mention Jamaica rum in the cellar. There was some shamefaced poohpoohing thereafter among the godly over this affair, but they excused the performance on the ground that "it was all privateering."

THE GLOBE MUTINY

The story of the mutiny on the Nantucket whaler *Globe* is as daubed with blood and diabolical heartlessness as any of the exploits of Blackbeard. This vessel left Nantucket for the Pacific in December, 1822, under Captain Worth, doubtless a relative of the Worth who fought on the decks of the *Bonhomme Richard*.

Among her boat steerers was a Samuel Comstock, a native of
Nantucket, who had left the island as a boy, and, let us hope,
learned his villainy elsewhere. Evidently, he had plotted his
mutiny from the beginning, if we are to trust his brother,
William, who wrote up the story afterward, and who had, at
least, a sneaking admiration for his hero. At any rate, while in
the Pacific in January of the following year, Comstock armed
himself with an axe and gave a boarding knife to a fellow con-
spirator, Payne, who had joined the ship in the Sandwich
Islands. The two then went about their bloody business. Comstock finished off Captain Worth in short order, and then, finding the first mate only seriously stabbed by Payne, smashed him
into eternity, likewise, with the trusty axe. Next he went to the
cabin to attend to the two mates. He first fired through the door,
then opening it stumbled and fell in. The second mate jumped
upon him, but on being promised his life, the man let Comstock
up again. This scoundrel thereupon killed the third mate with
several stabs of the bayonet, and then shot the second mate who
had spared his life. Thus all the ship's officers were disposed of.

There remained a boat steerer named Smith, who wisely
agreed to follow Comstock's leadership and thus was spared the
fate of the officers. Three days later, Comstock saw a negro sailor
loading a pistol. Thereupon he called a "court martial" and
sentenced the poor wretch to be hanged at the yard arm, re-
quiring all the crew to haul on the rope.

In the middle of February, the ship came near an island, and
Comstock decided to go ashore by means of a raft. In the course
of a short time, Payne and Comstock quarreled, and Payne shot
his leader down. In this mutiny, however, things were done with
due regard to form. Payne buried Comstock with great solem-

nity, and read aloud a whole chapter from the Bible to ease his old pal into the next world.

After this, Payne sent Smith with six men aboard the ship to take care of her, and Smith immediately took advantage of the opportunity to sail away. Despite his small crew, he managed to work the vessel to Valparaiso, where he turned her over to the American consul and told the story of the mutiny. Meanwhile, Payne managed to get himself into the bad graces of the natives by flogging and putting in irons a girl who had dared to run away from him. The natives arose and massacred, not only Payne, but all the rest of the men, except two youngsters, Lay and Hussey, whom some kind-hearted captors succeeded in saving. These lads were kept as hostages by the islanders until July, 1826, when the U. S. schooner *Dolphin* arrived to effect their rescue. They landed in New York in April, 1827, after living nearly two years among the natives. Presumably it was not long thereafter before they were welcomed back in Nantucket, having been absent five years. One may read in the Atheneum the little pamphlet they published about what they witnessed and experienced in this bloody affair.

THE ESSEX DISASTER

In the safe of the Atheneum there is also another pamphlet, written by Owen Chase, First Mate of the whaler *Essex*. This booklet is extremely rare. If in cleaning house in the garret of some Nantucket home, one were to run across another copy, it could be exchanged for a goodly sum of money. Indeed, it is said that the last one sold for $1600! But that was Herman Melville's copy with his own notes penciled on the margin. The story of the *Essex* has a special interest because it gave Melville the material for that terrible last chapter of *Moby Dick,* when the White Whale rams the ship and sinks it. Melville not only had the pamphlet, but talked with the author. The reason, they say, for the rarity of this booklet is the reluctance of the Nantucket people of that day to have others—benighted off-islanders especially—read an account of how certain Nantucketers were reduced to the extremity of eating their shipmates in one of the most dreadful disasters that ever befell the whaling industry. There were ships like the *Lady Adams* that were lost, no one knows how or where, with every soul on board; but this story was a long-drawn-out horror, with men dying one by one and the survivors mad with hunger, thirst, and the heat of the tropical sun.

Owen Chase, in his preface, states simply that he lost everything when the *Essex* went down and issues "this pamphlet in the hope of obtaining something of remuneration by giving a short history of my sufferings to the world." His title, as was the fashion in those days, is a summary of the entire story:

Narrative of the Most Extraordinary and Distressing Shipwreck of the Whale-Ship *Essex* of Nantucket; Which was Attacked and Finally Destroyed by a Large Spermaceti Whale in the Pacific Ocean; with an Account of the Unparalleled Sufferings of the Captain and Crew During a Space of Ninety-three Days at Sea in Open Boats in the Years 1819 and 1820. By Owen Chase of Nantucket, First Mate of Said Vessel.

This is the story in brief. On November 20, 1820, while in the southern Pacific, Chase was out with his boat in pursuit of a whale, as were two other boats from the *Essex*. Chase had just harpooned his quarry when it disappeared and suddenly rose under the boat, damaging it so badly that it could barely be kept afloat until it got back to the ship. As the captain and second mate were still out in pursuit of another whale, Chase altered the direction of the *Essex* to come up with them. Meanwhile, he began to work repairing the leak in his own boat.

Suddenly, a huge sperm whale broke the water ahead of the ship. It spouted, disappeared and then rose again to the surface. In a moment it charged directly at the *Essex*. The helmsman tried to sheer off, but the whale struck the vessel such a blow as nearly to throw every man on his face with the shock. It was as if the ship had run full speed ahead on a reef.

The whale dived again, this time grazing her keel. Again it rose alongside and made off. Meanwhile, the vessel was sinking by the head. Chase signaled the recall of the other boats. Suddenly the whale began thrashing about convulsively. It turned, as if in fury, came faster than before and a second time rammed the *Essex*. The whole bow was stove in by this blow. Again the whale dived under the vessel and then made off.

Chase barely had time to cut away the lashings of the one remaining boat, put in some nautical instruments and shove off, before the ship went over on her beam ends. When the other boats came up the men managed to regain the wreck and cut away her masts. This righted her and brought her up somewhat. Then they chopped through her decks to get water and ship's bread for the long voyage. The captain's and the mate's chests were saved, containing some useful instruments and tools. Chase found in his chest a few sheets of paper and a pencil, which enabled him to keep some sort of record of the experience.

The castaways lingered about the wreck for nearly two days

salvaging what supplies they could, including some turtles, and making sails and spars for their frail craft. The captain determined to head for the coast of Chile or Peru, two thousand miles away. There was land much nearer, to the west, the Marquesas Islands, but they were known to be inhabited by cannibals. Accordingly, the three open boats spread their sails toward the south and east, hoping to reach the line of the trade winds.

A month later they touched at a desert rock named Ducie's Island, where they were able to vary their diet with shellfish and birds' eggs and where they found some fresh water. Here they spent a week. Three men elected to remain and take their chances of living there. The others set sail again in the three boats.

Ducie's Island was 1500 miles from the scene of the *Essex* disaster, but actually farther to the west. Captain Pollard's decision to set a course east from Ducie's has been criticized because he might have reached the Society Islands by a short sail. The course to the mainland meant a distance of 2500 miles more.

On January tenth the second mate, Matthew Joy, died. He had been ill during the entire journey. Two days later a negro seaman was caught trying to steal an extra amount of ship's bread, but surrendered it at the point of a pistol and promised never to repeat his theft. That night a gale of wind and rain separated Chase's boat from the other two, and they never came together again. The small amount of provisions they had brought from Ducie's Island soon gave out. They ate a small species of clam found clinging to the bottom of the boat; they devoured stray flying fish that were caught in the sail—wings, fins, bones, and all—but were reduced in the main to the tiny allowance of hard-tack and water. They became so weak that they could not move an oar. One of the negroes died and was cast overboard. Then, on February eighth, Isaac Cole went mad from his sufferings and died in convulsions. Chase then made the suggestion that the body be used for food, and the other two men lost no time in complying. Chase describes with horrifying fidelity to detail how they fell upon the body of Cole and feasted. As the weather was hot they cooked the remainder of the flesh to keep it better. (They used the shell of a turtle as a hearthstone, and laid it on the sand ballast.) Ten days later, they were again on the verge of death from starvation. One lay down in the bottom of the boat to die. Just then a sail was sighted, and happily the ship's lookout spied the little boat at the same time. It was the English brig *Indian*. When the boat was brought alongside, the three surviving occupants were too weak to help themselves and had to be lifted into the ship. Indeed, one was so far gone that he was unconscious at the time of the rescue.

Meanwhile, the second mate's and the captain's boats were in no less straits for the want of food and water. The entire stock of food in the mate's boat was consumed by January fourteenth. A negro seaman succumbed and his body was eaten. Shortly after, a second negro died; and as the captain's boat also was at this time entirely without food, the body was eaten by both crews. Next a third African in the mate's boat and a white man in the captain's boat died, and their bodies were consumed. The next day the mate's boat became separated from the other and was never heard from again.

In a few days the situation became so frightful in the captain's boat that on February first it was determined to draw lots to see who should be sacrificed in order to prolong the lives of the others. The lot fell upon Owen Coffin, the cabin boy, who was Captain Pollard's nephew. The lad submitted to his fate without a murmur. The captain begged the youth to let him take his place, but Coffin insisted on his "right," as he called it, to make the sacrifice. The executioner was also determined by lot and the dreadful duty fell upon another young man, Charles Ramsdell. Thereupon he implored Coffin to change places with him, but in vain. Ramsdell finally put the pistol to Coffin's head, turned his face away, and fired. The body of Coffin kept the survivors alive for another ten days, but Captain Pollard refused to eat from his nephew's corpse. Then another man died, and his body kept life in the remaining two, Pollard and Ramsdell, until they were rescued by a Nantucket whaler. The two groups of survivors from the boats, five in all, met in Valparaiso shortly after.

The three men left on Ducie's Island also were picked up later by a ship sent from Valparaiso. When rescued, they had spent 102 days fighting for existence on that island. In one of their explorations for food they came upon a cave, where to their horror they saw the skeletons of eight men lying side by side, the grim testimony of an earlier shipwreck.

Of the twenty men in the crew of the *Essex*, just eight survived in all. It is a curious fact that in this trial of endurance five who died of exhaustion were blacks.

Captain Pollard made only one voyage after this experience, and that ended in shipwreck. He decided that he was born to be unlucky and never went to sea again. Chase, however, became master of a whaler and made several very profitable voyages. Both he and Captain Pollard lived to be old men. Chase's home, a little, unpretentious house on the northeast corner of York and

Orange Streets, may still be seen.

"There's where Captain Chase lived," said Mr. Wood, the driver of the surrey, as he pointed out the dwelling to me. "They say that after the shipwreck of the *Essex* he never suffered one single crumb to be wasted from his table." And in his declining years the old terror of starvation came back as an obsession. He would go to market and buy twice as much provisions as his housekeeper required. The surplus he would carry stealthily to the attic and hide it away under the eaves!

"WRECKED ON THE FEEJEES"

This is the title of another thin pamphlet in fine print which reposes in the Atheneum. It was written by William Cary, who was a boy on the whaling ship *Oeno,* and who was the sole survivor of its personnel. It is another one of those books to read on a rainy day.

The *Oeno* left Nantucket in November, 1824, and her voyage was uneventful until a fatal night the following April when she crashed on a coral reef among the Fiji Islands. Since there was no chance of saving her, the officers and crew took to the boats and made their way along the reef to a small inhabited island. There they were received in kindly fashion by the natives, but after a few days a visiting party of warriors in twenty canoes came down upon them. The newcomers shortly afterward massacred all the ship's company except Cary, who had hidden in a crevice of a rock.

There he lay until, tormented by hunger and exhaustion, he showed himself. Two men, he says, came toward him, one with a hatchet and the other with a knife. Cary sat down with his back to them, "expecting to have the hatchet driven into my head and not wishing to see the blow. They walked up until within a few feet of me and then stopped and looked at me a moment before they spoke. It seemed an hour!" But instead of murdering him, they addressed him in kindly tones. They proved to be the natives of the island, not members of the gang of murderous visitors. One of them was an old man who took him to his own hut and gave him food.

The invaders came to the hut where Cary was taken, but the wife of the old man put the boy behind her, indicating that he was under her protection and thus, perhaps, setting a taboo on him. At any rate they did not try to kill him. At last these savages departed from the island.

Thereafter Cary was transferred by the natives from one island to another. At the end of two weeks a canoe appeared, containing a white man. He looked at Cary and held out his hand.

"Hullo, William!" The boy gazed at him dumbfounded. "Don't you remember David Whippey?"

"Yes," answered Cary when he had recovered from his astonishment, "I formerly knew him. He was a townsman of mine and an old playmate."

"Well," laughed the other, "I am that David Whippey."

Naturally, there was a Nantucket reunion then and there. Whippey said that he had been left on the island to gather turtle shell, but his captain had apparently abandoned him, for he had never returned. By the end of a year, however, Whippey had become a chief himself, and was in high favor with the king of the tribe. Indeed Whippey declared that he so thoroughly enjoyed "going native" that he had no desire ever to return to civilization, not even to Nantucket.

Thereafter Cary wandered about in canoes among the islands, looking for a ship to carry him home. He seems to have had a genius for getting along with the natives, for they showed him every kindness. In return, he frequently went to war for his hosts, wherever he was, just to show appreciation of their hospitality, and was worth an army in himself because of his musket. He learned the language, and lived like a native; but, unlike Whippey, he was unwilling to stay. To cut a long, adventurous chronicle short, he finally boarded a ship homeward bound, and nine years after he left Nantucket he stepped once more on the old wharf and walked up Main Street.

William Cary lived "out Wauwinet way" in his later years. What pictures he must have seen in the fire as he sat before the hearth on a winter's night!

Of the shipwrecks occurring in the neighborhood of Nantucket the stories are so many that they would fill a book by themselves. In 1877 a pamphlet was written by Arthur Gardner of Nantucket telling the stories of over 500 wrecks about the island. Recently a New Bedford paper published the statement that between 1843 and 1903 over 2100 vessels had been wrecked on Nantucket shoals!

One of Gardner's stories is about the *British Queen,* bound to America from Dublin with 226 Irish immigrants aboard. On December 18, 1851, after eight weeks at sea, she struck on the shoals near Muskeget, in a gale. The wretched immigrants, packed into their narrow, cold and filthy quarters, suffered every discomfort imaginable as the ship pounded herself to pieces in the icy gale. Two of them died. Meanwhile, the steamboat *Tele-*

graph, towing two sloops, fought her way to the stricken ship. After great difficulties the passengers were brought to Nantucket in all stages of sickness and exhaustion, and there they were cared for by the townspeople.

Eventually, most of the immigrants sailed to the mainland; but one, Robert Mooney, who had left for the land of promise with his bride, preferred to stay. Indeed, he never left the island thereafter for forty-six years. He died at eighty-five, perfectly contented with his island home. When the *British Queen* went to pieces, her name board drifted ashore. It was rescued and given as a souvenir to Mr. Mooney. For years it could be seen over the barn door of the Mooney farm on the road to Wauwinet. His grandson is now Chief of Police in Nantucket.

In brief, Nantucket has known shipwreck as a commonplace tragedy from the first. Even in these days of lightships, buoys, charts, and wireless, it is astonishing how many vessels come to grief on the shoals. Another chapter could be written on the heroic rescues made from the shores of the island, and at least a passing reference must be made to the splendid work of the life-saving stations. What the men of this service have done in going out through winter storms, when the very oars would be blown out of the oarlocks and every wave threw a sheet of ice, fighting their way to some wreck where the crew hung in the rigging, would make an epic in itself. Once in a while, the rescue is so spectacular and so gallantly achieved that the men have been awarded medals, but it is safe to say that this recognition has never come too often.

The foregoing chapter has been a sort of "lucky bag," as the man-of-war's man says, filled with odds and ends of adventure. Recently, an adoring mother objected to her son's going on a summer cruise in a schooner because, she explained, "I'm afraid something might happen to him. He's only nineteen." It is true that Nantucket lads had little formal education; few, if any, went to college, but they were not permitted to grow up as precious darlings. "Only nineteen!" These boys were off to the Pacific at twelve or fourteen, and they had to take the hardships and face the perils of grown men from the first day out. It was a rough school, with no "Psychology of Adolescence," no snap electives, and a vacation only once in three or four years, but it bred men!

CHAPTER V

SOME OF THE "OLD BOYS"

THE graduates of any one of the famous boys' schools in England are known as the "Old Boys" of that school, and the alumni organization is called the "Old Boys Association." It is a good phrase, and it is used here to cover the Nantucket "alumni." As in the English usage, the term is applied here to these interesting men with a blending of affection and respect.

In this chapter a few of these characters will be briefly introduced. There are others omitted who might well be included, but these particular Old Boys are presented as representative of the different eras of Nantucket history, and also of a wide variety of personalities.

In a small island community, composed of men and women of the same English yeoman stock and removed from their fellow colonials on the mainland, it would only be natural to find a number of characters noted for their individuality. Not eccentrics, though there were such, but real personalities, not ashamed to be individual in their thought, their speech, their dress, their manners. The life, too, common to nearly all, which was spent at sea in pursuit of the whale, gave a flavor to their talk and their habits such as one could hardly find anywhere else. Even the women caught the nautical and whaling idiom which they added quite naturally to the "thee" and "thine" of their Quaker speech.

LUCRETIA MOTT LANE

PETER FOLGER 1617–1690

When Tristram Coffin stopped at Martha's Vineyard in 1659 to interview Thomas Mayhew, with whom he made arrangements for the purchase of Nantucket, he also obtained there the services of Peter Folger, whom he employed as interpreter in dealing with the Indians. This Peter had come from Norwich, England, in 1635. For twenty pounds he had bought Mary Morrill, an indentured servant who had crossed on the same ship with him, and whom he later married. She bore him two sons and seven daughters, the last of which female flock was Abiah, famous as the mother of Benjamin Franklin. The visitor who drives out toward Madaket will see the fountain by the roadside, dedicated to her memory, not far from the site of the old Folger homestead where she was born. This stood about a mile west of the present town. The country owes a debt of gratitude to Peter for being the grandfather of Benjamin, and to Abiah for being his mother, because Ben was a true Folger if there ever was one. By virtue of that fact he towered over the rest of his brothers and sisters who were plain, commonplace Franklins. There was something uncanny about the protoplasm that made up the old-time Folger. Every now and then, in later years, it would pop up in full force again, and produce a man or woman who was remarkable for precisely the same things that made the original Folger famous in his day.

These characteristics were independence, force of character and intellect, and an amazing versatility. The Folger type of mind was inventive, mechanical, scientific. One of Benjamin Franklin's biographers entitled his book "The Many-sided Franklin." That was Peter Folger all over. Tristram Coffin had employed him because, apparently, he was the only man available who had taken the trouble to master the local Indian dialect; but that accomplishment, valuable as it was to the white settlement, was only the beginning. He has been described as "the most useful man on the island." At a meeting of the inhabitants in March, 1664, "Peter Folger is excepted as a Tradsman namly as a Surveyor, interpretor and Millar." Three years later, it was stipulated in meeting that Peter should manage the mill for the landowners and other inhabitants at the rate of "two quarts of a Bushel for the Labor in grinding." He officiated, also, as schoolmaster and preacher; he tried his hand at prose and verse; he turned out to be a good blacksmith; he started weaving for the community; and no doubt if anybody had possessed a watch in those days he could have repaired it or made a better one. Apparently, when anything turned up that needed to be done, of a special and difficult nature, Peter Folger was the man who could do it. The others had so much faith in his accuracy and honesty that they not only made him one of the five commissioners, intrusted with the task of laying out the shares of land, but provided that three of them constituted a quorum, only if Peter Folger was one of the three.

Scientific as his tastes were, Peter did, on occasion, flirt with the muse on sedate, religious subjects. The following is from a poem on how the Baptists had been made to endure persecution. The title is "A Looking Glass for the Times, or the Former Spirit of New England Revived in this Generation."

> The cause of this their suffering
> Was not for any sin
> But for the witness that they bare
> Against babe's sprinkling.

That last line, especially, encourages one to believe that Peter's talents were not lyric, however excellent his intentions. Still it may be said that nobody in New England in those days was writing poetry that was any better.

In later years, when the factional dispute grew up between Coffin and Gardner, Folger, a "half-share man," sided with Gardner. By that time he had added to his many duties that of being clerk of court for the island. In this dispute, on being required by the Colonial Council to turn over the records to them, he refused and was haled to the bar of judgment for contempt. He was then required to deliver a bond of twenty pounds or go to jail. He either could not or would not produce the bond, and was accordingly put in durance most vile. His prison was, he says, "a place where never any Englishman was put, and where the Neighbors Hogs had layed but the night before and in the bitter Frost and deep Snow. They had only thrown out most of the Durt, Hogs Dung and Snow. The Rest the Constable told me I might lie upon if I would that is upon the Boards in that Case, and without Victuals or Fire. Indeed, I persuaded him to fetch me a little Hay and he did so, and some Friend did presently bring Bedding and Victuals." * Certainly this was no fit place for the worthy man and no proper reward for what he had done.

But he was not to suffer long because, on the triumph of Gardner and the downfall of the crusty Tristram, Peter came back into his own. To the end of his days his neighbors respected him as the master of many trades, and in character upright and brave.

* Quoted by A. Starbuck, *The History of Nantucket*, p. 54.

REUBEN CHASE 1754-1824

A running broad jump of a hundred years brings us to a picturesque figure of a very different stamp. This is Reuben Chase, whose name was mentioned earlier as one of the Nantucketers who had served under Paul Jones on the *Providence,* the *Ranger,* and the *Bonhomme Richard.* On the *Richard* he was rated as "midshipman." In those days it was not uncommon for a seaman to be raised to the rank of midshipman, a grade which did not necessarily lead to the quarter-deck as it does now. Jones selected Chase to serve as midshipman on the basis of his previous record, and, it is said, commended him highly. In the fight with the *Serapis* Chase happened to be second in command of a captured pilot boat, which lay becalmed at a distance during the action, and thus he was cheated of his share in the glory of the victory. He was on the *Alliance* later when she conveyed Lafayette to France, and was sent to the French privateer *Bonaventure* as second lieutenant. Finally, he was back again under Paul Jones on the ship of the line *America* at Portsmouth, together with his fellow townsman and shipmate Gardner. In her he made the trip to France at the close of the war. Since there was no American navy thereafter for many years, he went into whaling and became a well-known ship-master of Nantucket.

Reuben Chase is particularly interesting because of his being the original of the famous character, "Long Tom Coffin," in Cooper's *Pilot.* The following notes are written in pencil on the flyleaves of a copy of the *Pilot,* in the Atheneum Library, by Mr. F. C. Sanford, a well-known Nantucketer of the previous generation:

SOME OF THE "OLD BOYS"

The "Long Tom Coffin" of this story was Reuben Chase, born at Nantucket 1754 and died there in 1824. I remember him well, just such a man as Mr. Cooper describes, over six feet tall, boney and angular, very powerful. He fought on the *Bonhomme Richard* in September 1779 with the Heroic Paul Jones in North Sea, and it is here Cooper was made acquainted with him. I was in Sag Harbor in 1849 and purchased the ships *Fanny, John Jay,* and *St. Lawrence* for California and while there I became acquainted with the Hon. Charles Dearing who was an associate with Fenimore Cooper in the trips whaling from there. And he told me Mr. Cooper Said Long Tom Coffin of the Pilot was Reuben Chase of Nantucket who fought in John Paul Jones ship *Bon Home Richard.*

Just what Mr. Sanford meant by that statement, "and it was here Cooper was made acquainted with him," is not clear; for Cooper did not enter the navy until 1808, and Chase was not in the navy after the Revolutionary War. Cooper met him, as a matter of fact, when Reuben was master of a transatlantic packet on which the future novelist was a passenger. He describes Chase in the character of Long Tom Coffin thus:

The seaman . . . arose slowly from the place where he was stationed as cockswain of the boat, and seemed to ascend high in air by the gradual evolution of numberless folds in his body. When erect, he stood nearly six feet and as many inches in his shoes. . . . His whole frame was destitute of the round outlines of a well-formed man, though his enormous hands furnished a display of bones and sinews which gave indication of gigantic strength. . . . One of his hands grasped, with a sort of instinct, the staff of a bright harpoon. . . .

Cooper not only knew his man but knew his Nantucket background, too, for Long Tom is made to speak thus of the Coffin name in talking to the girl in the story:

"Ay, Coffin," continued the old sailor, his grim features gradually relaxing as he gazed at her bright looks; " 'tis a solemn word, but it's a word that passes over the shoals, among the islands, and along the Cape, oftener than any other. My father was a Coffin and my mother was a Joy; and the two names can count more flukes than all the rest in the island together; though the Worths, and the Gardners and the Swaines, dart better harpoons and set truer lances, than any men who come from the weather side of the Atlantic."

The novelist lets Tom drown in shipwreck on the *Ariel,* much to the distress of every reader, since he is the only character in the book that seems real. As for Reuben Chase, with that giant frame of his and prodigious strength, it does seem an anticlimax for him not to die with his boots on. But in time the infirmities of age laid him low, though throughout a long life British broadside and thrashing fluke had left him unscathed. He died in 1824, in the town where he was born, aged sixty-nine. His brother Joseph, also a famous whaleman, evidently possessed a salty sense of humor, for he devised these lines and had them cut on Reuben's tombstone:

HERE LIES
REUBEN CHASE

Anchored, who has stood the sea
Of ebbing life and flowing misery;
Though not dandy-rigged, his prudent eye foresaw
And took a reef at fortune's quickest flaw;

He luffed and bore away to please mankind,
    Yet duty urged him still to head the wind.

Rheumatic gusts at last his masts destroyed,
But jury masts * a while he still enjoyed.
    Laden with grief and age and shattered head,
    At last he struck and grounded on his bed.
    When in distress careening thus he lay,
    His final bilge expecting every day,
    Heaven took his ballast from his dreary hold
    And left his body a wreck destitute of soul.

Brother Joseph left that last line a wreck, too, with a particularly dreadful rhyme at the end. But the composition of that poetic epitaph must have used up a handful of quill pens, and Joseph's hand was almost as large as Reuben's. Indeed, the whole Chase family was famous for its size and muscle.

Noble as the above effusion was, Reuben Chase's son thought it much too flippant; maybe it seemed to emphasize too much his father's final aches and pains. At any rate, the son put up another more dignified gravestone in its stead, and it may still be seen in the Old North burying ground. But what an epitaph! It reads, "An honest man, a revolutionary officer, and a pensioner." That is some people's idea of climax, even today, but as a memorial inscription—well, no doubt the sturdy old tar would have preferred that of his brother Joseph.

ADMIRAL SIR ISAAC COFFIN, BART. 1759–1839

This member of the Old Boys Association was a genuine Coffin, but not a Nantucketer at all. He was a direct descendant of old Tristram the First, but his father, Nathaniel, held a gov-

* Probably this means crutches.

ernment job, being "Cashier of the Customs" in Boston. There Isaac was born and went to school. In 1773, at the age of fourteen, he entered the Royal Navy as a midshipman, just as his brother John had done. Naturally, when trouble arose between the Boston rebels and the King's ministers, the whole tribe of Boston Coffins remained staunchly loyalist. John, for example, won promotion for his gallantry at Bunker Hill and served with distinction all through the war on the British side. Isaac, too, made his mark. In 1778, he won his lieutenant's epaulet, became captain at twenty-two, and in that rank won the favor of his commanding officer, Hood, by his fine performance at the Battle of the Saints in 1781.

He got into hot water more than once by his independent ways, but kept going up the ladder until he had reached the highest rank of the navy, Admiral, and had been made a baronet with a coat of arms before that. He had crippled himself by going to the rescue of a sailor who had fallen overboard, and this injury retired him from active service some time before getting his final promotion.

He seems to have been a great old character; bluff, blunt in his speech, with a broad sense of humor, and famous for his Latin quotations. He was a close friend of the Duke of Clarence, who later became William IV, the "Sailor King." King William wanted Sir Isaac's name to appear on the list of the new peers that were to be created by the liberal House of Commons in order to jam the Reform Bill of 1832 through the House of Lords. At this royal suggestion, however, the Ministry balked, and the burden of their objection was that Sir Isaac was entirely too fond of his native land. Why, even then Yankee boys were learning to become master mariners at a school in Nantucket founded by this misguided man!

Evidently, despite the American Revolution and the particularly active part played therein by Massachusetts, Sir Isaac always cherished a love for the province where he was born. As he had no family to inherit whatever property he should leave at his death, he decided to look around and find some way of founding a monument to his name that would benefit the Coffin clan in the land of his birth, which he was always referring to affectionately as "my native land."

Meanwhile, he had sent over English race horses to better the breed in America, stocked American waters with British fish, such as the turbot, tried transplanting trees and shrubs from England which he thought would flourish in the New England climate. Then he made an elaborate will. "Holding in grateful remembrance the manifold blessings I have derived from the principles distilled into me while at Boston . . . and feeling that my success in life is mainly to be attributed to the excellent education I received at that place. . . . I give and bequeath all the personal property of which I may be possessed . . . for the establishment of three schools for naval education." One was to be in Boston, one at Newburyport, and one at Nantucket. Evidently, he realized that this was too ambitious and costly a project, and he destroyed the will but gave a copy to some American friends. Instead, he decided to concentrate his gift on Nantucket, the home of his ancestors.

In 1826, just after retiring from Parliament, he visited Nantucket for the first time. There he met a Mr. Jenks, of Boston, who had married a Coffin, and on his wife's death had moved to Nantucket with his two children. Jenks found, to his astonishment, no provision for public education, whereupon he sued the town on a state law. On Sir Isaac's arrival Jenks, as he says, "took the gouty old hero to 'Sconset"; and during the long drive over the commons, Sir Isaac told Jenks that he wanted to leave something to benefit his kinsfolk but didn't know just what to do. Jenks, boiling over with zeal on the subject of free education, pleaded for the establishment of a school. At all events, Sir Isaac made his decision to that effect while visiting in Nantucket. The result was the founding of a school for the benefit of the descendants of Tristram Coffin, together with the gift of a schooner for the instruction of the boys in the sciences of navigation and seamanship. A school building was erected on Fair Street, capable of taking care of 250 children. Since almost everybody on the island could claim descent from the original Tristram, the school became from the first open to all of the old stock. Sir Isaac, however, stipulated that a small tuition must be paid quarterly; "for," said he, "that which costs them nothing folk are wont to despise." The little red brick building on Winter Street, with its Doric columns, was erected later, in 1852–53. Until 1898 the school gave an academic course. Now it is used entirely for manual training and household arts, but it still perpetuates the generous thought of a Coffin who had never even lived in Nantucket.

The Sir Isaac Coffin School very nearly "died aborning," because the state legislature declared that the use of the donor's civil title was "an undemocratic vanity." The donor responded with some asperity that he could think of plenty of other places where he might put his money without being annoyed; whereupon the law makers climbed down from their high horse. When, finally, the new school was dedicated, Sir Isaac came for the ceremony, and as he walked up from the wharf to the scene of the exercises, young girls in fluffy muslin preceded him, strewing flowers in his path. That is a picture one would like to have seen!

The melancholy sequel to the story of this gift is that Sir Isaac's pet project, that of developing master mariners among Nantucket boys, long ago faded away into the limbo of forgotten things, because the American merchant marine went practically out of existence.

Upstairs on the wall of the school hangs a fine portrait of the benefactor, painted by Sir William Beechey. And nearby is a lithograph of him in his admiral's uniform, topped by a tremendous cocked hat, standing beside a gun on the ramparts of a fortification. To the story of his generosity should be added the fact that, during the War of 1812, Sir Isaac exerted himself for the liberation, by exchange or parole, of the members of the Coffin clan that languished in Dartmoor prison. Once, to his astonishment, a negro presented himself as a Coffin.

"Oh," observed the Admiral gravely, "you a Coffin, too?"

"Yes, Massa."

"How old are you?"

"Me thirty years, Massa."

"Well, then," sighed Sir Isaac, with a mournful shake of his head, "you are not one of the Coffins, because they never turn black until forty."

ROBERT RATLIFF 1794–1882

In contrast to Sir Isaac Coffin, baronet and admiral, resplendent in gold lace and ten gallon cocked hat, and the favorite crony of King William IV, this Old Boy is a very modest figure of a man. He, too, was not born in Nantucket, but he lived on the island sixty-two years and became as much a landmark of the town as the Old South Wharf where he had his shop. He, also, had been in the British navy, a contemporary of Sir Isaac; but he was, like the hero in *Pinafore,* only "a humble foremast lad," who doubtless more than once knew the stinging crack of a cat-o'-nine-tails across his back.

In a corner of the Old North burying ground, easily seen from the road, stands a headstone of polished granite, quite the handsomest one there. This was the last tribute of his many friends in Nantucket. The inscription on the stone reads:

Robert Ratliff, born at Newcastle upon Tyne, Feb. 25, 1794. Died at Nantucket, Feb. 28, 1882, aged 88. He was a seaman on board the ship Northumberland 84 guns, under command of Sir George Cockburn, that conveyed Napoleon Buonaparte to St. Helena, in 1815, and received marked notice from the great emperor. He was also a seaman in the Albion, 74, in the attack on the city of Washington, in 1814. In 1820 he was shipwrecked on the island of Nantucket where he resided the remainder of his life. He was well known as a successful master rigger for fifty years, honored for his integrity, respected for his uniform courtesy, and beloved for his kindness and generosity.

That is a considerable biography in itself, but it does not tell all. He fought in the Battle of Copenhagen under Lord Nelson. During the winter of 1813 his ship was frozen in the ice of the Baltic. He had scarcely received his discharge and reached home again, when a press gang pounced on him and dragged him back to the fleet. He was on a merchant ship, in 1820, when the wreck occurred on the South Shore of Nantucket which stranded

A DOORWAY ON QUINCE STREET

him penniless in a strange land. He tried one whaling cruise, and then set up his shop as a "master rigger." In the palmy days he had plenty to do; he owned his own home on Hussey Street and enlarged his shop and equipment. Then the great fire of 1846 swept away everything. After that the rapid decline of the whaling industry made it impossible for him to build his business up again to what it had been. Indeed, it was not long after the Civil War when there was no business at all for a rigger, and at the last he had to be admitted to "Our Island Home"—the poorhouse.

Mr. F. C. Sanford, who was a very public-spirited citizen, wrote a story of the old man's life for the Boston *Advertiser,* and started a public subscription, which bore among others the names of the Governor of Massachusetts, the Mayor of Boston, President Eliot of Harvard, and Henry Wadsworth Longfellow. Sanford also managed to get from the British Charitable Society a pension of fifty dollars a month, which, however, arrived only a few weeks before he died.

In the Whaling Museum there is a splendid portrait of this Ancient Mariner, painted by Eastman Johnson. It was done when Ratliff was an old man, yet the face that looks out at you, crowned with its odd, white cap, is strong, ruddy, and keen. The eyes have a humorous twinkle and he does not appear a day over fifty.

The most interesting fact about him is his contact with Napoleon, and it was the one great memory of his life. He had served under Nelson and fought at Copenhagen, one of the four important battles associated with Nelson's fame, yet that naval hero seems to have made little impression on his imagination. Perhaps he never even saw him. But that voyage on the *Northumberland* with the Man of Destiny! How often he must have told that story to his cronies in the tavern or on the wharf!

Once, not long before his death, a visitor came to see him. His sight was failing then, and sometimes his mind wandered, but when the talk came round to that memory the wrinkled old face lighted up with enthusiasm.

"Buonaparty pinched my ear once!" he exclaimed. "I was a lad of twenty then, sir. He asked me in fair English how I liked sailoring and whether they gave me enough to eat. . . . How did he look? Well, I'll tell you. He was full figured, you know, and wore small clothes and an old green coat. He never spoke to the English officers." Ah, but he did to a poor young bluejacket, impressed into the navy; aye, and pinched his ear and smiled! And when the ship arrived at St. Helena, Robert carried Napoleon's personal effects ashore with his own hands.

The fallen Emperor had been England's dreaded foe for many years, and yet this young English seaman fell under the spell of that personality like any grenadier of the Old Guard. To the end of a long life, that was his great, transcendent experience, his hour of glory.

Let us hope that Robert Ratliff has found his hero in the Elysian Fields, and that "Buonaparty" pinched his ear again!

WALTER FOLGER JR. 1765-1849

This member of the Old Boys Association was a direct descendant of the first, Peter Folger. He was the fourth of twelve children, and in him old Peter came to life again as he had in Benjamin Franklin. In fact, there is a marked resemblance to Franklin in Walter Folger's portrait hanging on the wall of the Atheneum today. In him, at any rate, the old Folger versatility, the love of things scientific and mechanical, the dexterity of hand, the inventive genius, the executive ability, all were reborn. Nor should it be forgotten that Peter's force of character and integrity were inherited as well.

The boy's childhood and youth came during the hurly-burly and misery of the War of Independence. He went to such schools as there were for his three R's; not, however, without astonishing his teacher by inventing new short cuts in arithmetic. One winter, toward the end of the war, he spent studying navigation in the evenings, with one Elisha Macy, who understood the science. Later, he and Elisha, with another friend, took up the study of algebra, without any instructor. He was sick in bed most of the year 1783, but apparently cured himself by studying a book on the new method of figuring longitude at sea by lunar observation. This he afterward taught the whale men of Nantucket.

The boy should have gone to Harvard, but the family funds were low because of the losses of the war, and Walter's father seems to have had some Quaker scruples against sending his boy to college. One biographer says that, in those days, higher education was "lightly esteemed" on the island.

When the French Revolution began, Walter organized a small group of his friends, including his sister Phebe, into a class to study French, with no teacher save an occasional stray Frenchman who had landed on the island. He learned the language so well that he could read French encyclopedias of science and master Lalande's work on astronomy, a copy of which fell into his hands from a shipwrecked French sailor.

At the age of twenty-two he devised a project for an astronomical clock which he built during the next two years. This ran without a hitch from 1790 until his death in 1849. It is the most complicated domestic timepiece on record. For example, the little golden ball, representing the sun, is made to rise and set at the exact moment for every day in the year. The sun's place in the ecliptic—whatever that is—is recorded by the same machinery, together with all the phases of the moon, indicated by a silver ball, and the times of full tide for Nantucket. The monthly changes are taken care of, including the extra day for February in leap years. Further up on the dial face is a slit to record the year. Exactly at midnight New Year's Eve the date changes, and the inventor had the fun, of seeing the century figure shift on January 1, 1800. In short, this clock did everything but predict the weather.

During Folger's lifetime the intricate mechanism worked perfectly, but after his death some clumsy hand tried to clean it and the clock never recovered from that experiment. It is still, however, in the proud possession of the Folger family, and is exhibited for the benefit of outsiders once a year at the Hospital Fair. Every piece of it was made by the inventor's own hands except the glass that covers the face. It is a miracle of ingenuity and exquisite craftsmanship, yet it looks at first glance like any other grandfather's clock.

Naturally, he was an exceptional watch and clock maker, and as a young man he followed this trade for a while. For diversion he taught himself medicine and surgery. He mastered all there was to know of these sciences and had some practice as well. During the epidemic of "putrid sore throat"—diphtheria, no doubt—he had among his patients two physicians, who apparently had faith in him, and he did not lose a single case. He also sent away for the virus of smallpox and inoculated without charge anyone who came to him.

The deft hand that built the clock was called into play while he was, even as a young man, director of the Nantucket bank, for it was Walter Folger who engraved the bank bills.

Meanwhile, having seen legal tangles come up in the bank's affairs, he set himself to learn the law, again with no outside help. At this he was so successful that his fellow townsmen sent him to the Massachusetts legislature, where he served for six years. After that he was the judge of Common Pleas for another six years. Next he served two terms in Congress, and while in Washington as a Congressman, 1817 to 1821, it was said that when his seat was vacant everyone knew where to find him—at the Patent Office.

All the while, during his self-education and the pursuit of his various trades and professions, he was corresponding on scientific subjects with other men of similar interests and attainments, among them Bowditch and Thomas Jefferson. Just for fun, too, he was always at work on experiments and inventions.

In the desperate days of the War of 1812 he set up a factory on Nantucket for the carding, spinning and weaving of cotton and wool. His was one of the earliest power-driven looms in the United States. When he went to General Court he was proud to be able to say that every stitch of clothing he wore had come from his little factory. He closed it down after the return of peace and the rebirth of the whaling industry made it unnecessary to create employment for the town.

In his fifties, he made with his own hand a reflecting telescope which was in that day the finest in the country. He invented improvements for it, and with this instrument discovered spots on Venus which even the great Herschel had failed to discern.

One of the most interesting sides of this man's character was his indifference to making money. For instance, it occurred to him that the casks used for stowing oil on the ships were not designed for the greatest economy of space. He calculated that in the right type of cask the diameter should be equal to the length. He persuaded a cooper, despite indignant protests, to make such a cask, and the inventor proved his point. Although this discovery saved millions for the whaling business, Folger's interest in the matter ceased as soon as he had demonstrated that he was right.

He was also ready at all times to welcome youthful disciples and admirers from off-island. Sometimes this hospitality must have been trying to his wife, for if some ardent young mathematician came to him, eager to learn, Walter Folger gave not only freely of his time but would take the young aspirant into his house and give him room and board.

Altogether, he was a remarkable man, and he made a profound impression on his contemporaries. In a memoir of Daniel Webster, published in 1831, there is an account of his visit to Nantucket to try a case. It contains this note: "On the island of Nantucket he met with a philosopher, a mathematician, and an astronomer in Walter Folger, worthy to be ranked among the great discoverers in science."

Of all the Old Boys Walter Folger has the only claim to real genius. If he had moved to Boston, Philadelphia, or New York, where there were scientific societies and universities, he might have been recognized as a second Benjamin Franklin and won a reputation that would have been nation-wide. But he cared as little for fame as he did for money. He preferred to live quietly in his home town among his old friends and neighbors. Thus did his philosophy triumph over his science.

CHAPTER VI

SOME OF THE "OLD GIRLS"

SINCE the term "Old Boys" has been borrowed for the alumni of Nantucket, it is appropriate to refer to the alumnae as the "Old Girls." The island town produced, as we have seen, some remarkably interesting men; and yet, in some respects, they were surpassed by the women. Indeed, it is probable that no other community in America of the size of Nantucket has ever given to the country so many extraordinary women. It has already been observed that the local conditions tended to develop individualities among the men. This was even more true of the women.

From one point of view, the isle must have been a land of lonely women, but from another it was a feminist's paradise. At any time the women outnumbered the men four to one. There were many spinsters, many widows, and the married women were separated from their husbands for periods of two to five years. Normal home life must have been almost unknown. "Society," also, in the usual sense, must have been impossible, for there never were half enough "suitors" to go around. The boys were schooled by women until twelve or fourteen; then off they went to the hard, masculine schooling of the forecastle. The girls just had to hope and pray.

The result was that, under these abnormal conditions, the fashionable eighteenth century and early nineteenth century theories about women's place could not work. What was the

STONE ALLEY

use of being a clinging vine when there was no sturdy oak to hang on to? The heavy home chores that normally were performed by men had to be handled by women, to get done at all. Home accounts had to be kept to balance with the results of the whaling voyage, and the duty devolved upon the women. It was not long before much of the business of the island also gravitated into their hands, and there it stayed until their little shops came in competition with the mainland. The tradition soon grew up that the woman was the home manager in the financial sense as well as domestic. The wives prided themselves on what they could save and also what they could make by household arts or little businesses "on the side."

For pleasure they "visited" each other and drank gallons of tea. And they didn't mind a good stiff walk, either. There is a story of some young women who started out on a day's visiting and wound up at home after twenty-two miles of tramping over sand and rutted roads!

The result of these conditions was a practical, forceful type of woman. In a letter dated 1815, a young lady of Nova Scotia, who was visiting Nantucket for a few days, made the observation that the women she saw were "Homely and Ungenteel." Catty, no doubt, but many of the portraits in the Historical Museum and elsewhere suggest that she may have had some grounds for that remark. Mary Gardner Coffin, for example, who went as a bride to the famous "Oldest House" in 1686, traveled six times to Boston before her portrait was completed. Doubtless the poor painter did his best, but Mary's lineaments, one might say, are painfully practical. Nay, the Nantucket ladies of the old days were not musicians, composers, painters, opera singers, poets, actresses, or queens of the salon. No one of them was a Serpent of the Nile. They were practical, intellectual, and moral. They won fame as mathematicians, abolitionists, philanthropists, suffragists, and preachers—reformers generally—and were all noted for their force of character. What tough old century plants they were! How many of them refused to die until they had reached the nineties, despite lives of the utmost activity! From these women have been selected the following as most typical and most important.

MARY COFFIN STARBUCK 1645-1717

First among these in point of time, and possibly in force of wisdom and character, was Mary, the seventh child of Tristram and Dionis Coffin. She was born in Haverhill, Massachusetts, in 1645, and was a girl of fifteen at the time her father settled on Nantucket. At the age of seventeen she married Nathaniel Starbuck and bore him ten children, of whom the oldest, also named Mary, was the first white child born on the island.

These ten children must have kept her reasonably busy, but she soon became noted for her unusual gifts of mind and character. Despite the prevailing seventeenth century notions of women's place in councils, the settlers soon learned to value her advice and ask for it. Her husband, realizing her superior gifts, modestly took the part of consort to the queen, but she, on her part, never gave an opinion without prefacing it with "my husband and I think." The pair were devoted to each other. For years she was the informally elected Deborah of the island folk, and was frequently referred to as the "Great Woman."

There are no special deeds to chronicle about her, for her dominant position was due entirely to her remarkable personality. She held no office, she was a busy wife and mother with a large family to care for, but her word carried almost the weight of a command.

Her most important single contribution to island history has to do with the Quakers. It was primarily through her that Nantucket became, more than any other town in the world, a settlement of Quakers. Her conversion to the faith occurred when she was fifty-six, at a time when her influence was at its height. An English Friend, John Richardson, left a detailed journal of his visit to the island in 1701, which was a few years after the earliest of the sect had preached there. On his arrival, he sought out Mary Starbuck as the most important personage. She welcomed him and offered to have his meetings in her own house. In due time she and her husband joined the Society of Friends. She herself was gifted with eloquence, and when she arose in meeting her hearers sat spellbound. There already existed a Presbyterian congregation, but with her conversion to the Quaker faith went all the force of her personal influence. The result was that a large proportion of the settlement joined the Society. For nearly two hundred years thereafter Nantucket was famous as a Quaker town.

In 1717, the "Great Woman" died. Her place as uncrowned queen of the island community has never been filled by another.

KEZIAH COFFIN 1723-1790

The next Old Girl on our list is one of the descendants of the doughty old Peter Folger. She may not have exhibited much of her ancestor's versatility and love of science and invention, but she had all of his practical, executive ability, and his fearless independence of character.

Something over a hundred years ago, a certain Joseph C. Hart arrived in Nantucket. He was a lineal descendant of Elihu Coleman, one of the early pillars of the Society of Friends, noted for his power of preaching and his stand for the abolition of slavery. At that time the old meeting house where Coleman held forth was being torn down, and Hart reverently removed one large cedar shingle, which he took home to frame in memory of his forbear.

On this same visit Hart gathered material for a novel, which he called *Miriam Coffin or the Whale Fisherman,* and dedicated, with a fine flourish, to his friend Sir Isaac Coffin. "This tale," he wrote, was "founded on facts and illustrating some of the scenes with which he [the author] was conversant in his earlier days, together with occurrences with which he is familiar from tradition and association." Hart came from his home in Westchester Co., N.Y., to avoid the cholera epidemic of 1832 and to visit the island home of his ancestors.

This book, published in 1834, went out of print and a new edition was published in 1872. Copies of that, also, are now extremely rare. At any rate, it seems to be a remarkably faithful picture of life on the island in the period of the Revolution, though heightened, of course, by the rosy light of romance. The heroine, called "Miriam" Coffin, is no other than the Keziah Coffin of real life. Apparently, Hart couldn't bring himself to give her such a name as she had to accept from her parents. To this day, therefore, there is much confusion as to her real name.

Keziah's outstanding characteristic seems to have been that she did not care a tuppence about other people's opinions. She was a Quaker, but she had to be summoned before the elders for the crime of keeping a spinnet in her house and letting her daughter learn to play upon it. She made no excuse about the matter, and when she was "set aside," which was their phrase for excommunication, it did not bother her in the least.

In the Frenchman Crèvecoeur's description of Nantucket during the years before the Revolution, he mentions her by name as "Aunt Keziah"; and cites her as an instance of the successful woman in business, for which the settlement was already celebrated.

The most famous period of her life was about the time of the American Revolution. Among the treasures of the Maria Mitchell library is a letter from Benjamin Franklin to Jonathan Folger, telling him that he is sending "Cousin Keziah" a box with his affectionate greetings. This letter was dated 1765. A decade later, Ben was not sending his cousin Keziah anything to speak of except maledictions, for she was an ardent Tory. In the dark days of the British blockade she wrote to Admiral Digby who commanded the British squadron on the coast. To him she expressed her loyalty to the King, described the hard straits of the islanders, and intimated that they were practically all Tories like herself. She begged permission to be permitted to have her own vessels trade between Sherburne and New York. All this while, by the way, her husband was off on a whaling voyage. This permission was granted by the Admiral and it resulted in giving Keziah a complete monopoly in trade. When every necessity of life was desperately hard to get, her ships were bringing in quantities of goods.

She had already built a town house on Centre Street which was by all odds the finest in Sherburne, and therefore quite the scandal of the Society of Friends. She flouted the local traditions still further by building that house just as she wanted it. She made it face north, an unheard-of thing, for no matter how the streets ran the houses had always faced south. She changed the traditional roof-line, also, in order to make her house look like the ones she had seen on the mainland.

In one of its rooms she had opened a shop, and now she proceeded to rake in the profits of her monopoly. She charged exorbitant prices, and her attitude toward her neighbors was "take it or leave it." If any buying was done, it had to be at her price; and though the good people groaned, they were obliged to come to her and impoverish themselves in order to get the bare necessities of life. She then took mortgages on their houses, wharves, warehouses, anything they could put up as real property, against the bills they could not pay.

At last, as may be remembered, the island people issued their proclamation of neutrality and were permitted to trade and obtain firewood and fish. This broke her monopoly. Her prices tumbled, but her fellow townsmen were not content; they combined and went after her to get revenge. Instantly, her grand financial castle crashed about her ears. Her neighbors naturally had no love for her and they showed no mercy. Every time she tried to sell a piece of property, such as a house or a ship, to meet her obligations in New York for goods purchased, she had to let it go for a song. There would be only one bidder, and he would offer an absurdly low price. In a short time she had lost all her fortune. Her handsome town house went for less than half what the stone foundation had cost. Her country home at Quaise, about which there had been many dark rumors, she lost also; her vessels, warehouses, merchandise, were all swept over the dam.

This was the state of the things which her husband, Jethro, discovered on his return from a long whaling voyage. He managed to salvage a few pieces of property and begin over again. The novelist Hart has him say this to his wife, "Thy unchastened ambition, not content with reasonable gains, hath ruined thy husband, stock and flock! Get thee gone to thy kitchen . . . woman, and do thou never meddle with men's affairs more!" Personally, I don't believe he dared to speak to her like that, but it is clear from the course of Hart's narrative that the author was no feminist, and he wanted to point the moral that woman's place was in the home.

It should be added that these irregular business ventures of Keziah in the Revolutionary War were not her first. Her house in Quaise, just mentioned, had been for some time before the war the rendezvous of strange sloops and schooners, which entered Polpis harbor abreast of the house, and, after tarrying some time, departed. The evidence seems to be that, some years before she showed her devotion to King George in the Revolution, she had been cheating him by large-scale smuggling. It is said that between the cellar of her Quaise house and the shore was a tunnel through which, after the cargoes were landed among the bushes under cover of darkness, bales and boxes and barrels were brought into the house, and from there to her place of sale.

After her downfall she left the island with her head high. She had put on black to signify her distress at the rebellion against her King, and now she vowed that she never wanted to set foot on Sherburne streets again. But in her latter years her daughter brought her back. At that time she was not in the least chastened by her punishment and exile. No sooner was she again among the familiar scenes than she hired a lawyer to try to win back in the courts some of the property she had lost. Of course, she hadn't a ghost of a chance, and her attorney told her so, but she replied sharply, "I want thee to keep this in court as long as I live." Indeed, it was while she was hurrying downstairs to attend court that she fell and broke her neck. She was sixty-six years old.

Keziah must have been a Tartar. She loved a fight and single-handed took on the Society of Friends, or the entire town united against her, or the State of Massachusetts. She was beaten every time, but would never admit defeat. It must have been a hard fall downstairs to break that proud neck!

DEBORAH CHASE 1750–1818

This member of the Old Girls sorority was a well-known figure on the streets of Sherburne when Aunt Keziah was waxing rich by smuggling or by her British monopoly. No doubt they knew each other by sight, anyway. But Deborah belonged to the younger generation and, like her brother Reuben in the navy, was a rebel; so perhaps Keziah looked scornfully past her when the great, strapping girl came striding down the street, though I am sure she never refused any money that Deborah brought into the shop.

As far as I know, this is the first time the girl has ever appeared in a list of eminent Nantucketers. Probably most of the other ladies would look down their noses at her, though they certainly could not look down on her in a literal sense unless they climbed to the second-story window. But Deborah Chase has my terrified allegiance, and here, at the safe distance of a hundred and fifty years, I lay this tribute at her feet.

There can be no mistake about it, Deborah was Some Girl. She was built on the same specifications as her gigantic brother, Reuben, and apparently was just as strong. Among those penciled recollections of Reuben Chase by F. C. Sanford inside the copy of the *Pilot,* mentioned in the sketch of her brother, is a notation as follows, "Reuben Chase had a sister Deborah who weighed 350 pounds and could fling a man of 160 pounds weight upon a house top." Evidently, Mr. Sanford remembered her too; or, at any rate, knew the fame of her. Let Mr. Fontaine Fox take his imaginary Powerful Katrinka away into outer darkness before the picture of this woman of fact! What a scene for the imagination! Perhaps some man is foolhardy enough to annoy her, or perhaps she feels just playful. At any rate, in the sight of her admiring townsfolk, she lightly tosses the poor fellow up on the roof. One cannot help wondering how he landed and what broke his fall as he came rolling down off the shingles. Clinging vine, indeed! What a pity that Fenimore Cooper did not see her as well as her brother. We might have had more interesting women in his novels.

It is too bad that we do not have more information about her. But there are a few stories that are eloquent of her prowess. At one time during the Revolution, the Tories, or "Refugees," raided the island town, ordered everybody within doors and posted armed sentries at the street corners. It happened that the Chase family needed water. The nearest pump could not be reached without passing a soldier on guard. Deborah announced to her father that she was going out to get some water. "Don't," he begged, "thee will get a bayonet in thee!" "I'd as lief die one way as another," she answered, and off she strode, swinging a pail in each hand.

As she came to the corner, there stood the sentry, who started to challenge her with the bayonet. With a quick overhand swing she slammed him on the head with a pail, and knocked the man senseless. Deborah continued her walk to the pump, filled her pails and returned, pausing only to note that the sentry still lay, bloody and insensible, where she had felled him.

There is another story of how she went to the store to buy flour, and there decided to get a whole barrel at once. To save time waiting for delivery, she picked up the barrel and carried it home, uphill all the way!

In those days there was a try works on the beach near the North Wharf for extracting oil from the blackfish that were still brought in from offshore. Nearby were vats where the oil was poured to cool off. One day the men who worked there sent a little girl up the street to get bread for their lunches. Since this was a heavy load for the child, Deborah volunteered to carry the basket back for her. As Deborah came down the street, high, wide, and apparently handsome, if we may judge from the sequel, one of the young men announced his intention of kissing her. This foolhardy wretch had recently been married and was still wearing the coat of his wedding day. Deborah warned him that he had better not try any nonsense on her. But there were the other men looking on who had heard his boast and the fellow made a try for a kiss. It did not get far. In a moment she had flung him like an empty valise into the nearest vat full of oil, wedding garment and all. It is quite probable that after that public oil bath, the man was glad to ship on a long cruise to escape the laughter of the town.

There is one other incident. It seems that a drayman made

himself a nuisance by constantly driving his wagon against the corner of the Chase house. Deborah's peace of mind was greatly disturbed. She expostulated, but the man was, even as truck drivers are today, singularly insensitive to suggestions. The collision with the corner of the house deliberately occurred again. Deborah strode forth and taking hold of the dray she tipped it bottom up in the middle of the street. It probably took ten men to right it again, and it would have been worth ten dollars to have seen the driver's face when he witnessed the performance!

Alas, we know too little about the doughty Deborah. I have looked in vain among the bushes and brambles surrounding her brother Reuben's grave to find her resting place. Evidently she does not lie there, or else her headstone has gone the way of many another. Did she ever marry? Yes, she did. Imagination staggers at the picture of anyone attempting a courtship of the 350-pound Brunhilde, but she met her Siegfried in Siasconset and married him in 1772, when she was twenty-two. Just how the wooing was conducted is not on record. I suspect that she Got Her Man after the forceful manner of a Canadian "Mountie."

It would, of course, be a privilege indeed if one could go back in history and see the other eminent Nantucket ladies, but for my part I should like most to be allowed to return to Sherburne on that day when, from a safe vantage point of a second-story window, I might see the Dynamic Debbie nonchalantly flinging a 160-pound man up on the housetop or tossing that other fellow into the oil tank. Ah, what an Olympic champion we lost by her being born too soon!

SOME OF THE "OLD GIRLS"

LUCRETIA MOTT 1793-1880

Henceforth in this chapter we must be prim and proper with prunes and prisms, for the two women that follow became national figures, both of them bursting with talents and virtues. The first is Lucretia Mott, born a Coffin, of straight descent from old Tristram, and by temperament another Peter Folger, being descended from him on her mother's side. She did not have, it is true, old Peter's scientific interests, but, like Aunt Keziah, she did inherit his fearless independence of character; only in her case, unlike Keziah, her independence and courage were devoted to humanitarian causes. Lucretia was the pure, unselfish flame of the crusading spirit. At the same time, unlike most crusading knights of either sex, she had a winning personality.

She was born in the house on the southwest corner of Fair Street and "Gardner's Lane,"—this was once called "Lucretia Mott Lane"—a large three-story, white house, now "Ship's Inn." The family soon moved, however, to the house next south on Fair Street, and this she remembered as the home of her childhood. While her father was off on a long cruise, her mother kept a little dry goods store in which Lucretia assisted at the counter by the time she was ten.

She did not live long on the island, it is true, for at the age of eleven she went to Boston to boarding school, thence to New York state, and thence again to Philadelphia. In that city, at the age of eighteen, she married one James Mott, "in whom," writes Douglas-Lithgow, "she met her hallowed affinity and brought up a family of five children with exemplary care and maternal affection."

Certainly she managed to be a good wife and mother—her "hallowed affinity" always stood by her in her advanced thinking and doing—while she marched in the forefront of reform in America. She went over to the liberal Hicksite branch of the Quakers, yet always wore the Quaker dress. She belonged to the first anti-slavery society and was probably the earliest champion of woman's suffrage. She had a beautiful speaking voice and a remarkable gift of address at a time when no woman was supposed to be able to speak from a platform, and it was considered manly to try to howl her down. In short, there was no cause for the advancement of the race in general or her sex in particular, that did not enlist her time and energy.

During her long lifetime—she died in her eighty-eighth year —she impressed all with whom she came in contact by her personality and her talents. Whoever knew Lucretia Mott and tried to write about her was bound to use superlatives. Douglas-Lithgow, for instance, completes his portrait of her thus:

She has been happily described as the "bright morning star of intellectual freedom in America." Who can estimate the beneficent influences of such a life? Can time or death destroy them? A thousand times No! For they are linked with divineness and immortality.

However, I think that sort of praise would have embarrassed Lucretia, for she was as modest as she was gifted.

Twice in her later years, in 1869 and again in 1876, the sweet-faced old lady returned to Nantucket, bringing children and grandchildren with her. She showed them with great delight the old, familiar scenes of her childhood, and picked up the threads of friendship that had been dropped for sixty or seventy years. Time has not robbed her of the position she held in her own generation. She still stands out as one of the noblest women of her time.

MARIA MITCHELL 1818–1889

This member of the Nantucket sisterhood, like Lucretia Mott, left the island, but not until she had reached middle age and had won her fame right in the old home town. At the risk of being monotonous I must start off with the statement again that she, too, was descended from Peter Folger by her father. And, in Maria, Peter's love of mathematics and science blossomed again. It might be added that she was not a whit behind him or any other Folger in independence of mind.

Her father was not merely fond of mathematics, he was addicted to that dismal science. Maria's brother also fell a victim, and as Maria, too, had inherited a taste for figures it is not surprising to find that at the age of twelve she was already assisting her father in his calculations. In fact, for many years she helped him in preparing the nautical almanac, or correcting the navigating instruments of the whaling captains. Among other apparatus was a much prized little telescope, and the study of astronomy, which was the major interest of the father in the mathematical field, was shared enthusiastically by the daughter. In her diary she tells of long night watches in their little observatory with her eye glued to the telescope. Sometimes the temperature outside registered zero, and inside probably not much better.

It was with this little Mitchell telescope that she made the discovery which gave her an international reputation. One evening, October 1, 1847, there was a party going on in the Mitchell's apartment. At the time, since her father was the cashier of the bank, the Mitchells had moved to the upper story of the bank building, and Maria's observatory was on the roof. As was her custom on such occasions, Maria slipped away to her beloved instrument just to see what was doing in the universe. She stayed longer than usual, and on coming back whispered to her father that she had seen a new comet. Mr. Mitchell went back with her and confirmed the discovery. The news was posted to Harvard as soon as possible. Two days afterward an Englishman also found the comet, and other observers followed, but Maria Mitchell of Nantucket had been the first.

There was a gold medal which had been offered by the King of Denmark for the discovery of a heavenly body by telescope, and very properly this medal was awarded to Maria Mitchell. That made her famous overnight, and she was made a Fellow of the Academy of Arts and Sciences, the first woman to win that honor. Old Asa Gray, who was the secretary of the organization, grimly erased the word "Fellow" and substituted "Honorary Member," though he had no right to do so after the formal action of the Academy, making Maria a "Fellow" in spite of her sex. Asa certainly did hate to see a woman come into that organization! Various incidents like that helped to make Maria a militant champion of the rights of women.

She was by temperament very independent anyway. Among the records of the Friends in Nantucket is a notation to the effect that on "8 mo. 31, 1843," Maria Mitchell was "disowned because she had neglected the meetings and told the committee that her mind was not settled on religious subjects and she had no wish to retain her membership." No sharper comment could be made on the hopeless conservatism of the Quakers of that day.

Ten years after her discovery of the comet she made a trip to Europe, and as her reputation had long since preceded her, she had a happy time with all the famous astronomers and mathematicians of the Old World. She even had a *tête-à-tête* with the "toothless old Humboldt," who entertained her with reminiscences of his friend Thomas Jefferson.

Meanwhile, for twenty years, she served as Librarian at the Atheneum, having begun her duties there when she was still in her teens. She looked after the reading of the young very carefully. If any book struck her as not edifying, she caused it to be "lost" until such time as the directors came round for their annual inspection, when the missing volume would appear, only to be lost again the next day. (What would she have done with *Huckleberry Finn*?) Among the young boys off on their first whaling cruises she had many friends, and helped them out with their Bowditch or taught them the use of the sextant.

Meanwhile, in 1861, the new woman's college, Vassar, had been founded, and what could be more appropriate than to appoint Maria Mitchell as the first professor of astronomy? She taught there with distinction for twenty-three years, at the end of which time she retired as Professor Emerita, in Lynn, Massachusetts, the city to which she had moved with her father after her mother's death. There she herself died in 1889.

The Quaker-grey house on Vestal Street where she was born is now maintained as a memorial to her, together with the observatory in the side yard. Likewise the building across the street, where her father once taught school, is now a Maria Mitchell Library of scientific books, especially those relating to Nantucket. There one may still see the little brass telescope—only a three-inch lens—with which she discovered the comet.

When Maria was invited to go to Vassar she demurred at first because she had never had any experience in teaching and was afraid that she might fail. There is many an institution today which would decline to employ her because she lacked instruction in pedagogy. But, somehow or other, she impressed herself on all Vassar, even among those who were not in her department, because of the combined charm and force of her personality. There are still white-haired women who come to Nantucket, making a pilgrimage to the museum, because they were in Vassar under Maria Mitchell. Perhaps colleges could stand more Maria Mitchells and fewer experts in pedagogy. All the while that she was teaching she continued her research work in astronomy, such as her studies of Jupiter and Saturn, and her photography of the sun.

It is to be regretted that she did not find in Nantucket her "hallowed affinity" like Lucretia Mott. Probably there were none to be had. But Maria would have made somebody a grand wife, and she ought to have passed on her fine qualities to another generation.

In the biography, written by her sister, Mrs. Kendall, there is a wealth of quotation from Maria Mitchell's diaries and letters that shows her independence and dry humor. But the authors of the *Nantucket Scrap Basket* tell one story which was not included by Mrs. Kendall, and which makes such a delightful picture that it must be repeated here, even if it isn't prunes and prisms.

While on her way to visit her sister in Cambridge, Maria remembered her doctor's admonition to take lager beer as a tonic. Suddenly the bar-keep at a corner saloon was amazed to see a tall, majestic Minerva of a woman, with white curls neatly arranged under her black bonnet, sail grandly up to the bar, and order a bottle of beer, which she carried off under her arm. When she presented the bottle to her brother-in-law to be opened, her sister asked in amazement, "Where did thee get it, Maria?"

"At the saloon on the corner."

"Why, Maria, doesn't thee know that respectable women don't go into such places?"

"Oh," she replied, with the air of one who had taken care of that aspect of the case, "I told the man he ought to be ashamed of his traffic."

Apparently, Professor Mitchell was not one who bore correction meekly. Miss Starbuck, in her book of delightful reminiscences, *My House and I,* says that one rash person called out to her, "Oh, Professor Mitchell, there's a hole in your stocking!"

"What," was her frigid reply, "only *one?*"

A Vassar girl once ventured to call attention to the fact that the famous astronomer's shawl was trailing on the ground, and was told, "I prefer it that way."

Of these Old Girls and Old Boys, Maria Mitchell carried off more degrees and honors than all of them put together, indeed, more than any other American woman of her generation. It would be tedious to list all the laurels that came to her in her lifetime. But it is worth noting that in 1893 the new Boston

Public Library bore among the names eminent in art, literature, and science, incised on its stone frieze, that of Maria Mitchell. In 1907, a tablet to her honor was placed in the Hall of Fame in New York University, and fifteen years later a bronze bust of her was unveiled there. She is one of seven women admitted to that Valhalla of national genius, a shining honor for her native town.

As one looks back over this roster of Old Girls, one characteristic stands out which is common to them all. As the saying goes, they were all "strong-minded." And this trait would naturally spring from a community which was left almost entirely in the hands of women as was Nantucket in the old days. These ladies salaamed to Almighty God, but they had only contempt and scorn for Devil or man, the last two being frequently lumped together. They loved Causes, and the smoke of battle was the breath of their nostrils. How can they be happy in heaven, where there is nothing to reform?

CHAPTER VII

TWO HUNDRED YEARS IN A QUAKER TOWN

AT the close of the seventeenth century, earnest apostles of the Society of Friends came to Nantucket, notably Chalkley, Richardson and Story. We have already seen the consequences of the visit of these Quaker missionaries in the conversion of Mary Starbuck, and the resultant swing of a great part of the settlement toward the Quaker sect. By the middle of the eighteenth century, there were two thousand belonging to Quaker congregations, and these included the wealthiest of the island.

There have been ungodly ones who have suggested that the reason for the amazing spread of this denomination was that it appealed to the thrifty instincts of the islanders. No way of getting to heaven could be, on the surface, so economical, primarily because there was no paid minister. While the Presbyterians of Sherburne had to figure out their pastor's salary as a major part of the budget, the Quakers preached to each other free. And what could be a better way of checkmating wives and daughters with yearnings for expensive finery than the Quaker rule of plainness and simplicity? At any rate, the people of Nantucket took up the new faith with warm enthusiasm, and probably the life of the island town would present a better picture of Quakerism in America than that of Philadelphia, which was always a city of fashion, the capital of the colonies, and constantly receiving an influx of new elements.

DOORWAY ON ORANGE STREET

TWO HUNDRED YEARS IN A QUAKER TOWN

That the first hundred years are the hardest was true of the rule of the Friends in Nantucket. No Puritans ever exercised more tyranny in the name of Divine law than the Quaker Overseers. Sometimes they came into conflict with the worldly powers. For instance, since the tax of 1757 was levied for the expenses of the French and Indian War, the Quakers of Sherburne decided that it would go against their conscience, as well as their purses, to pay it; whereupon the local tax gatherer entered the homes of the pious dissidents and extracted silver spoons, salt and pepper boxes, pewter platters, and other such valuables, by the process called "distraining," until he had what he considered the equivalent of the tax. There is no record of the Nantucketers trying to nullify any more taxes, no matter what they were for.

In 1772, Stephen Hussey was sent to the General Court of the Province of Massachusetts Bay. For some reason the elders decided that "no Friend can sit in that Assembly." Stephen refused to resign, and was promptly "set aside," or excommunicated.

In some of their practice they seemed to make unnecessary attacks on human impulses. For example, in the old burial plot of the Friends' Meeting House on Saratoga Street there are, it is said, five to ten thousand Quaker dead that have no marking stone and never had one, because any memorial to the dead was forbidden. The story is told of a young woman who lost her husband, and for fear that in time she might not be able to find the spot where he was buried, stole out at night and planted a wild rose on his grave. For this crime she too was "set aside."

The prejudice against the "world's people" seems especially hard to understand among Christians who certainly had their share of human kindliness. But if your neighbor was a Presbyterian and you became attached to him and his family, you were liable to be put "under dealings"; that is, receive a solemn visitation from the Overseers who would point out to you the error of your ways. If a Quaker married one of the World's People, it meant excommunication, too, without any further "dealings." And sometimes the Presbyterians resented this attitude. "Did they ever hang Quakers, Grandma?" asked one little girl of a non-Quaker Coffin family. "Yes, my dear," replied Grandma with grim emphasis, "and richly they deserved it!"

Then, for some unaccountable reason, the sect took the most hostile attitude against all forms of beauty, not only the vanity of personal adornment but everything that cheered the eye and ear. In one of the "Minutes" of the eighteenth century Quakers is a recommendation that the faithful plant the useful vegetable in their gardens rather than bright flowers! No wonder that the arts languished in Nantucket, and her citizens, who won distinction, men or women, had to turn to the "safe" science of mathematics.

In dress this plainness became a cult in itself, and what originated simply in a protest against the ridiculous and extravagant fripperies of the time of Charles the Second was a hundred years later the glum uniform of a Brahman caste, in which the materials could be as costly as money could buy, but the cut and color distinguished the wearer as a member of the Elect. The whole story of Quaker dress sums itself up in the unvarying formula, that the innovation in clothing was at first roundly denounced, then gradually accepted, just as everybody else was giving it up, and finally became a badge of the sect when no one else would wear it.

In 1803, for example, a young man in Nantucket was cast

into outer darkness because he had tied his hair instead of letting it hang lank on his shoulders. One of the objects of suspicion was the button. Because there were so many useless buttons on a man's coat in the seventeenth and eighteenth centuries the Quakers made a solemn attack on the button generally, in favor of hooks and eyes. Buckles, neckcloths, and wristbands also had to be carefully watched or one would be brought "under dealings" for frivolous attire. One old lady of Nantucket was taken to task because she wore gold-bowed spectacles. The "broad brimmed hat," which is supposed to be a distinguishing mark of the Quaker gentleman, belongs to the nineteenth century, and it amounts only to being a survival of an older fashion rather than anything designed especially as a Quaker uniform. The examples in the Nantucket Historical Museum are not different from hats worn elsewhere by conservative men of the period.

For the women, too, the famous "Quaker bonnet" was entirely a nineteenth century affair. In the previous century the women wore a wide, flat hat. But once set as a Quaker fashion, the hideous coal scuttle bonnet became standardized like that of the Salvation Army. In one of these typical bonnets a girl's face was completely hidden unless you came upon her bows on. Next to the bonnet was the shawl, which was an important item taken over by the Friends. They learned to cultivate the delicate art of adjusting it so that it "set" properly on the shoulders, and that other art of giving it a "flip" in order not to sit down on the rear corner. All in all, the costume which we are accustomed to think of as the typical Quaker costume of the women, follows that of the famous English Quakeress, Elizabeth Fry, whose full-length portrait was familiar on both sides of the Atlantic.

Another Quaker "testimony" was the use of "thee" and "thou" in speech. George Fox thought that the use of "you" was an affectation of flattery unbecoming a Christian of simple ways. Accordingly, as in the matter of hats, just as the fashion had died out of using the second person singular, the Quakers revived it and have perpetuated it until this day. But to the outsider it was a mystery, for there seems to be no grammar or consistency in it whatever. Among American Friends "thee" is used as the subject of the verb in the third person, "thee thinks." In England, I am informed, the Friends use "thou" correctly, but pronounce it "thu." Hart, in *Miriam Coffin,* makes his characters use "thou" with grammatical correctness all the way through the book. The Quaker poet, Whittier, used a quirk that seems to have been his own invention, "thee are." From Nantucket letters and diaries one may find other varieties, "thee hast heard me," "if thou wish," and that high priestess of learning, Professor Maria Mitchell, writes, "if thou thinks." Accordingly, Gentle Reader, if thee thinks thou wouldst write a novel on Old Nantucket, thee can use these pronouns as thou wills and nobody can possibly object!

The Quaker stand against art, poetry, and music, dancing, and drama, suffocated any yearning for beauty. Even family portraits seem to have been denounced as a vanity, though silhouettes were permitted, perhaps because they were in black and could never be very flattering. The objection to music was always hard even for a Quaker to explain. The minister Clarkson argued, among its other ills, that music "produces hysteria and weakens females for motherhood." We have already seen that Aunt Keziah was excommunicated because she introduced a spinnet into her house. A certain Elizabeth Black, who for years kept a little shop in Nantucket, refused to sell even a jew's harp.

"Cousin Elizabeth, has thee any jew's harps?" the children would ask.

"No, child, and no other harp that the Israelites used for diversion or devotion."

As if life were not glum enough without music, pictures, books, for these also were practically non-existent in eighteenth century Sherburne, the fashion prevailed of giving the children the most grotesque Hebrew names. When a baby was born the parents seem to have turned to one of the "begat" chapters of the Book of Numbers and picked at random. Culled from any Nantucket genealogical table one finds men's names like these: Amaziah, Antipas, Zenas, Zebdial, Barzillai, Jedidah, Abishai, Shubael, Zephaniah, Bethuel, Obed, Jared, Peleg, Libni, Micajah, Uriah. The women fared somewhat better, for in addition to Hepzibah, Hebzibeth, Puella, Merab, Bethiah and Keziah, there happily were Priscilla, Phebe, Eunice, Lydia, Lois and Love. These Old Testament names sound as if Nantucket were the place to find the Lost Ten Tribes of Israel, yet these strange labels may have been due to an effort to try to find something to distinguish one Coffin, Folger, or Starbuck from a hundred others of the same name. Yet even the Pelegs, Obeds, and Barzillais are duplicated over and over again. To this day the various Annie or Mary Folgers, Coffins, and Starbucks are distinguished from each other by the middle name or initial.

For a picture of life in the Quaker town during the eighteenth century there is Hart's novel, *Miriam Coffin,* already mentioned. Hart visited the town a hundred years and more ago, and made his notes when there were still many old people who remembered the life of the preceding century. A still more authentic picture was left by a French *émigré*, Hector St. John Crèvecoeur, in his *Letters from an American Farmer*. He was descended from a Norman noble family and was educated in England. He bought a farm in Pennsylvania and became an enthusiastic colonial American. He traveled extensively through the colonies before the Revolutionary War, and the *Letters* are the result of his observations.

Among the travels made by Crèvecoeur was what must have been quite an extended visit to Nantucket, the "Sherborn" of his book, and nothing in all his American scenes fills him with quite so much enthusiasm as the little Quaker town, at that time the whaling capital of the world. Here is an extract from his description of the place:

Would you believe that a sandy spot of about twenty-three thousand acres affording neither stones, nor timber, nor meadows nor arable, yet can boast of an handsome town, consisting of more than five hundred houses, should possess above two hundred sail of vessels, constantly employ upwards of two thousand seamen, feed more than fifteen thousand sheep, five hundred cows, two hundred horses; and has several citizens worth 20,000 pounds sterling! . . . Had this island been contiguous to the shores of some ancient monarchy, it would only have been occupied by a few wretched fishermen. . . . No, their freedom, their skill, their probity, and perseverance have accomplished everything. . . .

The buildings he describes as plain but serviceable. The streets were only lanes of sand, but after all there were few carriages to use them, for everyone walked. He did confess to a dreadful stench from the try works but he did not let a trifle like that disturb his enjoyment, because, he remarks cheerfully, "it is unavoidable."

This is what he has to say about the rule of the Quakers:

The Friends compose two-thirds of the magistracy of the island. . . . In all this apparatus of the law, its coercive powers are seldom wanted or required. Seldom is it that any individual is amerced or punished; their jail conveys no terror; no man has lost his life here judicially since the foundation of the town, which is upwards of a hundred years. Solemn tribunals, public executions, humiliating punishments, are altogether unknown . . . no gibbets loaded with guilty citizens offer themselves to your view; no soldiers are appointed to bayonet their compatriots into servile compliance. . . . How? . . . Idleness and poverty, the causes of so many crimes are unknown here. . . . The simplicity of their manners shortens the catalog of their wants.

He was struck, too, by the lack of dissipation when the whaling fleets came home, and attributes the fact to the custom of early marriages which, he says, is universal. Young people in this community, he adds, can marry as early as they like, since the girl does not have to have a dowry and the young man is secure in his employment. When the whalers returned from a long cruise, "the pleasure of returning to their families absorbs every other desire."

One amusing comment on the men is that they can be recognized by their gait as Nantucketers. It is "a peculiar agility which attends them even to old age," and he thinks this liveliness of the sinews may be attributed to the fact that they are "so copiously annointed" with whale oil all their days!

In general, he found an ideal democracy in the life of the town, and withal a "decorum and reserve so natural to them that I thought myself in Philadelphia." These people, he declared, "have all from highest to lowest a singular keenness of judgment unassisted by any academical light. . . . Shining talents and university knowledge would be wasted here; it would pervert their judgment." He is impressed by the fact that the two religious denominations, Friends and Presbyterians, kept a truce with each other, and he notes that the rich people are the Quakers.

Of the professions he found only two doctors. "What need of Galenical medicines when fevers and stomachs loaded by the loss of digestive powers are so few?" And there was just one lawyer. As for him, he got along because he had married one of the richest heiresses on the island, not because of his practice. This amounted only to a little collecting of loans on the mainland.

What struck Crèvecoeur most was the dominant position of the women and their handling of the business of the place, exemplified by Keziah Coffin. He could remember nothing like that in the France of the ancient régime! The Nantucket women were no flirting parasites, the sort of women that Addison satirized in his *Spectator* papers. "To this dexterity in managing their husband's business whilst he is absent the Nantucket wives united a great deal of industry." The men "cheerfully give their consent to every transaction that has happened during their absence and all is joy and peace. 'Wife, thee hast done well,' is the general approbation they receive for their application and industry."

TWO HUNDRED YEARS IN A QUAKER TOWN

Crèvecoeur does not remark it, but as a Frenchman he must have been struck by the absence of a lover in a society where husbands were at sea for years at a time. It is easy to imagine what a French novelist would make of the situation. There would be a touching farewell taking place on the "walk" atop the house between the beautiful lady and her lover:

"Armand, my beloved, I recognize my husband's ship in the outer harbor. Farewell, until the next cruise."

No, there was nothing of the sort in the traditions of the old Quaker town. However, the visitor observes that "the absence of the men leaves the town quite desolate, and this mournful situation disposes the women to go to each other's houses much oftener than when their husbands are at home; hence the custom of incessant visiting has infected everyone and even those whose husbands do not go abroad. The house is always cleaned before they set out, and with peculiar alacrity they pursue their intended visit, which consists of a social chat, a dish of tea, and ever hearty supper." The young men get wind of where they may be sure of a welcome and repair thither to "assemble with the girls of the neighborhood. Instead of cards, musical instruments or songs, they relate stories of their whaling adventures. . . . Puddings and pyes and custards never fail to be produced on such occasions, for I believe there never were any people in their circumstances who live so well even to superabundance. As inebriation is unknown, and music and dancing are held in equal abhorrence, they could never fill all the vacant hours of their lives without the repast of the table."

In short, whenever a young blade home from a whaling cruise had a mind to sow his wild (Quaker) oats, or have a good time with his girl Friend, he would repair with the other gal lants to somebody's house where he could spin a lengthy yarn about how he struck an eighty-foot spermaceti, and finally go staggering home stuffed with custards and "pyes."

In *Miriam Coffin* there is a chapter, which reads as if drawn from a tradition in the town, of a grand dance that was held surreptitiously in the loft of a candle factory, and it is quite possible that there were occasions when the young people kicked up their heels in spite of the Overseers. A dance had to be *sub rosa*, of course. Thomas Coffin was expelled from the Society of Friends for "allowing a company of young people to dance in his house in Siasconset."

Naturally, the men had no such pious atmosphere in the forecastle of the whaling ships into which they were pitched, at the age of twelve or fourteen, out of a strict Quaker home. Their companions were, too often, the scum of the seaports— Negroes, Kanakas, and what not—men whose ideas of pleasure were not modeled on custards and conversation. And when the ship was far out at sea doubtless some of the inhibitions insensibly let down. If, for example, a whale was sighted on "First Day," as they called Sunday, it is safe to say that there was often the same eager scramble to kill and cut him up as on any other day of the week. And among the natives of the Pacific islands there were no Overseers—quite the contrary.

One curious note which Crèvecoeur makes about the women of Nantucket (Sherburne) runs as follows:—

A singular custom prevails here among the women at which I was greatly surprised; and am really at a loss how to account for the original cause that has introduced in this primitive society so remarkable a fashion or rather so extraordinary a want.

They have adopted these many years the Asiatic custom of taking a dose of opium every morning; and so deeply rooted is this that they would be at a loss how to live without this indulgence; they would rather be deprived of any necessary than forego their favorite luxury. This is much more prevalent among the women than the men, few of the latter having caught the contagion; though the sheriff, whom I may call the first person on the island, who is an eminent physician beside, and whom I had the pleasure of being well acquainted with, has for many years submitted to this custom. He takes three grams of it every day after breakfast, without the effects of which, he often told me, he was not able to transact any business. . . .

The writer goes on to say that it is hard to see "how a people always happy and healthy . . . yet should want the fictitious effects of opium . . . but where is the society perfectly free from error or folly? . . . I can truly say that I was never acquainted with a less vicious or more harmless one."

The same Mr. F. C. Sanford whose notes on Reuben Chase were quoted in an earlier chapter, was so indignant at the opium story that he declared such a libel on the women of Nantucket was in itself proof that the Frenchman never came to the island at all. Of course, it was entirely possible that opium should have come back from China, together with the silks, porcelains, lacquer wares and teas that found their way into the Nantucket homes, and yet the story is not confirmed by any other testimony.

Speaking of tea, there is a little pamphlet, now long since out of print, entitled *A Nantucket Idyll*. It is the reprint of what was supposed to be a letter written in 1745 by a Nantucket girl, Ruth Starbuck Wentworth. It was edited by the well-known Unitarian

DOORWAY ON UNION STREET

clergyman of a generation ago, Robert Collyer, who believed that the document was genuine. Since then there have been those who cast doubt upon it, but this Higher Criticism is going too far! At any rate, it is a perfect little short story. The gallant young captain of a returned ship, who supplies the romance for the writer of the letter, brings a package of tea, and the interesting fact is that no one in the house knows how to brew it and the captain has to show them how. But it could not have been much later before tea was a common beverage in Nantucket. Certainly it was so in Crèvecoeur's day.

In the course of his visit the "American Farmer" made the rough trip over the "commons" to Siasconset and also out to the famous inn at Polpis. Here was the place for sport and entertainment for those islanders who owned a chaise. The guests amused themselves by "chatting and walking about, throwing the bar, heaving stones, etc." These, he says, "are the only entertainments they are acquainted with. This is all they practise and all they seem to desire." He escorted thither to an entertainment a lady, "one of the many beauties of that island (for it abounds with handsome women) dressed in all the bewitching attire of the most charming simplicity; like the rest of the company she was cheerful without loud laughs and smiling without affectation. . . . I had never before in my life seen so much unaffected mirth mixed with so much modesty. . . . What would a European visitor have done without a fiddle, without a dance, without cards?" In short, Hector had a grand time.

Of course, the Quaker conservatism was a strong obstructing influence in the history of the town. The first chaise was regarded as Babylonish luxury and for a long time the owner dared use it only for funerals or to give invalids an airing. The first umbrella, imported from France, suffered a similar condemnation. When inoculation was introduced, the Overseers put it strictly under the ban, so that all Quakers who took advantage of it should be "disowned." It was tampering with God's providence.

But this strict, drab view of life could not last indefinitely with the Friends any more than the Calvinism of Jonathan Edwards which flourished at the same time across the Sound in the rest of Massachusetts. Tom Paine made a shrewdly humorous comment on the sect when he wrote,

Though I reverence their philanthropy I cannot help smiling at the conceit that, if a Quaker had been consulted at the Creation what a silent and drab Creation it would have been. Not a flower would have blossomed its gaieties, not a bird would have been permitted to sing.

If Nantucketers wandered over the commons in October they must have admired the rich crimson and scarlets of the huckleberry bushes and sumachs, and maybe they observed to themselves that God could not be a Quaker. Or maybe their eyes were by custom so dull to color that they never noticed anything of the sort.

The second hundred years of Quaker history in Nantucket were not so hard; that is, not so hard on the members, but they were a progressive story of decay as far as the sect was concerned. At the end of the second century there was not a Friend left on the island which had been so long the undisputed stronghold of the faith. Like every other religion it thrived on persecution but could not survive prosperity. This second century really should begin with the time when the island began to recover from the suffering of the War of 1812. From that time on dates the distinctly newer period of the town's history. It is this era that furnishes most of the portraits of the sea captains and their wives which one finds in the Historical Association Museum, in the Atheneum, the Whaling Museum and in various homes. Already in the portraits of the eighteen-twenties one can notice the elaborate headdresses, turbans, side curls, and ribbons that show that the Quaker rule was losing its grip, at least on dress. The mere fact that one had a portrait painted would have been frowned upon a half century earlier.

To this period also belong the handsome houses and fine doorways of the town. In Crèvecoeur's day there was only one brick house, and that apparently was as plain as the frame ones. But it was not long after the Greek revival hit the rest of America, in or about 1830, that the new fashion in architecture spread to Nantucket. And this coincided with the high tide of prosperity in the whaling business. Quakers would still "thee" each other, but their costumes, and their customs, were getting steadily more like those of the "World's People." The leaders might even still wear drab, grey, and black, but their cellars had the choicest wines, and their tables shone with the finest china, glass, and silver.

Just at this time, about 1830, the great schism among the American Quakers struck Nantucket. A Long Island farmer, with a gift of eloquence, rebelled against the harshness and conservatism of the sect. He readily drew to himself many disciples who also had been getting restive under the rigid discipline of the elders, and the heresy spread to Nantucket, splitting the Quakers into two hostile camps. This division widened when, shortly after, the "Gurney heresy" carried away still more adherents than the Hicksite. The orthodox Quakers were known as the "Wilburites" after the American champion of the old order. From this time on, the liberals or heretics gained the upper hand, especially with the younger generation.

There are many documents to help form a picture of this later, nineteenth-century period. One of the earliest and most amusing is a letter written by a Mary Ann Hopkins, a visitor from Nova Scotia, who passed a few days on the island in the year 1815. A copy of her letter is in the Historical Museum. She was the guest of the Presbyterian minister, but no thought of Predestination or Foreordination weighed down her bubbling spirits. What she wanted was a Beau. Here are some extracts:

The packet landed at Long Wharf, where the Captain presented a young gentleman, handsomely dressed, and of fine countenance, and genteel and pleasing address. . . . Oh, my dear girl—I protest my Heart has received a Shock of which it will not easily recover, for Alas,—he is Married. . . .

This place far exceeds any idea I had formed of it. . . . We have just set out from a walk through the South part of the Town. . . . The houses generally have an appearance of Neatness and Comfort. . . . The soil is of sand which rendered walking quite a fatiguing exercise. . . . In the evening a gentleman came to call, and he distinguished himself by conversation at once easy and polite. . . . When we parted for the night we were all equally delighted and some half in love with him. . . . Oh my dear Frances, why are we not favored with (at least) One or Two such Gentlemen? . . . The ladies here are all uncommonly Homely and Ungenteel. . . .

There seems to have been a decay of beauty since Crèvecoeur

took the lovely girl to the party at Polpis!

The diary and letters of Maria Mitchell, as quoted by her sister in her biography, furnish especially interesting material for a picture of the early part of the century. There were those bleak days in winter when the mercury went to zero and the island was blockaded by ice, such as the January and February of 1857, when Nantucket was cut off from all communication for seven weeks. February was referred to in the old language as the "trumpery" month, because so little news could come to the island, and people had to talk about "trumpery" things. On more than one occasion news had to go all the way to London and back again to Nantucket. Maria, during the long cold snap of 1857 killed time by memorizing long passages of poetry. And those little frame houses must have been chilly places when the gales howled down from the northwest. One girl correspondent complains that as she writes the ink is constantly freezing on her pen. There were no furnaces, of course, in those days, and although there were fireplaces in the bedrooms nobody thought of building a fire in them unless the occupant were ill. Going to bed and getting up again during the winter must have called for magnificent will power!

It is interesting to note the change coming over the Quaker thought and habit in this early nineteenth century. Maria's mother was of the most conservative temperament, but her father was for stepping out a bit. He loved bright colors, bought a gay carpet and flowered wall paper, chose red bindings for his books, and even went so far as to paint the supports of his telescope vermilion! The great act of daring in the Mitchell household had to do with a piano. The first piano in Nantucket, by the way, had been imported by Captain Seth Pinkham for his daughter, in 1831. Maria had no musical ear, but she conspired with her sister to buy a piano and keep it in a neighboring building, where the sister could practice secretly. After a while, knowing full well what her father would think of the matter, Maria and her sister contrived to have their parents invited out one afternoon, while the piano was bootlegged, so to speak, into the house. When the father and mother returned they heard the gay worldly notes of the instrument.

"Why, of all things!" gasped the scandalized mother.

"Come, daughter," laughed the unregenerate spouse, "play something lively!"

The result of this heresy was that Professor Mitchell was put "under dealings" by the Overseers. But he was at that time cashier of the Bank, which held the mortgage of the Meeting House. He pointed out to the committee sent to wait on him that it was very improper to put under dealings a member who held a note against the Society. This reasoning seemed to satisfy, for Friend Mitchell kept the piano in his house, where no doubt his daughter played him all the "gay tunes" he wanted to hear.

Maria did not learn to play the piano but she did something far worse—she learned to play cards. In her diary of those dreary days during the ice blockade she has this entry: "Last night I took my first lesson in whist playing: I learned in one evening to know the king, queen, and jack apart, and to understand what my partner meant when she winked at me." Of course by this time she had been out of the orthodox congregation for many years. And it might be added that Walter Folger had withdrawn long before the "disowning" of Maria Mitchell. The old order was fast cracking up. It is interesting that before 1835 advertisements appeared in the local paper of lectures on dramatic literature, philosophy, of quadrille parties and schools of dancing and music, of concerts by the Handel and Haydn Society, and similar worldly follies.

But the orthodox congregation did not surrender without a struggle. As late as 1864 Narcissa Coffin, an eloquent preacher, was silenced because she "went ahead of her guidance"; that is, she prepared her sermons beforehand instead of trusting to the inspiration of the moment. For twenty-five years the poor woman was under the ban of silence, both in this country and in England. There are still people who remember seeing her come out of meeting on First Day and stand on the steps, her eyes suffused with tears. When the ban was lifted, all of her accusers being dead by that time, she went to Europe and preached there with great success. Narcissa is the last notable example of the Orthodox discipline in Nantucket.

All these changes in the thought and life of the community were hastened by the rapid decay of the whale fishery and the scattering to the mainland of so many of the old families. Dancing, cards, music! And then toward the end of the century a daughter of the Coffins and one of the Folgers went to the "Continent," even to Paris, to study painting, and with eminent success. The girls of the old Quaker families took to wearing first hoops, then bustles, with their hair in "Chignon" and "waterfall" and bangs, according to the fashion—ah, well, let the curtain fall on the Quaker tradition of Nantucket! In 1867, the last formal meeting was held and the local congregation of Friends became extinct. For another score of years a handful of old people still crept to meeting on First Day, but, it is said, no one was ever moved to speak. In 1900, Eunice Paddock, the last member of the Society, died, just at the close of the two centuries of its history in the island town. In Nantucket gardens there was a "Quarterly Meeting rose," so called because it bloomed at the time of the summer Quarterly Meeting of the Friends. The rose still blooms, they say, but there has been no quarterly meeting on Nantucket for two generations.

The sect passed out because it was hidebound and unreasonable in its conservatism. A communion that could drive out such characters as Walter Folger and Maria Mitchell was doomed. But it is not fair to lay too much stress on that aspect of the Quaker rule. It should not be forgotten that from these same Friends sprang the earliest opposition to slavery, the first declaration against war, and also the first demand for equal rights for women. In their way of life there was a beautiful sincerity, wholesomeness, and simplicity, against which their conservatism need not weigh so heavily after all. Perhaps there is nothing so much needed in this twentieth century as the return to something of the Quaker attitude toward life.

CHAPTER VIII

OLD NANTUCKET IDIOMS AND CUSTOMS

ANY community cut off on an island thirty miles from their neighbors of the "Continent," and making their livelihood in waters seven to ten thousand miles away, would naturally develop not only individual characters but peculiar ways of speech and local customs. Ten years ago the late William F. Macy and Roland B. Hussey published a little book, the *Nantucket Scrap Basket*, into which the writers put many curious details about the old speech of the Island. Some of the words are survivals of speech of the early English settler. Others seem, like Topsy, to have "just growed" in the sandy streets of Nantucket. Some of the idioms quoted in the *Scrap Basket* may be found elsewhere in New England, and still others are common to sea-faring men wherever English is spoken on quarter-deck or in the forecastle. But there are many more which are peculiar to this island. A few may be noted here, practically all of which are now obsolete.

One of these, "coof," denoting an "off-islander," was probably the old Scotch word meaning a fool or a simpleton. At first, "coof" was applied to visitors who came over from Cape Cod; then it came to be applied to any "foreigner." All who were not Nantucketers were "coofs." Following is a list of other idioms:

A "squantum" was a picnic.

To "flax" meant to hustle, "get busy."

BAPTIST CHURCH, SUMMER STREET

To "fudge" was to fool or bamboozle.

To "perceive" was to recognize, as when one "perceived" his friend on the street; used of all the senses.

To "whittle" was to fuss unnecessarily, or to waste time.

"Always a little astern of the lighter" meant being always just behindhand or too late.

To "gam," participle "gamming," was to visit between ships at sea.

Where any other Yankee would "guess" and the Southerner would "reckon," the Nantucketer would "presume likely."

A "porch" was the ell attached to the house in which stood the kitchen.

Nantucketers always sat "under the window" in order "to watch the pass," that is, the going to and fro of people in the street. Perhaps "under" came to be used because Nantucket windows tended to be high from the floor.

"Rantum-scooting" was a word meaning rambling at large with no particular place to get to. This was derived, apparently, from "random" and "scouting." If a party went off on the commons for a day's picnic, just wandering about at pleasure, that was "rantum-scooting."

Since the farmers of Polpis were supposed to be distinguished by their rustic manners, "Don't act Polpisy" meant "don't be so countrified"!

When anyone was insincere one said of him that he was "all teeth and outwards."

If a man were on the island from the Continent, he was referred to as "on from off."

These are only a few specimens from a vocabulary that would make a little *Dictionary of Phrase and Fable* all its own.

CUSTOMS

The most characteristic custom has already been touched on several times; namely, the fact that it was the women who handled the business of the town, even in the eighteenth century, when such a thing was unheard of elsewhere. Indeed, out of the fact that at any time there were in the town four women to one man, grew customs peculiar to the feminine society of the community. For instance, the perpetual round of visiting, noted by Crèvecoeur, arose from houses empty of companionship.

Yet, despite the scarcity of eligible men, aggravated by the fact that no Quaker girl might marry a Presbyterian, there was in the eighteenth century a secret society of young women pledged to refuse to marry any young man who had not yet struck his whale. That is, if Hart's testimony may be trusted in *Miriam Coffin*. Mary Folger, in that story, addresses her suitor, Julius Imbert, M.D., an off-islander, in these portentous words:

"I am the youngest member of a certain female association whose rules I have promised to observe. . . . I cannot, under my vow, accept thee as a suitor of mine until thou hast well and truly proved thyself worthy of alliance with a whale-fisherman's daughter."

"How can I prove it to you?" asks the young man.

"By going on a long voyage and killing thy whale!" answers she.

This makes the young physician extremely angry, but he says nothing. He goes aboard a whaler, makes his long voyage and kills his whale. Then he returns, the wedding is arranged, and while the bride waits on the appointed day, Dr. Imbert leaves her and the island, sending her a letter to explain that this is his revenge for what she inflicted on him. The young woman "falls senseless," which in those days was the approved thing to do under the circumstances.

The author goes on to say that "the reasons assigned by Imbert in his letter, for the desertion of Mary, gave the deathblow to that extraordinary association of women upon Nantucket, whose secret meetings took on the semblance of freemasonry." It is a good story, anyway.

The same William F. Macy, who was a storehouse of information about the old days on Nantucket, says in his *Story of Nantucket* that the quaint custom of "bundling" flourished in the town, and indeed, according to very old ladies whom he knew, lasted on the island long after it had disappeared from the mainland. Of course, it must have been much more comfortable when courting Hepzibah for Zephaniah to stick his cold feet under the quilts during those icy winter evenings. But somehow it does seem rather at variance with the Quaker tradition for the young people to get into bed together, even if they were fully dressed and there was a little fence between them. It is noteworthy that Macy is the only historian of Nantucket who has remarked the custom.

Marriages, in the Quaker practice, were simply a matter of standing up before witnesses. Afterwards, there was a wedding party at the house, to be sure, but it had to be very seemly. If Quakers were invited to the weddings of Presbyterians they waited in an adjoining room while the service was read by the minister, but came back in plenty of time for the refreshments.

Childbirth was the occasion for a grand female holiday. All the women relatives and friends that could pack into the house arrived to offer their services and their advice, also to eat whatever the "expectant mother" had on her shelves. Macy tells of one occasion when eighteen women were settled in a house for a grand visitation among themselves while their poor friend upstairs was in labor.

There were plenty of children born to those whaling families, and the midwives must have had a good practice. There was one of special fame, Rachel Bunker. When she died at the age of eighty, in the year 1795, she had had twelve children of her own, one hundred and twenty-two grandchildren, and ninety-eight great-grandchildren. Thirty-three years of her life—probably after she had finished with her own dozen—she devoted to helping other women bring their offspring into the world. Her record stands at 2994 children, including thirty-one pairs of twins. Just how many died under her hands is not mentioned. There should be a bronze tablet somewhere to a woman with a record like that.

The first object to greet the eye of the returning whaler was the group of four windmills on the hill. In the War of 1812, by the way, these were used to signal home-coming vessels of the proximity of British ships of war, by pointing the arms in the direction where these ships lay. From this point of vantage the landsman could sight the distant sail on the horizon better than anywhere else in the town. Accordingly, it was the custom for the millers to report the ships, read their signals of identification, and pass the word to boys, who ran as fast as they could to be the first to reach the home of the captain on the ship sighted. For this service a boy would receive a dollar. In every whaling captain's home shiny new dollars were saved for the purpose. In some families it was also the tradition to bake a large loaf of gingerbread in honor of the return just as soon as the ship was identified. In a later period of town history a blue flag was hauled up on a pole, bearing the word "ship." This meant that a vessel had been sighted, and everybody scrambled up the "walk" to see. In those days, before telegraph and wireless, the Nantucket whaling ships had a code of flag signals which could report to the watchers on shore the company to which a vessel belonged and the size of its cargo of sperm oil. When a ship flew its flag at half mast, it meant that the captain had died during the voyage.

Another tradition was that of putting a black cat or kitten under a tub or bucket the night before a ship was due to sail. This was supposed to create a head wind that would make the setting out of the harbor impossible. In 1825, the Governor of Massachusetts visited the town. To be sure, his packet was stuck on the bar at the entrance all night, but the rising tide got the Governor's party clear and he was received in state by the town officials; indeed, he had the honor of being welcomed in Latin by Micajah Coffin. At any rate, there was a young aide in the Governor's party who was greatly struck by the beauty and liveliness of the girls. One in particular impressed his heart deeply. When it was announced that the party must be off at daybreak, the girl put a kitten under a bucket and, sure enough, a stiff head wind arose which compelled the Governor and his staff to spend the next day on the island. That happened to be "First Day," and the young aide went to the Quaker meeting. Whatever it was in the exhortations that the women and girls made in meeting—including his inamorata—the young man was disillusioned, or frightened, and fled. Perhaps after that broken romance the number of deaths by suffocation among the black cats on the island fell off.

Of the social life of the women left to themselves for such long periods of time, Crèvecoeur has drawn the picture of what he saw in the years just before the Revolutionary War. Another, of the next century, is furnished by the record of a club of young married and single women and men. This record, made by the secretary of the society, is a precious document treasured among the possessions of one of the First Families. The entries are made in an exquisitely fine hand—how did they manage quill pens like that? Interspersed here and there are comical little drawings in pencil, interesting for what they show of the contemporary dress of the members; also the carpets and other furniture of the rooms, which are faithfully rendered.

The first entry is of November, 1829. On the fly leaf in pencil is a memorandum, evidently of the members of the club, and it is interesting to see that by 1829 Friends and Non-Friends mingled in the same social organization. The "world's people" are distinguished by having surnames, while the Quakers are listed only by their given names. There happened to be two Quaker Williams, so "William the Jeweller" is distinguished from "William the Teacher."

Strictly speaking, the club was the "Social Reading Society," but the title was too formal for general use. It was informally the "Budget Club." The girls and young married women met weekly on Wednesdays during the winter, bringing their knitting and listening to a reading. At nine o'clock the male members came. Then original literary contributions were read and discussed. After that the whole company moved into the dining room for the "Budget." This was the name for a good, hefty repast, consisting of chowder—of clam, chicken, or fish—pork and beans, coffee cakes, "puffs," and cakes known from their shapes as "hearts" and "rounds." Once in a while the entire club would go on a picnic to Siasconset for a chowder, cooked there, or a light refreshment of crackers and wine taken over in the chaises.

If there had been any Quaker gloom over the assemblies of young people in an earlier day, the record of this club shows that there wasn't much left in 1829, for the temper of all the contributions is humorous and satirical. They have fun with each other and poke particular ridicule at the newly elected President Jackson. There is a clever burlesque inaugural address supposed to be delivered by Old Hickory. In this connection, there is a sly dig at the editor of the *Inquirer* for his trimming sail to the new administration. What is most surprising is that the style most frequently parodied is that of the Old Testament. Every now and then there is a chapter of diverting "Chronicles." For example:

1. Now in those days there sojourned in the land two young women—and the name of one was Lydia and the other was called Abby.
2. And on the 31 day of the month called December, they arrayed themselves in pink and fine muslin and wore curls upon their heads, —curls of their own wore they, for had they not paid for them?

There was also a set of epitaphs on the members, of which the following is an example:

> Here Philip lies, his praise let others *dis*cuss
> He had black eyes and a huge pair of whiskers.

The Budgeteers were not too particular about rhymes.

There is a strong note of aggressive feminine spirit with all the fun. One poem, for instance, suggests that the women be allowed to run things for a change. It begins thus:

> It seems that the lords of the earth can't agree
> Who they shall choose for the Presidency.
> What if we take the lead and oust both Jackson and Adams
> And instead of Messieurs let's be governed by Madams;
> I'm thinking we'll rule with a great deal less pother
> Of jarring and sparring from one to the other.

And this is a most excellent suggestion at the end,

> And instead of Congress to meet every fall,
> We'll think it much better to have none at all.

The "literary" contributions are not very valuable to be sure; nobody took them seriously anyway, but the record makes one sure that anybody who was privileged to belong to the "Budget Club" was in luck, because they were clever people and they must have had a great deal of fun.

THE CENT SCHOOLS

Whatever grudging concession was made by the Selectmen toward public education after the time of Mr. Jenks and Sir Isaac Coffin, all through the first half of the nineteenth century dame schools flourished on the tuition plan. These were for younger children. Also some girls, hardly out of their teens, made a little pin money by holding what amounted to nursery schools for very little children on Wednesdays and Saturdays to give tired mothers a chance for an outing.

The regular cent schools were for the purpose of teaching the three R's to youngsters of beginning school age. In some of the earlier schools teachers cheerfully accepted goods in lieu of currency. One mother paid her child's tuition by homemade yeast and another by a present of some andirons.

The cent schools got their name for their rate of pay, which seems to have been uniform for a long time. This was a cent a day per pupil. Frequently, so as not to be oppressed by a colossal bill of twenty to twenty-five cents coming in at the end of the month, the mother would put the penny into the lunch pail or tie it in the corner of the child's handkerchief every day, from which place the teacher would extract it. At one school it was customary for the children to carry their pennies to the teacher in their mouths, and on arrival discharge them into a tin cup, the same cup which was used by the school afterwards to assuage thirst. But that was before germs had been invented! Of course, in the early days the cent was a huge copper disk not so easy to lose or to swallow as the corresponding coin of today.

Other people paid their bill in one lump, as witness the following quoted by Helen A. Gardner in a paper to the Historical Association:

Job Coleman 2d

To Anne Macy, Dr.

For care of Ann Maria
from 5mo. 17 to 10mo.2

19 ½ weeks at 11	$3.25
Absent 4 weeks	.66
	$2.59

Received payment

Anne Macy

Nantucket
10 mo.2, 1841

Apparently, Miss Macy's rates were higher than the traditional cent, for it is seen from the foregoing that she charged all of eleven cents a week. But she gave a refund for absence!

The author of the paper just quoted says that the discipline in the school which she remembered was not more severe than a tap on the hand with the pointer or a few minutes spent on the "repentance stool." If a boy got too noisy at one recess he was kept in at the next. In this particular school, which was held like the rest in the teacher's home, he would then be held in the lap of a blind invalid member of the family, who would first lecture the boy on the error of his ways and then, that painful duty done, invariably would regale him with adventures of his whaling cruises!

It might be added that, along with the ciphering and copying of maxims in a Spencerian hand, the children of the cent schools were taught lessons in manners, a department of education that is all but neglected in our schools today.

THE TOWN CRIER

Probably longer than any other community in the country, Nantucket kept the town crier. This functionary served to advertise the wares, special sales, and so on of the shopkeepers of Nantucket, and interspersed these items with bits of news.

The most famous of these criers was Billy Clark. He is described by W. F. Macy in his history as "errand boy, window washer, bill poster, distributor of almanacs and handbills," in short, "a general factotum." In addition to his advertising, he announced the news. As soon as the bundle of newspapers was dumped on the wharf from the steamer, he would skim the headlines, or get someone to read them for him, since he was not a scholar, give a blast on his tin horn and then bawl his news items, following them up, from a sense of duty, with the advertising blurbs.

When the present moving-picture house stood on Main Street, operating as a roller skating rink under the management of two young Harvard students, they, as well as the townspeople, were astonished to hear Billy Clark deliver himself as follows: "President Garfield assassinated! There will be a grand carnival at the roller skating rink tonight. Everybody come!"

Billy Clark assumed certain duties of his own accord for which he was paid nothing. Every day he climbed the tower of the South Church to get the first glimpse of the incoming steamer. As soon as he spied it he thrust his tin horn through the slats of the belfry and tooted loudly to give everybody due notice of the great event of the day. Also, it must be added, he climbed up there at dawn on mornings after a heavy storm to scan the horizon for shipwrecks or vessels in distress, and that, in winter gales, was no mean service.

In a book on the *Nooks and Corners of the New England Coast,* published in 1873, the author, S. F. Drake, gives the following description of Billy Clark at the height of his glory:

This functionary I met, swelling with importance, but a trifle blown from the frequent sounding of his clarion, to wit, a japanned fish horn. Met him, did I say? I beg the indulgence of the reader. Wherever I wandered in my rambles, he was sure to turn the corner just ahead of me, or to spring from the covert of some blind alley. He was one of those who . . . knew all the other inhabitants of the island; me he knew for a stranger. He stopped short. First he wound a terrific blast of his horn. Toot,

toot, toot, it echoed down the street like the discordant braying of a donkey. This he followed with lusty ringing of a large dinner bell, peal on peal, until I was ready to exclaim with the Moor

"Silence that dreadful bell! It frights the isle
From her propriety."

Then, placing the fish horn under his arm, and taking the bell by the tongue, he delivered himself of his formula. . . . "Two boats a day! Burgess's meat auction this evening! Corned beef! Boston Theater, positively the last night this evening!"

He was gone, and I heard bell and horn in the next street. He was the life of Nantucket while I was there; the only inhabitant I saw moving faster than a moderate walk.

These town criers were self-appointed. Sometimes there were two to four in Nantucket at the same time, for a visitor in 1885 notes that there were in that year two other criers beside Billy Clark. This odd character died in 1909. One other crier survived him but not for long.

SHEEP SHEARING

The one great festival time of the whole year in the olden days was the sheep shearing. This took place on the "Second and Third Days" (Monday and Tuesday) nearest the twentieth of "6 mo." (June), on the shores of Miacomet Pond. In *Miriam Coffin* there is a full and picturesque description of the celebration as it took place in the eighteenth century, and in all important particulars it remained unchanged for generations. People came from Martha's Vineyard, Cape Cod, and elsewhere on the mainland to enjoy the spectacle. It was the chief occasion for family reunions with those who had left the island.

This shearing time necessitated rounding up the flocks which all the year had been roaming over the commons. They were next accounted for as to ownership and then washed and shorn. The poor animals led no easy life. It was early decided that grubbing for their own food and shelter made the sheep healthier. Besides, this policy was cheaper for the owners. So all the year through the creatures had neither shepherd nor fold. Sometimes, during the winter storms, they would huddle together on the edge of a bluff and get pushed off into the sea. Sometimes they were buried in snowdrifts. But evidently enough sheep survived this treatment to make the policy profitable.

There must have been plenty of work in the business of washing and shearing some ten thousand sheep and keeping them in order. Often rams would break loose and romp through the tents of the shearers and their families, or they would charge through the streets of the town and jump the fences into the gardens. The women folk had to provide vast pyramids of food for the men, and it could not have been all play for them, either.

But the shearing festival came nearest to being a circus that the island people ever enjoyed. There were gaudy catchpenny devices brought from the mainland, gypsy fortune tellers, flying horses, and so on, which gave the shearing ground a real circus appearance. There was also a famous character called "Blind Frank, the Fiddler," who furnished music for worldly people who enjoyed dancing. In short, it was the one season of the year toward which everyone, especially the young people, looked forward with the greatest anticipation.

The program of the shearing was simple; the first of the two important days was set apart for the washing and the second for clipping the wool. By daylight on Monday there were swarms of "tip carts" creaking over the route to Miacomet Pond. These tip carts were two-wheeled contrivances without springs or seats. The grown-ups rode sitting in kitchen chairs and the driver usually stood, as did the children who hung on to a bit of rope to keep from going overboard while the cart lurched and jounced. One of the time-honored practical jokes was to offer a ride to some girls, and then when a soft sandy place was reached to unfasten the hook that held the front end down so that the cart would suddenly tip up and dump the screaming young ladies on the ground.

At the shearing place sails were laid on the turf to catch the fleeces, and other sails were spread to give shade to the workers. Families erected their own tents, and poor widows and spinsters would set up stands for the sale of their cookies, cakes, and preserves. This was their one opportunity for a holiday sale, and it was the proper thing to do to buy liberally from poor "Cousin Nabbie" or "Aunt Debbie" as the most tactful way of giving charity.

Meanwhile, others of the town poor lingered on the outskirts of the festivities to glean the stray fluffs of wool that blew away during the shearing and clung to the bushes. This meant a good deal to them and it was not taking charity, either. When the shearing was done, the tip carts were filled with wool, and the children had to foot it home all the way along with the able-bodied adults. Tuesday night all hands were glad to get to bed.

It was also around shearing time that the Selectmen used to set a day for their annual "Perambulation." This meant that the elders would go round and about the town to see if everything was shipshape. It must have been an entertaining spectacle, for the solemn procession of Selectmen in their beaver hats was always accompanied by all the small boys and dogs. But it was a very good idea, which many a board of aldermen would do well to copy.

Finally, among the customs of Nantucket, should be included a homespun tradition of respect for manual labor. High thinking and hard muscular work were supposed to go together like butter and parsnips. Every boy, and also every girl, whether the parents were well-to-do or not, was expected to learn a useful trade. For example, Captain Seth Pinkham was able to retire at thirty-seven, a rich man for those days, yet his daughters had to to learn dressmaking. The idea was that a girl must not be found helpless if a reversal of fortune made it necessary for her to earn her bread. It is interesting to remember, too, as one looks at those three brick mansions on Main Street which Joseph Starbuck gave to his sons, that he required each one of them first to become a master cooper.

So much for the traditions, the turns of speech, and the old customs that made Nantucket distinctive in her early history, some of which survived to the close of the nineteenth century. They have now vanished with the fleets of whalers and the flocks of sheep. Only a few are left who can remember a sheep shearing or who were brought up on that odd mixture of nautical phrase and Quaker speech. These things, too, have long since faded into the mists of legend.

CHAPTER IX

THE MODERN TOWN

HAVING ambled in a leisurely way through considerable history and biography in order to get the right background for what the visitor sees in Nantucket today, we may now do some exploring among the streets, wharves, and old graveyards, and look more closely at some of the interesting buildings. It has already been remarked that Nantucket was a town "all of a piece," because it suffered from a severe depression that protected it from the horrors of the factory. But it was not only mills and slums that it escaped. Those years of financial doldrums were just the ones in which the rest of the country suffered a succession of architectural epidemics of the most noisome kind.

In the middle of the century, from the fifties to the seventies, came the fashion of Mansard roof and cupola, which was the gift to the United States of French culture from the Second Empire. Nantucket did not entirely escape this architectural blight, for here and there one may see an occasional Mansard roof, but the examples are rare and, during the summer, they are mercifully shrouded in the trees.

After the Mansarditis plague, there came a worse one, the "Victorian Gothic" or "Queen Anne." What this had to do with Queen Anne has never been explained, but it was just what Queen Victoria thought beautiful. This style has bay windows galore, wide, projecting roofs over the doorways, and all kinds

THE BARNEY HOUSE

Now Owned by Mr. C. E. Satler

of lace edging, scroll-saw work, and dribbles tacked on to anything that would hold them up. Alas, there are too many of these, but even one would be too many. For example, on one of the principal streets there are two of the most imposing specimens of this fashion of the eighteen-eighties. There they sit facing each other like two parvenu dowagers at a ball, too big, too white, bulging fore and aft, wearing a tiara atop their heads and hung with decorations at every joint.

Then, about the time of the World's Fair at Chicago in 1893, there arrived the worst pestilence of them all, what might be called the Tumor style. Buildings erected in this period of the gay nineties sprouted boils, turrets, verandas, bay windows—in short, excrescences of what the doctors call a "malignant growth." Happily there isn't much of that. This style was adopted by some people who built cottages along the sea, but there are very few in the town.

Next came the suburban bungalows, the familiar eyesore of every city in the United States. Indeed, ghastly specimens may be seen even in the beautiful countryside of England. Only a few are visible on the outskirts of Nantucket, for most of these, also, betook themselves to the vacation colony along the bluff or by the beach. And the latest fad of all, the kind of things one sees in the modern architectural journals, the sort of house that looks as if it had started out to be the turret of a battleship and then changed its mind—thank heaven, no one has fallen as low as that in Nantucket yet.

In short, the ugly exceptions are so few that the visitor has the delightful sensation of walking through a town that might be Cranford. It is still old New England at its best. And that explains the charm that is inescapable for anyone above the Broadway and Coney Island type of mentality.

Moreover, the town has an architectural history of its own; and it is a pleasant diversion to ramble in and out of the lanes and streets, noting the characteristics of the Nantucket home, and identifying them by their periods.

THE HOUSES

The earliest, or seventeenth century type of dwelling, was very simple. The outstanding example is the "Oldest House," built in 1686, which is now one of the proud possessions of the Nantucket Historical Association. On the hill near the windmill is another similar house, which was rebuilt from two derelict remnants of dwellings dating from the seventeenth century. Miss Gladys Wood's house on Upper Main Street is also a reconstruction from the remains of a home which belongs in this earliest period. Doubtless, too, in other old houses there are portions of seventeenth century dwellings which have been built into the newer structures. Such a one is the Tobey house, opposite the Civil War Monument on Main Street, of which one part dates probably from the seventeenth century, and is a whole generation older than the other part.

This oldest form of the Nantucket dwelling is known in Connecticut as the "salt box," but on the island it is called the "lean-to." It was a single house with two stories in front and with the roof sloping down to the first story in the rear. In the middle of the roof was a huge clustered chimney. The windows were casements with diamond panes; often no two windows were the same size. Some of these seventeenth century houses had only a one-room width in front and the chimney at

A LEAN-TO HOUSE WITH END CHIMNEY
Owned by Miss Gladys Wood

the end. Miss Wood's house just referred to is an example of this.

The next type was still a "lean-to" in shape, but less rough and massive in its structure and more roomy. The casements gave place to windows. The houses of this style were built in the early eighteenth century up to about 1730. Examples are the Elihu Coleman homestead, on Hawthorn Lane; the Josiah Coffin house on North Liberty Street; the Brock house on West Chester; the Tobey house just mentioned, and the Gardner house at the end of Upper Main. All these have the characteristics of the "lean-to," the long back roof sloping down to the first story in the rear and the large chimney in the middle. The lean-to type was perpetuated in Nantucket for fifty years. The internal arrangement and structural detail of all these earlier homes follow closely the cottage architecture of England.

The third type still had the door and chimney in the middle, but the back roof was raised to the full two stories, and there was often an ell. In this style of dwelling the inside structure has become still less massive than the earlier "lean-to." Number five Liberty Street, called the Paul West house, is a good example.

The fourth kind of Nantucket house represents the building boom in the prosperous era just before the War of Independence. This became the most distinctive type, for it was the favorite. Literally hundreds were built on this plan, and the style continued to flourish as late as the eighteen-forties or the time of the Great Fire. This was a "one-sided" house. The door was not in the middle, being flanked by a single window on one side and two on the other. The chimney, too, was a little off center. Usually there was a long ell on the rear. Inside, the exposed beams of an earlier design had disappeared, and there was often much handsome paneling. At first, this type seems very severe and plain, but it grows on you, because of its dignity and simplicity. There are countless examples of this kind of house but a well-known one, easy to identify, is the birthplace of Maria Mitchell on Vestal Street.

The fifth type developed as business revived after the Revolutionary War. Again the houses were built "double breasted," as someone has called them, with doors and halls in the middle. These homes began to show a real elegance; they became more spacious and stately. The Baxter house, 117 Upper Main, the Varney house, 100 Main, and the Joseph Starbuck house, on New Dollar Lane, are specimens of this fashion. It flourished between 1780 and 1820.

The last period of Nantucket architecture, which coincides with the golden age of whaling, from 1820 on to the Civil War, developed handsome houses of various styles. But all of them were classic in their ornament, after the late Georgian tradition or the neo-Greek. The houses characteristic of this period may well be called mansions, for they reflect the fortunes made during this generation.

Brick dwellings were rather late in coming to Nantucket. Dr. Chas. Congdon's house, at 5 Orange Street, is an example of a late eighteenth-century house that was built of brick. Even this had brick only on three sides and a wooden front until the fire of 1846, when the front was scorched and later replaced by brick. It was fortunate that there were some brick buildings at the time, for that conflagration was checked by four of these, the dwelling on the southwest corner of Main

THE TOBEY HOUSE

An Early Homestead of the Starbuck Family

and Orange, the Pacific Bank, the Coffin home—now the Ocean House—and the Mitchell house on North Water Street. After that, brick was held in high respect.

Dr. Congdon's home is also an example of the gambrel roof, which is rare in Nantucket. This kind of roof, which was so popular during the eighteenth century on the mainland, was never generally adopted on the Island. The Baxter house, mentioned above is the only one which has the "Dutch Cap" roof, one that slopes in four directions. This house dates from 1790.

Before leaving this last period of Nantucket domestic architecture we must mention that neo-Greek fashion that swept the country in the eighteen-thirties, leaving houses and churches that looked as if they had been begotten by the Parthenon. This fad was known to Europe too, but no other country in the world took the Greek pediment and pillar so enthusiastically to its bosom as the America of the eighteen-thirties. Perhaps this was largely due to the wide popular sympathy for the Greek war for independence. This style has been ridiculed, but there are those who find infinite charm in these graceful white churches with their Doric, Ionic, or Corinthian columns and classic spires, and the similar temple-like mansions of the well-to-do, which still survive in many a small town, North and South.

In Nantucket the best examples of neo-classic homes are the two well-known pillared mansions on Main Street. In others the classic style is more modestly restricted to the doorways and interior mouldings, as in the handsome entrance to the Hallet house, 72 Main Street, now known as Wallace Hall, after its present owner. Many people refer to the pillared style as "Colonial" or "Southern Colonial." Of course, it is not colonial at all and no more characteristic of the South than of the North. The fashion happened to coincide with a period of prosperity for Southern planters following the development of cotton-raising on a large scale, and many planters were able to afford to build stately mansions of this sort. This style held on for a long time in Nantucket, as witnessed by the present Atheneum, built in 1847 after the first had burned down, and the Isaac Coffin School building which dates from as late as 1852.

While many of the foregoing remarks about the types of architecture would hold good about most of the old settlements on the Atlantic seaboard, particularly New England, Nantucket developed its own characteristics in addition. In the first place, Nantucket houses, like those of the Southern town dwellings, such as in Annapolis, Maryland, or Fredericksburg, Virginia, planted themselves right on the street instead of standing far back on a lawn, as in most New England villages. Also, as in the Southern practice, the Nantucket householder preferred to have all the available space in the back, where he could enjoy his gardens and his privacy. And this, by the way, was also the old English tradition. And for neighborliness in a town where the husbands were at sea for such long periods, the dwellings snuggled close together.

Next, one notes the almost uniform dove-colored shingled sides and fronts which give the town its peculiar soft greyness. But in the first decade of the nineteenth century it was the prevailing style to paint the houses red (sometimes grey) for there was no white lead. The Quakers could not object to this ruddy hue, because that was the most economical paint one could use.

As we admire these old dwellings with their satisfactory proportions and their charming entrances, we marvel that the carpenters of that early day, working in an atmosphere of Quaker drabness, soaked in whale oil, could create such works of art. At that time Nantucket boasted no architects. The explanation generally given is that these builders possessed very fine books of house plans with all measurements and working drawings included. These books were published in England and represented the best of the Georgian and classic tradition. All one had to do, then, was to flip the pages and say to the builder, "I want that." Even so, the Nantucket carpenter must have had a feeling for beauty that wasn't in a book, for there are individual touches that distinguish the dwellings here from those on the mainland.

One of these is the projecting shelf that may be noted everywhere. This is a board, seven inches wide and seven-eighths of an inch thick which extends over the tops of the doors and windows. The effect is to break the blank surface of the house by casting transparent blue and lilac shadows in the brilliant sunshine.

But long before you remark this detail, you have noted interesting things about the Nantucket roof. First is the wide chimney in the middle of the ridge pole. Along the Connecticut River, in Vermont and New Hampshire, you may see many a house that resembles in other respects the late eighteenth and nineteenth-century houses of Nantucket; but where the mainland roofs have two slender chimneys, gaunt, red, and angular like English governesses, the Nantucket chimney is portly, usually washed with plaster, and it placidly dominates the house like a dowager Duchess in an armchair. The Nantucket builder used bricks with a lavish hand, both in the cellar and in the wide chimney that gives character to the Nantucket roof. On the other hand, a charming "double breasted" house on Orange Street (number 37) is an example of one dwelling that erected its chimneys after the mainland tradition rather than that of Nantucket.

The most famous characteristic of the Nantucket dwelling is the "walk" or platform which surmounted the ridgepole. This top deck is often referred to as the "Nantucket walk," the "Captain's walk," or the "widow's walk"; but when it was built and used it bore no such sentimental titles. It was simply the "walk." Here one mounted through the scuttle in the roof next to the chimney, and from that point of vantage could scan the sea for incoming ships. When the whaling fleets vanished, many householders took their "walks" down as being of no further use, but fortunately a large number survived.

Another detail which is noteworthy in the Nantucket house is the doorway. Of course, one must not expect such entrances as adorn the grand, planter type of mansion in Maryland and Virginia, or the imposing houses built by the rajahs of the clipper ship era in Salem or Portsmouth. Even if the Nantucket whaling men could have afforded homes like these their Quaker discipline would have made such showy architecture impossible. Hence one will look in vain for the highly ornate doorways with "Palladian" windows above them which are the glory of many a house on the mainland. But there are good entrances, nevertheless, in which the builder seems to have delighted in creating a doorway that would be simple, as befitting the Quaker tradition, and yet would be so carefully proportioned and so delicately modeled that it would charm anyone. As in

A TYPICAL NANTUCKET DOORWAY

the device of throwing shadows from the window tops, these doors seem to have been designed with a special eye for the play of sunshine and shadow. Since most of the houses stand right on the sidewalk, these doorways are often raised and approached by steps with railing and platform. If the house is set back somewhat, there is a fence of slender white palings which gives it the effect of wearing a little lace collar. These white fences are very characteristic of the Nantucket scene.

There are a wide variety of doors to be studied. Cape Cod houses of the same period have a little projection in front resting on slender pillars with a "pediment" overhead. On the Island this is the exception rather than the rule, but one such exception is the charming entrance to the Mixter house on Academy Hill—what the architect calls an "open pediment" porch. Much more typical of Nantucket is the door with carved molding on top and sides, flanked by slender pilasters, with side lights and a fan at the top. But there are all varieties of entrances that belong to the different types of houses, from the very plain and simple to those with elaborate carved decoration. This decoration may follow a variation of Greek ornament, or it may branch out into something of the builder's own fancy. Above some doorways a decorative pattern has been made by the simple device of boring holes with an awl or gimlet. Sometimes, too, it is a running, interlaced design. Often the most pleasing effect is obtained by a pattern that is very simple but delicately proportioned.

While we are on the subject of doorways, it is worth noting that in the older Nantucket houses the inside doors had panes of glass over the top. The purpose of this was that if a fire started in a shut-up room it would be discovered at once.

NANTUCKET

The sad part of the story of Nantucket architecture is that so many of the old houses are in pathetic need of repair, adorned by "for sale" signs and ragged with falling shingles, peeling remnants of paint and rickety railings. The hopeful sign is that, more and more, people who appreciate old New England houses are buying these and restoring them with intelligence and taste. Only rarely, praise Allah, has the new owner taken it upon himself to "improve" the original by adding bay windows and porches.

As with all antiquities, the present generation prizes them much more than their contemporaries. It rather shocks one to read in Maria Mitchell's journal the offhand way in which she refers to the old houses of her time. During the period of the ice blockade in 1857 she writes cheerfully that there will be no fuel shortage because there are "plenty of old houses to burn up." In fact, this was actually done on previous occasions when firewood was scarce. And it is sad to reflect on the many fine Nantucket homes which were taken apart, sliced up, laid on the decks of schooners, and carted away off to the mainland to be set up anew in a strange land. The Nantucket houses were used to moving! When the settlers shifted their habitation from "Wannacomet" to "Wesco" after the Capaum harbor became blocked, many picked up their houses as well as their goods and transplanted them to the new site. This moving was comparatively easy because the frames were held together, not by nails, which were too expensive, but by oaken pegs, which could be knocked out and hammered back.

Although the temptation to list the interesting houses in Nantucket must be resisted, or the subject would bulge out into a chapter of its own, attention must be called to a few. One

THE MACY DOORWAY

should know the three brick houses in a row on Main Street, built by Mr. Joseph Starbuck for his three sons. This was the Joseph Starbuck whose ship ledger was quoted in the chapter on the whaling era. His own house stands on New Dollar Lane, not far away. These three brick dwellings were exactly alike at the time of their construction, and were known as "East Brick," "Middle Brick," and "West Brick." The Middle Brick is still owned and occupied by a descendant of Joseph Starbuck, the granddaughter of the son to whom it was presented.

Opposite are the two Greek temples already noted. These were built in 1845-46 by William Hadwen, a partner of Mr. Starbuck, who married his daughter Eunice. The one on the corner of Pleasant Street (number 96) is generally known as the Barney house. The other next to it has columns with unusual capitals, copied from the portico of the "Tower of the Winds" in Athens. This used to be known as the Wright house, after the man who married a niece and adopted daughter of Hadwen. At one time, six children of Joseph Starbuck were living in this section of Main Street, three sons in the brick houses and three daughters opposite.

By the way, on the opposite corner of Pleasant Street from the Barney house, is the former residence of Benjamin Coffin (number 98) now owned by his granddaughter. This was built on the site of the old Quaker meeting house in which Elihu Coleman preached, and from which Colonel Hart obtained a shingle as a souvenir a century ago.

Directly across the street is the beautiful Macy house with the most famous doorway in Nantucket. A little further on, opposite the Civil War monument, is the Tobey house, already

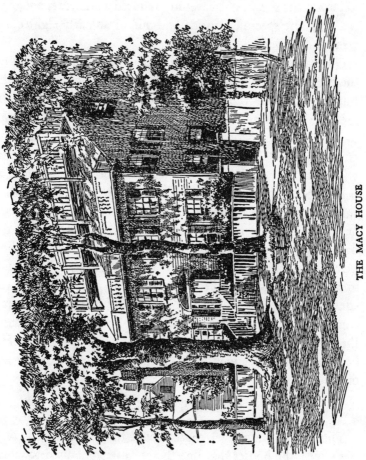

THE MACY HOUSE

referred to as one of the most ancient houses in Nantucket. This was originally built out in the old settlement and later moved to its present site. It was carefully restored some years ago, and is a very fine specimen, inside and out, of an early eighteenth-century dwelling.

One more house should be mentioned in passing. This is on the corner of Broad and Federal Streets. It belongs now to the municipality, and though greatly in need of repair could be preserved as a fine example of the old-time Nantucket ship-owner's mansion. Moreover, it was the home of an outstanding citizen, Mr. F. C. Sanford, the man who knew Reuben Chase, who as a boy watched the wounded of the *Neufchâtel* fight being operated upon in the tavern, and who as an old man came to the rescue of Robert Ratliff in the poorhouse. Sanford never went to sea himself but he was a ship-owner. In the dark days of the seventies and eighties he was the leading citizen, often referred to as the "King of Nantucket." A handsome man, he quite looked the part as he drove through the streets behind his span of glossy black horses. His portrait was painted by Eastman Johnson, and hangs in the Atheneum, the institution to which he gave liberally in his lifetime. His house is a fine specimen of a Nantucket home of the period of the forties.

THE STREETS

There is an individual charm about the streets that is of a piece with the houses that line them. To anyone used to cities, planned with an eye to efficiency, like the gridiron of New York, it is a joy to discover that Nantucket is not laid out that way. Little lanes and alleys and even streets wander at their own sweet will, like brooks. The newcomer who starts out to do a bit of exploring is likely to find himself completely turned round in regard to the points of the compass, and must pick his way home by keeping an eye on the gilt dome of the Unitarian church. Even Main Street, though it starts off in a decorous, straightforward way as it leaves the Bank, soon takes a meandering course as if trimming sail to keep to a winding channel. It luffs up and bears to port, then, when it reaches the Civil War monument, decides to take a look at the sunset and comes about on the other tack, steering west. It still is Main Street, Upper Main if you like, and what looks like the proper continuation of this street becomes Milk Street.

The prize example of whimsy in streets is appropriately named Liberty. This goes along decorously enough until it joins Gardner. Then it turns sharp right, as if pretending to be a continuation of Gardner Street, but bursts out as North Liberty, a little way to the west, and then goes gaily off on a rantum-scooting of its own. After various twists and bends it crosses West Chester Street and finally stops on Cliff Road, heading in the opposite direction from where it began. Indeed, it couldn't gallivant any further without falling over the cliff into the sea. Liberty is, among streets, the world's champion wriggler. West Chester, very properly, checks Liberty's exuberance, being the most ancient thoroughfare on the island. It led from the village around Capaum to the Great Harbor, and is named in the records as early as 1671.

Sidewalks in Nantucket also have as much individuality as the streets. None of your long ribbons of cement for them! Sometimes a corner will be quite impressive with brick sidewalks and granite curbs, as at the corner of Main and Pine, but after a few paces the east sidewalk gets tired and quits entirely. On the opposite side the bricks give out, leaving the curb for a while to carry on alone. Then the brick returns, only to vanish again. Lily Street, which was named after a now extinct Lily Pond, is a good example of sidewalks that change their minds frequently. Even staid old Main Street shows an extraordinary variety of flagging—asphalt, brick, and plain dirt. But may the Foul Fiend fly away with any Board of Selectmen that tries to make them uniform!

In 1837, the sandy stretch of Main Street in the business section was first paved with cobbles. Later these cobbles extended in different directions. Some of these have since been covered with asphalt, tar, or concrete, but let us hope that no profane road machine will desecrate any more of them.

Even in those early days of sandy streets there seems to have been a traffic problem, as suggested in the following excerpt from a petition to the Selectmen: "To see if the Town will take some order to prevent people from Riding through the streets so fast as some are in the practice of Riding; as that practice is attended with great Danger to Children and Other Inhabitants of this Town."

It was not until the year 1797 that the streets were named. One of the delightful characteristics of Nantucket is its roster of street names. Some of the signboards bear an older name and the newer. Occasionally the alterations are for the better, but mostly not. For example, Vestal Street is much more appropriate for the *via sacra* on which that shining Vestal, Maria Mitchell, was born, than its original name, Jail Lane, even if the rickety old house of detention is still visible at the western end. But Pearl is no improvement on India Street. The latter name had a significance because on that street lived so many captains who made trading voyages to India. A certain peddler, appropriately named Cash, once went the length of that street without making one sale. He returned, chanting loudly for the benefit of the thrifty housewives:

"Some calls it Injy Street;
I calls it Stingy Street!"

Sunset Pass, also, is too sweety-sweety compared with the original Break Neck Alley. But let us be thankful that no one was rash enough to change the title of Tattle Court, so named because of the gossip that used to go on there. There is much more local flavor, too, in names like Rose Jenkins' Lane or Nabby Bailey's Lane than the present Flora Street or Hillers Lane. (The modern street signs, by the way, dispense with the mark of the possessive.) Recently there has been a move to change Hussey Street to Hollyhock Lane, but that would be a questionable improvement. At any rate there should be a black mark set down against the man who changed Gingerbread Lane (where Aunt Somebody-or-other used to bake and sell delectable gingerbread) to its present flabby name of East Chestnut Street.

The stretch of Centre Street between the Bank and Broad Street is often referred to as Petticoat Row because it has long been an avenue of shops. Now, because none of the younger generation know what the word means, the street should be designated as Avenue des Shorts, which is far more appropriate.

Finally, Main Street used to be State Street, as the faded old sign still reminds us, and it ought to be State Street always.

All in all, the street names are remarkably flowery and picturesque for a staid Quaker town. Here are some of them: Quince, Orange, Lily, Rose, Flora, Bloom, Pearl, Pleasant, Fair, Darling, Gay, Joy, Vesper Lane, Stone Alley, and Step Lane (which used to have steps). One attractive lane, named by Joseph Starbuck, who built his own house there, is called New Dollar Lane. This probably was in allusion to the bright new dollar which in every home was the symbol of the safe return of the whale ship. There is also an Easy Street, if you please, and the unique glory of that seductively named avenue is that it has a gallery for the benefit of Nantucket artists. It has been remarked that Nantucket is the only place in the world where art flourishes on Easy Street.

In the alluring names Gay, Joy, Darling, one may identify former citizens. Certainly the Joy family was one of the pillars of the old days. Mooers Lane, a pretty little byway, is not, as it might seem, named after the lowing herd that used to "wind slowly o'er the lea," but after the captain of the Nantucket whaling ship that was the first, at the close of the Revolution, to show the new flag in the port of London.

Reminiscent of old days are Whale Street, and Whaler's Lane; also Trader's Lane, as one might expect. At one end of Pine Street there is Hay Scale Lane, where the farmers used to come in from Polpis way.

There are evidences that this town had its share of patriotic enthusiasm as well as any other, and we find streets called Federal, Independence, Liberty, Washington, Madison. Finally, there is a Coon Street, and this is not in the Ethiopian quarter either. Very early in the town's history there were negroes who had shipped on the whalers and brought their families to Nan-

ORANGE STREET

tucket. Nantucket, also, was a station on the Underground Railroad in slavery days. New Guinea, the area south and east of the old mill, is still the negro section. Egypt was the name for the region about North Liberty Street, which was lonely and "dark as Egypt."

A hundred years ago Orange Street was unique in having on its five-eighths of a mile length more whaling captains' homes than any other street in the world. The curious may read the list in the Whaling Museum. It used to be regarded as the avenue of the aristocracy of Nantucket. But no residential street suffered so much as Orange in the depression after whaling died out. At the southern end, especially, many a fine old house was torn down or so changed as to be unrecognizable. In the same period Main Street held its own remarkably well.

Before leaving the houses and streets, observe that this is the one town which has the unique distinction of never having been visited by either the Father of His Country or by his aide Lafayette. Accordingly, there is no house to point out as the place where these worthies stayed, or any four-poster beds where they slept!

THE CHURCHES

Of the old Quaker meeting houses there is scarcely a trace left, which is perhaps fortunate, as they were painful to look upon. The little one next to the quarters of the Historical Society is kept as a museum exhibit, but it was originally a schoolhouse which was taken over by the Quaker congregation after the disintegration and splitting up began. Another is now the dining room annex of the Roberts House, but that, too, has no great antiquity.

As evidence of how the village has pulled itself gradually eastward, it is said that in the days when the old Quaker meeting house stood on the site of the present ancient burial ground on Saratoga Street, more worshipers came from the west than from the east. The burial ground now stands on the very westward edge of the town.

The most interesting church building, as well as the most

CONGREGATIONAL CHURCH

conspicuous, is the South Church or Unitarian, which dominates every view of Nantucket. Here, too, is the town clock, and the bell which rings a wide-awake notice at seven in the morning for everybody to get up out of bed. The bell is rung again at noon to remind people that it is time to think about the midday meal, and finally there is another protracted ringing at nine, as a warning that all good people should be indoors or be prepared to give a good reason why they are not—in short, a curfew.

This familiar clock-tower was used before the days of fire
alarms as a watch-tower for fires. The watchman would signal
by waving a lantern in the general direction of any blaze that
had been sighted. The most famous object in the tower is the
bell. Even the dull of ear cannot fail to note the singular sweet-
ness of its tone. This bell was cast in Portugal, intended to be one
of six bells for a local institution of the church. For some reason
the order fell through, and the Nantucket captain who was
looking for a bell for his church bought it for five hundred
dollars. Later, a Boston church tried to buy it at a handsome
figure, but the Nantucket Unitarians would not consider such
a thing, and it has continued to charm the ear of both islanders
and off-islanders for well over a century. Anyone who wants a
full history of the bell has only to climb the tower and read
the printed account that hangs near the bell. One may obtain
admission from the sexton who guards the shrine and pulls the
bell rope, and who may be found ready to unlock the door just
before noon. The church is not beautiful, as are the lovely white
pine or brick meeting houses all through New England. It has
no such spires as the ones at Old Lyme and Avon in Connecticut, or such treatment of the little gilt dome as Bullfinch
gave to the Unitarian church in Peterborough, New Hampshire. It is painted a Quaker grey, and stands rather with its
arms akimbo like a schoolmarm looking down at the town.
Still, it is full of character, and of course one would not have
it changed.

The present Congregational church on Beacon Hill, or
Academy Hill, dates from 1834. In the rear is the old, plain
meeting house that preceded it as the place of worship. This
originally stood two miles west of its present location and was

moved east in 1765. Finally, it was pushed back to make room for the present new building. This church also has its charm, having a square tower with simple and dignified ornament.

The Methodist church standing on Centre Street is a Greek temple that suffers from being crowded in by its neighbors. This was built in 1823, but the Parthenon front was not added until 1840.

For sheer beauty, the spire of the Baptist church carries off the prize. Here is one of the white New England meeting houses of the old time. It is true, the front is not so impressive as it might be, because the early Baptists apparently felt that they could not afford a complete pillared portico, and the builder did the best he could with four pilasters. But the little white spire, simple in design yet graceful and slender, lends beauty to every vista in which it stands. It was designed by a Nantucket architect, F. B. Coleman. Long life to it, and may the Baptists always be able to afford a coat of white paint when it is needed! They are to be congratulated on their treasure.

The Episcopal church, the only one built of stone, is not in the Christopher Wren tradition, as it might have been, but it has its own charm. The Catholics worship in a plain, wooden structure with no special historical or architectural interest.

GRAVEYARDS

Churches naturally suggest burying grounds, but in Nantucket these do not lie in the churchyards as they do in some New England villages. The famous old Quaker cemetery looks now like an old pasture, for the thousands of Quaker dead interred here had no marking for their graves. The few stones that may be seen in one corner belong, it is said, to the heretic

Hicksites and Gurneyites who had no pangs of conscience on the subject. There are also a few very modern graves as well. The two burying grounds that are most interesting to ramble in are the ones that lie at opposite ends of the town—the Old South and the Old North.

The Old South may be reached by the road that leads behind the South schoolhouse. This burying ground is in good order, for it is still used. But it has considerable antiquity, and its stones bear the names of all the First Families of Nantucket, as well as the Second and Third families, down even to the Portuguese, all of whom are apparently named Silvia. One of the treasures of this burial place is the headstone with the inscription to Huldah Snow, composed by her sorrowing husband:

> Huldah, wife of Benj Snow
> However dear she was not laid here.
> Some private grief was her disease
> Laid to the north her friends to please.

In other words, his wife's relatives insisted on burying her in the North cemetery, whereas he was determined that her headstone, at least, should stand in the South. In the same burial ground is another epitaph with this brief but poignant inscription, "Father gorn home." And you may discover this bit of mortuary verse on the stone of two little brothers who died within a day of each other in the year 1856. Their parents must have thought the occasion apt for preaching a sermon to the young and heedless. Here it is:

> Brother playmates, here we lay,
> Once so happy and so gay.

THE MODERN TOWN

Now God has called us to his home,
No more with you to play or roam.
So look to God without delay
And be prepared to come our way.

On still another gravestone is the following rhyming admonition:

Stop, my friends, as you pass by,
As you am now so once was I;
As I am now so you must be,
Prepare for death and follow me.
Follow me and be you wise,
And up to heaven you will arise.

Anyone who cultivates a taste for graveyard sculpture and poetry may have a still better time in the Old North cemetery, which may be reached from West Chester Street by a little sandy thoroughfare, which is still called New Lane. But it is more difficult to get at the tombstones there because the place is so overgrown with bayberry bushes and prickly wild rose. This lot is no longer used as a cemetery.

Many of these graves have been obliterated, stones and all. The town has put up several wooden boards to call attention to the resting places of forgotten dead. One such tablet mentions the grave of Reuben Chase. Another is a memorial to Captain Robert Inot, who navigated the first steamship across the Atlantic.

Except for the fact that there is no ivy-mantled tower—the water tank on the distant horizon being hardly suitable—here is the ideal place to recite the *Elegy Written in a Country Churchyard*.

NANTUCKET

Perhaps in this neglected spot is laid
Some heart once pregnant with celestial fire.

Perhaps. But it isn't likely that these old whalemen had hands that could have "swayed the rod of empire"—though their wives might have done so—and most certainly they could not have "waked to ecstasy the living lyre." For we have many of their efforts at verse. Even that great mathematician and philosopher, Walter Folger, once wrote an ode to be sung by school children. But none of this output will push Byron or Shelley off their pedestals.

Some mute, inglorious Michael Angelo left his art here, too. In the oldest slate headstones may be seen some very remarkable angels in voluminous robes, and grinning death's heads, often equipped with wings, too.

No one can miss the headstone of Robert Ratliff with the inscription already quoted in the Old Boys chapter, and there stands farther back in the burying ground the grave of Reuben Chase with the reformed epitaph written by his son. Many of these graves are so badly overgrown with brambles as to make investigation difficult, and yet there probably is buried here many an old worthy of long ago. Perhaps some day when the Historical Association is rich it will do a job of restoration and make this old cemetery one of the interesting historical shrines of Nantucket.

WHARVES

With all the interest in shingled houses, winding lanes, and deep, tangled graveyards, it must not be forgotten that Nantucket is a seaport. Accordingly, this ramble about town must take in the wharves. There are five of these still in use; from north to south they run as follows: Steamboat, Old North, Straight (Killen's), Old South (Island Service), and Commercial. The earliest of these is Straight, so called, it is said, because it went straight out from the end of Main Street. This dates

THE FOOT OF OLD NORTH WHARF

from 1723, which was soon after the settlers moved to the shores of the Great Harbor. In the early days, these wharves were merely a structure of planks and piles, not the solid piers of today. The one exception was the last one to be built, the Commercial, which was begun in 1800 and was not completed until 1820. This was the pride of the harbor because it had a solid foundation of Connecticut granite. During the whaling era this wharf was the busiest of all, and here was where the earliest steamboats docked. The decayed outer end of this—as also that of the other wharves—may be seen at low tide, when the foundations are still visible. One wharf has disappeared completely: This was "Peleg's Wharf," so called after its owner Peleg Macy. This was near the end of Fayette Street.

What these wharves were like in the days of whaling is described in the following reminiscences of Mr. J. E. C. Farnham in his *Boyhood Days in Nantucket,* which was published in 1914:

I wonder if the younger residents at Nantucket have any conception of the changes which have taken place along the harbor water front. I am sure that they have no adequate realization of the lonesome feeling which possesses one who was a boy there upward of fifty years ago as he now looks over the locality. . . . Not one of those wharves at that time but was a hive of industry, where, upon, or near them, there were located many shops of the different lines of business of the town, especially in connection with the fitting of whale ships for sea. On the Old South was the pump and block-making business of my father, and close neighbors to it were five blacksmith shops; the old rope walk, under the direction of Robert Ratliff, where rope and cordage were spun, and over it the sail loft, where thousands of yards of canvas were fashioned into sails; at the head of the dock the lumber yard and buildings of Isaiah Robinson and Peleg Macy, besides numerous small shops in different trades.

Probably the most startling change that would strike the old-timer would be the perfect silence that now prevails on these wharves as compared with the ringing of the blacksmiths' hammers, the blows of the coopers, the booming roll of the barrels along the wharves, the clatter of the drays, the creaking of tackle and the shouts of men at work—a babel of many sounds from daylight till dark. Nor should it be forgotten that along the shore near Brant Point, where now the children wade and dig, was a shipbuilding yard where more hammers were ringing and a medley of shouts and groaning blocks was going on in a little overture of its own.

No doubt a boy can still have a grand time on the wharves, but the old-time youngster would turn up his nose at the small fry of boats that tie up alongside now. Not only have the square-riggers vanished these many decades, but, nowadays, even a two-masted schooner is a sensation. If one of these comes in, all the local artists flock down to "do" her before she puts out again. For a long time the ancient *Ada C. Shull,* a schooner with rich green sides, was the faithful standby of the painters, who knew her affectionately as the *Ada Seashell.* Alas, poor Ada, she is dismasted now and desolate, waiting to go to the boneyard.

All the rest are "otter trawlers," most of which have discarded sail entirely and chug in and out with gasoline or Diesel engines. Probably the next step will be to get halibut, plaice, bluefish and scallops by hydroplane, so that there won't be a mast left to stick up anywhere. Those old whaling captains in the North Cemetery must be turning in their graves like turbines.

But gasoline can never beat canvas for fun, and if there is a better sailing ground on the coast than the inner and the outer harbors, it will have to speak up quickly to get a hearing. So, during the summer, one looks out from the ends of these wharves upon a scene of gay coming and going among pleasure craft of all sizes from the humble catboat to the elegant

AN OTTER TRAWLER

yacht which looks snootily down its bowsprit upon the little fellows. And gayest of all are the sails of the rainbow fleet, which put flecks of the most unexpected colors against the blue of the harbor. Then, when the races are held with the neighboring yachtsmen of Martha's Vineyard, there is a spectacle that might even cheer the gloomy ghosts of the old skippers. A goodly place still, Nantucket Harbor!

CHAPTER X

SPECIAL SHRINES

HAVING just made a leisurely tour of the town, we shall now stop in at some of the special places of interest. The first thing any visitor should do, after signing his name in a hotel register or moving into his cottage for the season, is to pay one dollar for membership in the Nantucket Historical Association. This modest price delivers to the member a ticket which admits him free to each of the four important places of historical interest, the Whaling Museum, the Oldest House, the rooms of the Historical Association (with its museum and old Quaker Meeting House) and the Mill. Further, a member may visit these places as often as he likes on the same ticket. This small payment to an Association that labors under great difficulties to preserve the historical treasures of the town should be made compulsory, just as in Switzerland the tourist pays a *Kurtax* of so much a day to help support the local casino. Since it is primarily the historical atmosphere of Nantucket that attracts visitors, they should be glad to have at least a small share in keeping the relics of the past safe from decay. It is to the credit of public-spirited people like members of the Historical Association that so many of the following shrines have been preserved. Let us take a look at them.

THE OLDEST HOUSE

For the first of these relics of old Nantucket we select the most ancient. This is called "Oldest House," "Jethro Coffin House," and "Horseshoe House." All of these names are accepted and proper. It is the oldest of the Nantucket houses, having been built in 1686. It was a wedding present to Jethro

THE OLDEST HOUSE

Coffin and his bride; hence the name. And finally, on the great clustered chimney there is a curious inverted ornament called a horseshoe. As to whether this is a horseshoe, or a tuning fork, or a wishbone, or what not, may be open to debate, but since that was the title selected for the booklet on the house prepared by the late William F. Macy for the Historical Association, it is at least official.

To reach this house we must start from the Square, along Centre Street, past the Congregational church, bearing left on West Chester Street, past the Cottage Hospital until we come to the little lane that ambles up the slope to the right, called Sunset Hill. This has a white signboard marked "To the Oldest House." A few steps further will bring you to its door. This relic may be recognized from a distance, also, because it is the one house which boasts the old-time well sweep.

This is typical of the late seventeenth-century "lean-to"; it is not at all beautiful, standing grey and stark against a treeless skyline. But it is well worth more than one visit. Briefly, its history is as follows:

The wedding between Jethro, the grandson of old Tristram Coffin, the first settler, and Mary Gardner, the daughter of John Gardner, was a great event in more senses than one. The chief point of interest for us is that it united the two factions on the island that had been warring ever since John Gardner and Peter Folger and their friends rebelled against the autocratic rule of Tristram and his followers in the interest of the small landowner and the landless. This same John Gardner had been invited to settle in Nantucket in 1672 to teach the art of cod-fishing—his brother Richard had come six years before —and John developed the fishery into a very important means of livelihood for the island.

At the time of her wedding Mary was just sixteen. It was a grand house for those days, and the couple kept it until they left for the mainland early in the following century. Thereafter it changed hands as time went on, and grew more and more dilapidated. Then a Mr. Tristram Coffin, of Poughkeepsie, became interested in buying and preserving it, after coming to the home of his ancestors for the grand Coffin reunion which was held on Nantucket in 1881. From him it came into the possession of the Historical Association. Finally, another member of the Coffin clan, Mr. Winthrop Coffin, of Boston, generously offered to pay for all the repairs needed, provided they were undertaken by experts. For this, Mr. Sumner Appleton, antiquarian of Boston, and Mr. Alfred F. Shurrocks, a specialist in New England architecture, combined forces and achieved a beautiful job of restoration, completed in 1928.

Before leaving the ancient building, we should notice that it faces due south, as was the custom of most dwellings for so many years. Also observe the small diamond panes of glass, which were used in the seventeenth century, together with the casement type of window. Finally, note the huge fireplaces, the one in the east room measuring seven feet wide, five feet high and three feet deep. And, if you like ancient portraits, don't miss the one of Mary herself, the one which cost her, not only the painter's fee, but six different trips to Boston for sittings. Mary was not beautiful, but she was a woman of character. She looks rather fragile in that picture, but she lived on to the age of ninety-seven.

Leaving the Jethro Coffin house and turning back into Upper Main Street, the traveler strikes the road to Madaket. This passes through the site of the older part of the Sherburne of the eighteenth century and the original settlement of the seventeenth. About a mile out of the present limits of the town there stands by the road a memorial fountain which commemorates the site nearby of the Folger home where Benjamin Franklin's mother, Abiah, was born. This fountain, set up in the days when there still were horses who got thirsty, is now a relic. Continuing further to the point where the highway swings left, we come upon some rutted roads which lead north and east. One of these wanders down among the bayberry bushes to a little valley, at the bottom of which stands a granite post. This marks the site of the original Tristram Coffin homestead. From there we can see the Capaum harbor— now a pond—which the earliest settlers used for their fishing vessels. Probably what is now marsh land was in those days a tidal inlet, also useful for small boats. Except for a few summer homes on the shore, all this area is now bare of habitation, though once it was thickly settled. The town stood here when Franklin came to visit his Folger relations, and it stretched from Capaum on the north to Hummock Pond on the south. On the hill overlooking Maxcy's Pond (which lies below the water tower) stood the original burying ground.

So far we have been looking to the right of the Madaket highway. Soon after leaving town we passed the Elihu Coleman house, standing at some distance to the left of the road. We should now turn back to a signboard near the highway reading "Elihu Coleman Homestead." The rutted road at that point leads directly toward it.

ELIHU COLEMAN HOUSE

Elihu Coleman was a descendant on his mother's side of Tristram Coffin. He was a carpenter and builder by trade, and a Quaker preacher by inclination, as his mother had been before him. He is noted for the fact that, as far back as 1729, he wrote a pamphlet denouncing slavery, the first in New England, that home of abolition sentiment. This house was planned

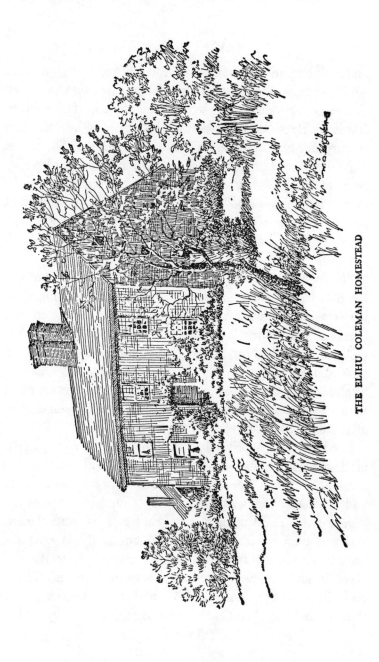

THE ELIHU COLEMAN HOMESTEAD

and built by him as a young man, and he lived here sixty years. The little grassy road that runs behind the dwelling was known as late as a hundred years ago by the name of Duke Street. It was thickly settled with houses on both sides in the eighteenth century, for at that period it was in the heart of Sherburne. Now there is not another dwelling for a mile in any direction. Next to West Chester, it is the oldest thoroughfare on the island. It is now called Hawthorn Lane, from the jungle of twisted hawthorn trees that line it on both sides, the most gnarled, thorny hawthorn trees that ever defied the approach of man.

The legend is that they are the reincarnation—if one may use that word—of all the unhappy old maids who lost their lovers at sea, or who fell in love with boys who were not Quakers, or had their lovers taken from them by girls at other ports, or never had any lovers at all, and lived long, thorny, gnarled lives ever after. Once a year, in May, they bloom a virginal white. Once a year, in October, their branches are hung with red berries like drops of blood from a deep wound. And all the year they stretch forth their savage thorns.

The house is now privately owned, but it deserves a full page of description because it is so distinctive. Both outside and inside it is easy to see the resemblances between this and the Oldest House. Both of them face south, and both are of the lean-to type. The Coleman house, however, is much larger, and was built much later, in 1722; but it shows how the seventeenth-century type persisted for a whole generation or more. It has the great, clustered chimney in the middle of the roof, the same two stories in front and the slant back to one story in the rear. The Coleman house varies from the Oldest

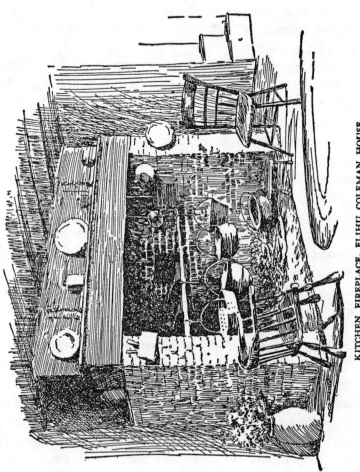

KITCHEN FIREPLACE, ELIHU COLEMAN HOUSE

House in having square panes of glass and large windows instead of the diamond panes and small casements of the other. It has also an overhanging cornice. The board underneath that cornice, called by architects the "cornice soffit," was once painted a bright green.

Inside, there is much of interest to lovers of old houses as well as to the architect and builder. As in so many other Nantucket homes, the woodwork suggests the ship's carpenter— doors with slanting tops, and beams supported by "knees," which were brackets formed by the trunk and root of a white oak; also "lapped sheathing" on the sides to keep out the weather. It is said that the oak corner posts are so toughened by time that it is impossible to drive a nail into them.

The chief glory of the old house is its great fireplaces. The one in the kitchen projects several feet into the room and is six and a half feet in width. The magnifico of all fireplaces in Nantucket is the one in the "keeping room," nine and a half feet in width, and so high that it is easy to step into it and look up at the sky. Each of these fireplaces is built of home-baked brick and is held together by clay instead of mortar.

There are several details worth noting, such as the decorated "H" hinges, the front door called the "Christian door," because the panels form a cross, the latch and latchstring on all the doors, the ventilator over the door of the parlor to let heat upstairs, the small cupboard beside the big fireplace in the "keeping room," a "Bible box" where presumably the family Bible was stowed away, the wide floor boards, some measuring as much as twenty-two inches across. Many of the roof boards are fully as wide, and the kitchen door has a panel twenty-five inches in width. Some of the little window panes are said to be the original ones that Elihu placed there, and from these one views miles of rough, tangled country, in the midst of which the old house stands austere and alone as a landmark, a stark grey monument of the Quaker tradition.

It was in front of that great fireplace in the "keeping room" that Elihu Coleman wrote his pamphlet to prove that the principle of human slavery was wrong: *A Testimony Against That Anti Christian Practice of Making Slaves of Men*. This was published the following year, in 1730. It made no great impression in its time; but over a hundred years later, when the issue had become acute, the abolitionist, William Lloyd Garrison, made a pilgrimage to this house as to a sacred shrine, and met and talked to Elihu's son, William, who was still living there.

In the course of time this old manse passed out of the family into the hands of another Friend, William Hosier, who took good care of it and willed it to the town with the idea that it should be preserved as a memorial to Elihu Coleman. This was in 1899. But the Selectmen were not interested, and it remained deserted for years. Windows were boarded up, birds nested in the chimney and upstairs rooms, weeds grew tall, and it became a "haunted house." To save it from desecration, Miss Annie Barker Folger, the artist, bid it in at a public auction and began the slow task of restoration. This was continued by Mrs. Rose Forbes, the next owner, who did much of the work with her own hands. It is now in a fine state of preservation.

The value of this relic may be judged by the fact that it was selected to represent Nantucket architecture under the recent Federal survey, which chose one house in each of the old villages of New England as the best example of the local architecture.

of the bygone age. The detailed measurements of the Elihu Coleman house are now filed away in the Library of Congress to be saved for posterity.

THE OLD MILL

For the next shrine we must return to town. This landmark looms so conspicuously on the hill that it cannot be missed. It is the last of four such mills that used to stand on the hill west of the town. It was built in 1746. A good many years ago, when townspeople had little interest and no money to devote to local monuments of the past, this mill was offered for twenty dollars as firewood. A kindly Providence saved it, and it is now under the beneficent wing of the Historical Association, which has done so much for the preservation of Nantucket antiquities. There were some things done to it which are regrettable, and which may be repaired some day when the Association has a full treasury. One is that the great spar and wheel that stretch out behind are fixed in place so that the arms of the mill can revolve only when the wind is due west. However, they whirl merrily then and in a good stiff wind have to be checked by a brake.

Another mistake was to set the lower millstone in cement so that it cannot revolve. Nevertheless, the old mill has been made to work, grinding cornmeal, which is sold for the benefit of the Association. And it is amazing how much is sold. Of course, the chief interest locally in such cornmeal is as a souvenir, but we are informed that the meal is in considerable demand because of its superior quality as compared with that ground out by the big flour mills. It is supposed to have all the

THE OLD MILL

proteins and carbohydrates and roughage and what not that the doctors claim are so good for whatever ails you. Certainly there aren't many eighteenth-century windmills still grinding cornmeal for sale, and may its business thrive!

Another attraction is the superb view from this situation over the entire island. Here, in the old days, many a home-coming ship was sighted, and the good news sent to the waiting families as fast as a small boy's legs could run. Once, during the Revolutionary War a cannon ball is said to have gone through the mill, uncomfortably close to the miller's head. There is a story, too, of a girl—there wasn't anything that Nantucket damsels would not do!—who caught hold of one of the arms while it was revolving and treated herself to a free ride three times round. Her frightened companions ran in and told the miller, who in a panic did the worst possible thing by stopping the arms suddenly, flinging the poor girl to the ground with shattering consequences to her arms and legs.

THE MARIA MITCHELL HOUSE

On the way down from the mill, following Milk Street, we soon reach Vestal, a lane that turns off to the left. There, at the corner, is the little grey house in which the astronomer, Maria Mitchell, was born, and which, as already noted, is now preserved as a memorial to her by an association that exists solely for that purpose.

The house itself has already been mentioned as an example of the old-time "single" dwelling which was so popular in Nantucket. Also, though it was not the scene of Maria's famous discovery of the comet, it is the place where she spent her girlhood and studied with her father. The house dates from 1790, and was originally a square structure with the chimney off center. Note, by the way, the long, wooden latch on the front door, so characteristic of Nantucket houses. This one happens to be a bit of mahogany from a wrecked ship. In the kitchen is an example of elaborate "graining," once the vogue, of which this is a remarkable example. The original walk on top of the house was blown away by a gale in 1855, but was replaced in 1915.

In the little yard, somewhat to the rear, is a small observatory which also is maintained by the Association. The observatory is presided over by a professional astronomer. And directly across the street is a building that used to be the school in which Maria's father taught and where the girl studied under him. This also is part of the shrine. It houses a scientific library and reading room, also a stack room containing the Mitchell relics, such as the little telescope with which the young astronomer discovered the comet, her scrap books and personal library, and odds and ends of souvenirs and letters.

The beginning of the Maria Mitchell Association was made by a group of loyal admirers who bought the house in 1902. Six years later the observatory was built, and its telescope is one which was presented to the astronomer by the women of America in 1859.

Under the present director in charge, Miss Margaret Harwood, the work goes on, both in research (on a particular cluster in the Milky Way) and in popular astronomy for school children and summer visitors. Occasionally Miss Harwood contributes an interesting column to the *Inquirer and Mirror* on the pictures that the night sky is billed to offer for the coming month. Maria Mitchell would be pleased to know the work that is being carried on there in her old home and in her name. The house may be inspected during the summer season for a small fee, and it houses an annual free exhibition of the wild flowers of Nantucket.

The leading spirit in the founding and maintaining of the Maria Mitchell Memorial was Mrs. Charles S. Hinchman. She was Lydia Swain Mitchell, born in the very same house as her cousin Maria. Ninety-three when she died, and ever since 1864 a citizen of Philadelphia, she always cherished a keen interest in everything that benefited her native town.

HISTORICAL MUSEUM

Continuing down to the monument, from the Maria Mitchell house, we should turn right and follow Main Street as far as Fair; thence walk a few steps to the Historical Museum. This is the headquarters of the Historical Association, which houses the collection of antiquities. Adjoining it stands the last Quaker meeting house, maintained just as it used to be when the worshipers sat there waiting for the Spirit to move them to speak. It is eloquent of the old Quaker tradition, with its hard benches, bare floor, and candles on the walls.

Many visitors to Nantucket miss the interesting things in this museum. It is true that the present quarters are too small. Anyone who likes antiquities of any sort, whether they are ancient costumes, or china, or pictures, or what you will, can keep his or her nose flattened against the glass cases for a goodly part of an afternoon. It isn't possible to enumerate all the items, but a few may be mentioned to give an idea of the variety. There is, for example, a broadside, dating from the war of 1812, and illustrated with a crude woodcut, entitled, "The Horrid Massacre in Dartmouth Prison."

A tragic story you shall hear, from Britain comes the news
Of Yankee sailors there confined and how they have been us'd.

The ballad tells of an incident that caused the most bitter resentment in this country, of prisoners being shot down in the jail yard.

If you are interested in the unhappy story of the Dauphin at the time of the French Revolution, there is a life-sized wax image of the child which some sentimental whaler captain bought in Paris and brought back in 1786. At that time the child was six months old, and as yet the tumbril and the guillotine were not dreamed of.

In the upper gallery is a collection of portraits of early Nantucket worthies. Some of these are sufficiently grotesque in drawing and painting to be rated as masterpieces of modern art. These poor artists were only ahead of their time!

There is nobody on hand to paint a coat of arms for you, but if you yearn to belong to the Colonial Dames, or the Daughters of Pequod War, or something, there is a cozy nook lined with books on Massachusetts genealogy and an obliging secretary who will help you.

In one of the cases is a curious little item that is easily overlooked. This is the famous cherry stone containing twelve dozen silver spoons. The legend is that a whaling captain, who had unsuccessfully wooed a girl, was finally put off with the declaration that if he could bring her back twelve dozen silver spoons in a cherry stone she would marry him. The captain returned from his next cruise and showed her the microscopic twelve dozen spoons in a cherry pit wrought with his own hands. She, being a good sport, kept her promise and they lived happily ever after. That is the story of the origin of the spoons as it was told to me, and I intend to believe it; though there are people who say that it isn't true! The set of spoons on exhibition is not the original, which is treasured in a private home, but a replica, and until very recently one could buy a similar set made by a skilful hand in Nantucket.

One of the most valuable possessions is a portrait that stands out from all the other paintings on the wall. It is Eastman Johnson's picture of an old man in a beaver hat, resting his chin on his cane. This is a Mr. Myrick, who is said to have been a great beau in his youth, and, as a picture of old age, it might be the original of Holmes's "Last Leaf."

The Association hopes before long to erect a building, adequate to house its collection, on the lot next to another one of its interesting shrines, the Whaling Museum, and there is where we shall turn now.

THE WHALING MUSEUM

Probably the most popular of the Nantucket historical exhibits is the Whaling Museum. This is housed in the old brick building at the foot of Steamboat Wharf. It was built in 1847 as a sperm candle factory, and was used later as a warehouse, and an office building for shipping firms. Fortunately, this building was sold to the Historical Association by a former resident, Mr. E. F. Sanderson, together with his own collection of relics from the whaling era. These made the nucleus of the present exhibit.

The outside, attractive as it is, with its ancient doorway and mellowed bricks, gives no hint of the interesting objects within. There are, even in summer, dour "no'theasters" that drench the streets with a rain that drives horizontally and keeps up,

THE WHALING MUSEUM

with a persistence worthy of a better cause, for three whole days. When one of these comes along, there is no refuge so inviting as this whaling museum.

It would be impossible to describe the exhibitions in detail, but the visitor may pick up a folder at the entrance which will tell him all he wants to know. For example, in the large room are the jawbones of a huge sperm, the press used to make the candles, and spades for cutting blubber—sometimes used also as weapons against South Sea Island cannibals. In the middle of the room stands that "camel" which was invented to carry ships over the bar, and which worked all right but, like many another perfect invention, cost too much to be profitable. At one side is a complete try works such as was set up on the deck of every whaler, and one wonders how that boiling oil and fire behaved when the little vessel heaved and pitched in the long swells of the Pacific. At one end of the room is an original whaleboat, the most seaworthy craft that ever was designed by the hand of man. Look on this and imagine that voyage of 3500 miles in 93 days made by the crew of the *Essex*. Nearby, on the east wall, are harpoons of every conceivable variety, ending with the ones shot out of a gun. Gaze on one of those hand harpoons and imagine what Long Tom Coffin could do with his right arm when he declared that he used to plunge his harpoon into a whale "right to the seizing"—that is, up to where the rope was fastened at the end.

This main room is the center of interest, and under the skilful and tireless direction of William F. Macy, it has been admirably arranged to interest the visitor. But there are other rooms, too, where one may see portraits of whaling captains, sea chests, medicine chests, relics from the Pacific Islands, and log books—some of them with comical illustrations. Especially absorbing is the collection of scrimshaw in the small room at the left of the entrance.

A snug haven on the northeasterly day referred to is the Reading Room. Here are shelves loaded with the literature of the sea, especially the literature of whaling. Among these are stacks of ancient log books, the oldest bound in ship's canvas instead of leather.

Fortunately, this museum of whaling is in charge of Captain George Grant, son of the famous Captain Charles Grant mentioned in the chapter on the whaling era. Captain Grant can remember more about the old whaling days than anyone else in Nantucket, or perhaps, for that matter, anywhere else. He is also very patient and obliging about answering the kind of question that landlubbers are wont to ask. Indeed, who wouldn't ask questions in that great loft, packed as it is from floor to roof with the most mysterious gadgets of the sea? At any rate, it should be clear by this time that if a visitor has only a few hours to see the town, the one place he cannot afford to miss is the Whaling Museum.

CHAPTER XI

SIASCONSET

"THE Newport of the Nantucketoise," wrote a highly genteel author for *Scribner's Magazine* in 1873, "is Siasconset." It is high time that we see what this "Newport" looks like. To reach Siasconset—and, by the way, it has to be pronounced " 'Sconset"—we take a bus or drive eastward from the foot of Orange Street, past Our Island Home, the commodious poorhouse, and follow a fine state highway across the island for a distance of eight miles.

Siasconset has been for a long time "the Newport of the Nantucketoise," but the present highway is comparatively recent. It was built in 1910 and widened in 1933. The old-fashioned way for a stranger to get there was by hiring a conveyance of some sort, from a Coffin or a Folger, or take the stage driven by Captain Baxter, and then crawl and lurch and jounce for two or three hours over the commons in any one of a series of deep-rutted tracks. These could hardly be honored by the name of roads, and yet they were the only roads that existed. Their sandy ruts were often worn down to the depth of a foot or so, and once the vehicle was in the channel there was no turning out until one came to what was called a "soft place," an open spot of sand where the carriage might make a turning. If by accident one's chaise or "box wagon" turned into the road to Polpis or Wauwinet, it had to stay there until it reached that destination. When these ruts became impossible, someone would start

"SHANUNGA"

another route which in time would become as bad as the old one. Thus the commons were streaked in every direction with wheel tracks.

The box wagon, by the way, which was a favorite Nantucket vehicle in the nineteenth century, was a four-wheeled affair with two seats. Usually, however, the back seat was taken out, and low chairs, even rockers, were installed in its place.

In spite of these uncomfortable forms of travel between Nantucket and Siasconset, the trip apparently was greatly enjoyed. Whenever there was an occasion for a picnic or a squantum the only thing to do was to go to Siasconset. And when notables visited Nantucket they could not escape off the island without being jolted over the commons to see this resort of fashion. Sir Isaac Coffin had to endure the trip, in spite of the fact that the old gentleman was then suffering from gout.

The modern highway is marked by a series of milestones, the gift of Peter Folger Ewer, a native son, as far back as 1824. They have been moved twice since then in order to follow the routes, which had a way of shifting. Some of these stones are now hidden in the scrub oak, but they can all be accounted for. The groves of pines on either hand are the result of planting begun in 1912 by the State; hence the name "State Forest." As late as the middle of the nineteenth century, when Thoreau visited Siasconset, there was nothing to see in all directions but low bushes.

The highway we travel today is a fine, straightaway course. The traveler has scarcely left the town before he is vaguely conscious of a pleasant sensation to which he has been a stranger. He soon realizes that this is due to the fact that there is not a single billboard to desecrate the landscape. Whatever mistakes the Selectmen have ever made, for this achievement they deserve a large gold medal. May they never flinch!

For a few years there was a railway that ran between the steamboat wharf in town and Siasconset. The trains were few and far between, but it was always very clubby on board, and you could hail the train anywhere to stop and pick you up. Alas, it never made money, and it was "sold down river" to the Allies in the middle of the War, when rails and rolling stock were at a premium.

As we come over the crest of "Bean Hill," the outline of Siasconset is spread out ahead. To the extreme left is Sankaty Lighthouse with its bright red girdle. Straight ahead is a tall, dismally black water tower which marks the village. Nearby are the famous cranberry bogs, said to be the largest cranberry plantation in the world. Just beyond are flocks of sheep in the last remaining sheep pasture on the island.

Still further, on the left side of the road, lie the "old" golf links, the scene of many a hard-fought battle to break a hundred or win a five-dollar bet in the heyday of the actor colony twenty or thirty years ago. It is now a public course, and is shorn of its old-time glory since the swanky golf club was established near Sankaty Light.

Opposite the club house, on the other side of the road, is a little pool inhabited by a mud turtle of reflective frame of mind who has sat on the same log and contemplated the universe for at least a score of years, from my own observation, and nobody knows how many eons before that. This pool is known as "Corn Pond," for the reason that anyone afflicted with corns needs only to wade in its magic waters to be completely cured. They say this treatment is infallible, though I have yet to observe anyone testing it.

The little golf course, with its club house and Corn Pond, is all that is left of a once beautiful estate, Bloomingdale. This was laid out as a pleasure ground for parties from Town by a wealthy Nantucket shipmaster, the original owner of Moor's End on Pleasant Street. Flowering shrubs, fruit trees, ponds, and lawns made the place the pride of the island. Lavish hospitality was extended there in the old days of plenty. Bloomingdale witnessed many a gay dinner, chowder party, and fancy dress ball. In spite of the long, rough ride, these were festivities to which the young people were glad enough to come all the way from town.

Leaving the old golf course, the site of Bloomingdale, behind us, we now enter the village of Siasconset. "Slow!" says the sign at the entrance, and it is a sign to obey, for, in the summer season especially, cars driven by exuberant boys and girls have a way of dashing out unexpectedly from side streets. Straight ahead is the center of the village, where the post office stands; and in front of it is a tall flagpole, rigged as a mast, a memorial in honor of the late David Gray, a generous benefactor of Siasconset. To the right is a branch road leading down to the shore. It bears a sign "To Spain, To Portugal, 3000 Miles." The custom is, however, to conclude the journey at this point, and we shall dismount from the bus or park our car for the present in order to see Siasconset on foot, as it was intended we should. Indeed, it would be a wise provision if all cars were forbidden to drive through the lanes of the old village, and were routed around it instead.

The old village referred to lies to the left of the post office and it really is an "old" village. Before there was a single house on the site of the present town of Nantucket there were fishermen living here. There is an interesting historical pamphlet written by Roland Hussey on the *Evolution of Siasconset*. According to Mr. Hussey, there were houses here as early as the seventeenth century. In those days and, for that matter, during a century thereafter, the fishermen built their shanties along the bluff as a refuge and a shelter to come back to after their trips in boats, fishing offshore for cod and bluefish. The cod season ran for about six weeks in the spring and again for another six weeks in the fall. Then there was the bluefishing season in August and September.

At first these shanties were very crude, with board chimneys, and the roughest accommodations for sleeping, cooking, and eating, all in one room. The table hung by hinges to the wall, a three-legged stool was the only chair. Frequently the kitchen was housed in a lean-to called the "porch," which at first had no walls. It was all very rough and untidy, a man's paradise, a masculine club, separated from the females by eight miles of rutted roads.

But those eight miles were not enough; into this salty and fishy Eden, Eve insisted on coming. She wondered why the men had such a good time in Siasconset and was determined to find out. So Eve brought with her the serpent of New England and Quaker tidiness. The men might grumble but the shacks grew clean and respectable. The wives stayed to do the cooking, for they liked Siasconset too. Soon the kitchen "porches" were walled in and chimneys came to be made of brick. By 1820, the last board chimney was gone. Old windows were brought from town, and old doors utilized, the latter always hung so that the wind would swing them shut. Ells and other additions began to sprout. Plaster appeared on the walls, and Siasconset became the favorite resort of Nantucketers for the summer. Fishermen, during the off season, were glad enough to rent these little cottages to the townsfolk.

The broad state highway by which we entered Siasconset used to be known, from Bloomingdale to where it ended in the village, as Main Street. This was where the fashionable people of old Nantucket built their summer homes in the days when the fishermen's huts still had little to commend them. Here they would come for their chowder parties and squantums, or stay for the summer season. Sometimes, much thought, taste and money were lavished on their cottages. For example, the estate on the main road, now called Green Chimneys, was formerly the summer home of the Barneys, the same Barneys who occupied the pillared mansion on Main Street in Nantucket. A landscape architect who had been imported from Boston to lay out the Macy garden was employed by Mr. Barney to develop the grounds of his place in Siasconset. That was a hundred years ago. The present owner, while adding to the buildings, has skilfully preserved the character of the original place.

Most of the vacation homes, however, were small and unassuming. Some of them were buildings brought all the way across the island. For example, the charming cottage directly opposite Green Chimneys, readily distinguished by the two magnificent sycamore maples in the dooryard, was originally a cooper shop on one of the Nantucket wharves. It was picked up, put on rollers, and hauled all the way to its present location. Several other Siasconset cottages also were moved in whole or in part from some other site.

Practically all of these old houses look today very much as

they did when they were built, except for the background of trees, flowers, and little white fences. Just as in Nantucket, nobody thought about planting trees for a long time. Photographs of the village taken in the Civil War era show it not nearly as attractive as it is now. The huts were unrelieved by a tree or flower. Ugly board fences divided one lot from another. Even twenty years ago, the first impression a stranger received was that of a glaring, treeless settlement. What has been said of Nantucket is quite as true of Siasconset. It never looked as beautiful as it does now.

In order to scan more closely some of these little old houses, which have a character unmatched by any other in America, let's turn up Broadway. The first little cottage on the left is Nauticon Lodge. "Nauticon" is an Indian variant of the name Nantucket. Many of the cottages date in their present form from the War of 1812 when so many Nantucketers had to take up offshore fishing in order to eat. But this cottage goes back a long way before that time. It used to have the date 1735 over the door, but Mr. Hussey believed that it was much older than that. This is a fine example of the Siasconset house. It is exactly ten feet from the ground to the ridgepole. The roof line has been extended to make what they used to call a "wart," a projection just big enough to hold a bunk. Sleepers in these warts had to learn not to get up too suddenly in the dark.

Next beyond is Auld Lang Syne, the patriarch of the village. Alas, it looks the part now for, on account of complications about inheritance, so they say, it is rapidly crumbling to decay, and more is the pity. The accompanying sketch is intended to show the way it used to look when it was the pride of the village rather than its pathetic appearance today. Nauticon Lodge originally belonged to a Coffin, and Auld Lang Syne, also was in the same clan, the property of a Micah Coffin, who was noted for the fact that he hired Indians to do his fishing while he stayed ashore and tended the cook stove. This house is thought to date back to the close of the seventeenth century. In the door

"NAUTICON LODGE"

there are four keyholes, all worn out with long usage, one after another.

A few steps beyond, on the same side of the street, is another one of the ancient treasures of the village. This also shows the need of repair. It is now called Shanunga, after a ship that was wrecked on this shore about eighty years ago. But it is better known as the Carey house or the Baxter house, after its former owners. This is not so typical of Siasconset in style as the others just considered, because it has an upper story, but it is equipped with ells and warts in the true Siasconset manner. It is also more redolent of local history than any other. This used to be the village tavern, with a tap room measuring eight by ten, where

"AULD LANG SYNE"

the whalemen could drink themselves very rapidly into a stupor on New England rum at three cents a glass.

In the middle of the nineteenth century the tavern was run by a Mrs. Carey; hence the name frequently given to the house even today. For a picture of what the place was like, and above all what Mrs. Carey was like, the reader should turn to *Harper's Magazine* for November, 1860. In those days an artist named David H. Strother, who bore the pen, or rather pencil, name of

Porte Crayon, went about the country writing up and sketching the pre-Civil-War Americans in various sections of the land. His travels brought him to Nantucket. Apparently, he brought a friend with him, and the two men spent several days on the island. They went bluefishing out Madaket way, and again off the beach at Siasconset. Before setting out from the village they came into Mrs. Carey's tavern and bought some provisions, not forgetting to fortify themselves against the cold and wet. In fact, Porte Crayon relates that Mrs. Carey, who was in a bad humor at first, became quite chummy after a drink or two. Indeed, he drew a picture of the estimable lady for his article, a dreadful one, representing her as having a black eye, wearing a sloppy dress, and sitting in the midst of an assortment of bottles, one of which she is fondling.

This tavern became the Baxter house to the next generation, because Captain Baxter, who drove the stage between Town and Siasconset married Mrs. Carey's daughter. What Homeric combats between him and his mother-in-law must have rocked the walls and started the shingles of that old house! At any rate, Baxter as the self-appointed postmaster of Siasconset made the old tavern his post office. When he came over the hill into the village in his stage, he would blow mighty blasts on his horn to inform the inhabitants that the mail was arriving. Then he and his daughter Love—a pleasant name—sorted out the mail and handed the letters through the window to the waiting cottagers. No matter what your mail was, you paid one cent for each piece, which was Billy Baxter's reward for the service rendered. There used to be a rail fence about the house, and long before mail time every day it would be packed with all the children of the village sitting on the top rail like a flock of birds awaiting their turn at the window.

When he was ready to set forth to town again, he blew his horn once more. This was a five-minute warning to all who had last-minute errands to give him or letters to post. And it was exactly five minutes—no more—by a large silver watch, which he always declared was a gift to him from President Grant on the occasion of his visit to Siasconset.

In 1872, a post office in Siasconset was formally recognized by the United States. Love Baxter was appointed postmistress at a salary of twelve dollars a year, and her father received, for carrying the mail to the boat, eight dollars annually. There seems to have been a lapse in the post office history, from the official point of view, for there was a "reopening" of the Siasconset post office in 1883, with a Mrs. Almy as postmistress, which sounds as if the position, with its princely emoluments, had passed out of the hands of the Baxter Dynasty.

The house looks now as it did in 1811, but the low part was built all of two hundred and fifty years ago. This little one-story portion was brought on rollers all the way from the other village of Sesacacha, which has now completely disappeared, but which was once as big and important a fishing center as Siasconset. It lay between Sesacacha pond and the sea out beyond Sankaty Light.

Just by Shanunga, on the side opposite from Broadway, the other two streets open together into a little town square, and in the heart of it stands the famous village pump. This is a monument of antiquity also, for here the inhabitants dug their community well in the year 1776, after passing the (cocked) hat around for subscriptions. This well served the village for a hundred years or more. Everybody went to the pump with a bucket and drew his water for all needs. In the eighties it was the custom to pay one cent a pailful to boys who made a business of carrying it. The water was supposed to have some extraordinary properties, but, whatever they were, they are now lost to the world, for the pump is in chains, merely a relic of the past. Rain water in barrels was used for ablutions. A guest was sometimes taken to the barrel and told, "You can stay here as long as the water lasts."

The odd-shaped cottage used in the illustration as a background for the pump is another relic of the past. It was doing duty during the hard years of the War of 1812. With its mantle of trumpet creeper, it, too, has been an artist's favorite.

From this little dwelling there runs to Broadway a typical Siasconset thoroughfare, stretching away to a length of almost fourteen feet. It is named after the illustrious Maria Mitchell, and does seem a bit skimpy for her.

From this point on the visitor may ramble about the lanes at his own will and find his own little gems of Siasconset architecture without further help. About mid-July, when the pink ramblers are still blooming over the roofs and the hollyhocks are just beginning to lift their heads over the palings, is the time when these little houses show off at their best.

Of course, we must walk to the edge of the bluff on which the village is built, and look down at the beach and the sea. In the early days the ocean came right to the foot of the bluff, so close, in fact, that, during one storm, a whole street with its houses tumbled into the surf. There were old people, not so long ago, who used to say that they could remember when one "could toss a penny from Broadway into the sea." Now the coast line has retreated far out. The beach is famous for its surf

THE OLD PUMP

bathing. Fifty or sixty years ago, life lines were rigged out to buoys, and only the hardy swimmer was bold enough to let go. That *Scribner's* article of the year 1873 tells of the terrible quicksands and deadly undertow on the Siasconset beach!

The life lines have long since gone, and with them all the legend about undertow and quicksands. A life guard lolls on the sand all the summer long, but he never has anything to do except to rake up the seaweed. Even twenty years ago there were still bathhouses to rent on the beach, for in those days no one would think of walking through the village in a bathing suit, even if shrouded in a voluminous and flopping bathrobe. All genteel ladies cultivated a mystery about their "limbs" and struggled in the surf, hanging desperately to the life line, swathed in bloomers, stockings, and skirts. Rumor hath it that fashions have changed since, and bathhouses have become superfluous.

Between the village and the beach is the settlement of the squatters, known as Codfish Park. This in recent years has spruced up amazingly and is growing flowers and flaunting new shingles and fresh paint as gay as you please. But it was not always thus. There are still little cabins in the Park that suggest something of the way all the Siasconset houses were built, with a stray window here and an old door there and a piece of tiling for a chimney. In the days when offshore fishing flourished, the Park was somewhat *dégagé*. Entrails and heads of fish were blithely tossed about, which under the summer sun became extremely obsolete. Now that the fish refuse to be caught off this beach any more, the inhabitants grow nasturtiums, clip hedges and take in washing for the "summer people" up the bank, and the place is nothing if not genteel.

The visitor, if he has not forgotten the use of his legs, will now stroll along the path at the edge of the bluff toward Sankaty Light. This is the finest short walk on the island, at any time of the day or night. Of course, for invalids there is a road-

ATLANTIC AVENUE, CODFISH PARK

way that parallels the walk some distance back from the bluff, but we have left our car parked at the post office.

It was not so long ago that the lighthouse was considered far from the summer cottagers, but now they have crept right up to the government reservation. Obed Macy in his history describes the view from Sankaty as he saw it a hundred years ago. At that time there was no lighthouse:

A view from Sancoty Head, at a clear sunset, can hardly be surpassed in beauty and grandeur. The rich coloring of the sky, reflected by the distant waters, the distinct outline of the town, with its steeples and busy windmills, the repose of the surrounding plain, contrasted with the gloom which broods over the rolling and roaring ocean in the rear give rise to sensations, which can be felt indeed but not described.

Obed must have had a fine pair of eyes! Any ordinary person by knowing where to look may strain his vision and make out a tiny speck on the western horizon, but he will have to climb the lighthouse in order to distinguish the arms and know it to be a windmill. At that he would not know whether it was "busy," and the church steeples are still harder to discern.

But Sankaty Head is a great place for a view in any direction. If you are lucky you may hit upon a day with one of those "dry northeasters" which the island knows in summer, when a wind that is supposed to bring rain instead sweeps the sky clear of every cloud, and makes the horizon a keen razor edge against the sea. On such a day one can easily see the shore of Cape Cod in the neighborhood of Chatham and the lightship at Handkerchief Shoal.

The scene as Obed Macy described it from Sankaty Head, with his telescopic vision, is not much changed. Of course, the cottages of Siasconset have since stretched out along the bluff, north and south; and below, directly to the west, lie the attractive, rolling links of the Sankaty Head Golf Club, an amazing achievement built from a wilderness of scrub oak and sand.

After all, the finest view is seaward. Just at the edge of the bluff is a wooden bench cut up with the initials of forty years of visitors. Sit down on the ground and lean your back up against this bench. Obed Macy says the view "can hardly be surpassed in beauty and grandeur," but there is nothing staggering about

SANKATY LIGHT

the scene. The surf is breaking only about eighty-five feet below. Sankaty Head is no Dover Cliff, but your eye does sweep a magnificent expanse of ocean and sky, and the more you look at it the more you like it.

According to tradition, Bartholomew Gosnold, the English navigator, landed on the beach at this spot, in 1602, the first white man to set foot on the island. It is not hard to imagine him standing here on the edge of the bluff and looking seaward to where his little ship *Concord* rode at anchor among the shoals. The view is little changed today.

There are all sorts of days when it is good to look at that prospect, but for sheer vacation feeling I commend one of those warm August days—it *can* get up to 85° in the shade—when there is a gentle wind, south by southwest, which seems to be trying to muster enough clouds to make up a shower. And these clouds, like fat, lazy conscripts in white uniforms, line up very slowly and reluctantly along the southern horizon. Perhaps you have wondered sometimes where Mr. N. C. Wyeth gets the romantic cloud shapes that he puts into his illustrations. You can see them off Sankaty Head on just such a day.

Below that sky is an ever-changing sea. Sometimes it is a pure cobalt; other days it is crossed by dark tracks that seem to come from nowhere. Again, thanks to the cloud shadows, it is a deep violet with insets of pea green, and that violet is just purple enough to suggest why the Greeks called the sea "wine dark." At any rate, with the pageantry of sea and sky and a soft-scented breeze off the moors, Sankaty is a place of all places to loaf away a whole afternoon.

For the farthest view climb the seventy-five steps to the top of the lighthouse. A knock at the door will bring you the courteous lighthouse keeper, Mr. Eugene N. Larsen, who will unlock the lighthouse door for you and show you the lantern. Mr. and Mrs. Larsen were both born in Norway. Mr. Larsen went to sea at sixteen in the British merchant service, sailing square-riggers. Then he entered the American Revenue service and became quartermaster. Ask him to tell you about when he was on the cutter *Gresham* at the time they went to the rescue of the *Republic* after her fatal collision in a fog back in 1908.

Persons who have a yearning for statistics are hereby informed—this on the word of Captain Larsen—that the light shows 166 feet above water; it is electric, having 720,000 candle power, and is flashing. Forty-two miles southeast is the famous Nantucket lightship, marking, on the edge of these shoals, the steamer course to Europe. Fourteen miles due east is the edge of the Rose and Crown shoal, which marks the boundary in that direction and beyond which ply the United Fruit steamers and the New York to Boston boats.

The lighthouse was built in 1850, and for awhile it was confused with the Gay Head light on Martha's Vineyard, which also is a flashing light, with the result that several ships went on the shoals. Now it is managed entirely by electricity, but Mr. Larsen will show you the clockwork device which preceded it, and a contraption that had to be wound up every hour—fifty-five turns. It is still something to fall back on in case the electrical outfit goes wrong.

While strolling back toward supper time, supposing that we have loafed on Sankaty for several hours, let us hear some more from Obed Macy about Siasconset. Even in his day the village was better known as a summer resort for the residents of Nantucket than for its fishermen, for the offshore codfishing had sadly declined even as early as 1835. Here is the way he writes about Siasconset:

As a summer resort, no place in the United States presents greater attractions for the invalid than Siasconset. It is not, indeed, the focus of fashionable life; but the fine bracing air, the excellent water, and the unique customs and "laws" of the place are adapted to refresh and invigorate both mind and body. At Siasconset, all are on a level, or rather on an equal elevation. Useless forms and ceremonies are laid aside, and the little community, for the time being, indulge in a reciprocity of good feeling and interchange of civilities, which can be found in no place but one situated precisely like Siasconset, and no other such place exists in the known world.

In front, the eye rests on the broad expanse of the Atlantic, and below, the surf, rolling and breaking, gives animation to the scene by day and lulls to repose by night. Fleets of fishing smacks are frequently anchored or sailing near the shore, catering for distant markets; and larger vessels on longer voyages are continually passing. The sea bird is ever skimming over the ocean, now eyeing the waters beneath, and now darting headlong at his prey. Shoals of small fishes may be seen blackening the surface, sometimes floating leasurely [*sic*] with the tide, at others fleeing from the pursuit of the shark; and occasionally the majestic whale comes so near one may see his breath and hear his breathing.

Times have changed enormously, or else Obed tended to draw the long bow when he plunged his quill into that passage of description. The visitor can now stand every day and all day throughout the long summer with the finest pair of eyes and scarcely ever see so much as a dory on the surface of the ocean.

As for the whale coming close to shore to entertain the off-islanders with his heavy breathing—even a Realtor would not dare to advertise that attraction now!

The unique charm of Siasconset to the eye is its grassy lanes and low, picturesque cottages, hemmed in with little white fences and gay with flowers. After reading about the numerous

"CASTLE BANDBOX"

fires in Nantucket, one of them devastating enough to be the major cause of the downfall of the town, it is hard to understand why this little huddle of wooden houses, soaked in fish oil and lighted by candles, managed to survive with never a fire of any consequence in its history of two hundred and fifty years!

There was another charm to Siasconset besides that which delighted the eye. As Macy says, there were certain customs of simplicity and democracy about the summer colony there that were unwritten but frequently referred to as the "laws of Siasconset." Anyone who dared to build a house that went his neighbor one better in modern improvements was forced to run the gauntlet of disapproval. There was no dressing up. Colonel Hart in collecting material for his story *Miriam Coffin,* so frequently mentioned in these pages, made the journey to Siasconset and was fascinated by its air of simplicity. Indeed, he went so far as to pretend in his introduction that the whole novel had been given to him, in a bundle wrapped with a tarry string, by an old fisherman in the village. When one reads the highflown, elegant language in which that story was written, the pretense is rather droll. Literary codfishermen were never plentiful anywhere, even in Siasconset!

Hart particularly praises the "laws" of the village and holds up to scorn somebody who had the effrontery to build a modern house, as a traitor to the Siasconset tradition. Everyone, whether the daughter of the richest whaling captain or the orphan girl who "worked out," met at the same old pump and gossiped about the same subjects. The latchstring of every door hung outside, and everyone knew everyone else by his first name. It was the sort of community that the ardent French republican, Crèvecoeur, would have thought a bit of heaven on earth.

Forty years after Hart's visit, another lover of the village published a ballad in the *Inquirer and Mirror,* entitled the "Laws of Siasconset." The sentiment of the whole is well expressed in one of its stanzas, thus:

> Here kings and compliments are done,
> And all your Boston fashions,
> The song, the jest, the smile serene
> Amuse the friend that haunts it;

SIASCONSET

Here old simplicity is seen,
In ancient dress at 'Sconset.

Something might be said about the curious old-timers of Siasconset, the fishermen and the retired whalemen who lived there, and were famous as "characters." But the following last will and testament of one of them, Obed Gardner, serves better to sketch such a personality than a whole chapter of description. Without knowing it, he left in this document a character sketch of himself and a picture of his time. Here it is as quoted in *The Evolution of Siasconset,* by Roland B. Hussey:

Siasconset, May 30th, 1841

I, Obed, Gardner, master mariner, now livin in Sconset, write down this will.

Item.—I have cruised with my wife, Huldy Jane, since 1811. We signed articles in town before the preacher on Independence Day. I want her and my oldest boy Jotham to be captain and mate in bringin to port whatever I leave and to see that every one of the crew gets the lay as writ down on this paper. I put mother in command. I know shell be captain anyway, for six months after we started on our cruise I found out that I was mate and she was master. I don't mean that she ever mutinied, but I no that whenever we didnt agree she manoovered to work to windward. May be it was all right for she could sail closer to the wind than I could and could manage the crew of little ones that she had as much to do with shippin as I did. She always wanted me to do the swearin when there was any trouble. I no that when she and Jotham break bulk the cargo will be got out as well as I could do it myself.

Item.—In 1838 Captain Ichabod Worth got tired of the old

Nancy Rotch and wanted to get rid of her so he got me to take a piece of her. When I last saw her she was lyin at the wharf in Valparaiso moren half full of oil. Mother never liked her. I want Jotham to have that piece as extra pay for what he does in settlin up my affairs for heel have to steer things while mother is takin observations, watchin the weather and lookin over things below decks.

Item.—I want Mother to have the house in Union street until she goes aloft. Then I want it to go to the children in equal lays and if any child dies I want the lay of the parent to go to the parents young ones. But I dont want my daughter Belindy to have anything as long as her husband is livin. He is a lubber, but she has been cruisin with him for years. I havent got anything agin him but he doesnt no how to navigate the sea of life. I do believe if he wanted to stop a leak board ship it would be just like him to go into the hold with an auger and bore a hole threw the plankin to let the bilgewater out to the sea. But Belindy likes him. Thats just like a woman. If I should give the lay out and out to her, I am afraid her husband would manoover to get hold of it. So I want mother and Jotham to put it out at interest and give what comes out of it to her until her husband ships for a corpse below decks in the grave yard. Then she can take the lay and do what she wants with it.

Item.—I dont want my son Ezry to have anything from what I leave. All the children except him was good ones. They looked out for mother and me. He didnt take after either of us except the time he took after me with a fid and hit me over the starboard eye. He new what was to come and was smart enough to jump into Johnny Gibbs catboat, haul in the sheet and steer for the continent. When he got to Bedford he shipped as boat steerer on the old Falcon. I was glad he did. I dont know where he is now but I herd he was master of a steamboat runnin between

Canton and Whampoa. I havent got any news of him and I guess he hasnt got any for me. The black eye he gave me is outlawed and I dont now lay anything up agin him for that.

Item.—I want mother and Jotham to settle up things as soon as they can, break bulk and make a fair divide between the children. But dont forget what I have writ down about mother and Belindy. I dont think Belindys husband will make any fuss about the way I have taken care of her unless she runs head on the shoals of a lawyers office. Then look out for squalls. I hope sheel stand off if she sees a lawyer comin thort her bows.

Item.—I want mother to have half of what comes from what is left of my property besides the house on Union street. She deserves it. Every time I was around the Horn she did her duty to the young ones and I want her to have enough to live on until she goes aloft. Then I want her lay to go to the children except that Belindy shall only have what comes from it until her husband dies. If mother wants to marry again thats her business I never did like to cruise without a mate, and I guess she would not like to either.

Obed Gardner

Master Mariner

Captain Obed Gardner ast us into his porch and opened his locker. He then ast us to take a drink of rum that was fetched to him from Boston by Captain George Swain, in his schooner. It was masterly warmin to our insides. Then he pulled this paper out of his pea jacket and signed it and said it was his will and he ast us to sign it as witnesses. We done so, and then he ast one of us to write down what took place and as they said I was more of a skoller than they, I did so.

Jethro Coffin 2nd

Eleazur Paddack

Shubael Starbuck.

CHAPTER XII

SIASCONSET: CONTINUED

IN the middle of the last century a carpenter and builder, discouraged by the lack of business in Nantucket, shut up shop, moved to Siasconset and made the best living he could by fishing. In the seventies a New York gentleman approached him with the request that he build a cottage for him at Siasconset in the traditional style. The builder nearly dropped dead of surprise and joy. It was his first order in twenty years.

These same seventies that saw a revival of interest in Nantucket were the years when its little neighbor began to perk up with summer visitors, too, and what had been merely the "Newport of the Nantucketoise" became more and more the resort of the "Strangers." The prevailing rental rates in the eighties was seventy-five dollars a season for a cottage. At the same time, new homes and summer hotels began to sprout. The newer village tended to grow up, either along the bluff toward Sankaty or over the area to the south of the old village, called Sunset Heights, for no apparent reason except that it faces the sunrise. Here is where the hotels were built.

Southward along the low bluff from Sunset Heights is another pleasant walk toward Tom Never's Pond, and Tom Never's Head, rising just beyond. Tom, thus immortalized, was an Indian who lived two hundred and fifty years ago on the bluff that now bears his name. His job was to keep a lookout for stranded whales. Next to Sankaty, Tom Never's Head is the

"HEARTSEASE"

finest place on this side of the island to scan the sea and sky. A building was put up there many years ago, and in 1916 there was an attempt to boom the surrounding property for cottages, but it did not thrive. During the war it was whispered that German sympathizers were using the building to signal to U-boats off the shoals. There was supposed to be a secret passageway among the shoals direct to Tom Never's, and many believed that the Germans actually got their supplies of gasoline there. And if this seems absurd, it must be remembered that in 1916 a German submarine did sink six steamers off Nantucket. The building stood empty a long time and then was burned down, but it does seem as if someone with imagination and a little capital could do something with this splendid site. From Tom Never's Head several rutted roads meander over the moors, leading back to Surfside, where the government radio station is located. On their winding way they pass ideal picnicking and bathing places on the South Shore.

To return to Siasconset, there is another charming settlement which is worth a look. Years ago a Mr. Underhill built a whole village of his own along three or four little lanes. It consisted of tiny houses built in the manner of the fisherman huts in the old village, without being literal copies of any of them. Covered with their climbing roses, their windows bright with flower boxes, they, too, delight the eye. They belong in the Siasconset scene.

Some taxi driver with sight-seers from town may point out these Underhill cottages, saying: "There's the actor colony." And the response is a gush of "Oh how quaint!" and that sort of thing. But alas for the truth! The actors don't live here in these little houses any more. But there once was an actor colony in

Siasconset, and its story is worth telling.

Thirty years ago Siasconset was famous as the greatest actor summer colony to be found anywhere. Apparently it all began at the turn of the century with Mr. George Fawcett and his wife, Percy Haswell, who were among the earliest to come here. Mr. Fawcett sent his family ahead of him, and when he landed on his first visit to Nantucket he says he discovered that, while his ticket from New York had cost him only about six dollars, he "had to pay a local pirate four dollars" to drive him over to Siasconset. Next morning a northeaster started in. He was completely disgusted and ready to return to civilization, but he hesitated, on the strong protests of the family. It was a fatal hesitation, for he and Mrs. Fawcett became Siasconseters for thirty-five seasons thereafter. And they made their permanent home in Nantucket.

In his cottage on that first visit were Mrs. Hopper, mother of the late DeWolf Hopper, and Mrs. G. H. Gilbert. The latter was a greatly beloved actress of the nineties whose playing of old ladies' parts is still a delightful memory among the greybeards and baldheads of today. She had been for thirty years under the management of Augustin Daly. That summer Mr. Daly died in Paris. Mr. Fawcett then wired to Mr. Frohman that Mrs. Gilbert was available for a new contract, and received back word to engage her at her own terms. When this was accomplished, Mr. Frohman made considerable publicity out of the fact that the popular actress was henceforth to be under his management. Newspaper men and photographers found their way to Siasconset for their publicity and feature articles. All this was particularly interesting to the actor guild, and members of the Lambs' Club asked each other, "Where *is* this Siasconset?"

NANTUCKET

Since Mr. Fawcett was the supreme authority on the subject, his actor friends came to him for the answer. Of course, after he had described the place, they arrived, bag and baggage, to see for themselves. First were "Billy" Thompson, the actor and producer, and his wife, Isabel Irving, and Digby Bell, the famous comedian. After that it was only a matter of a short time before *their* friends came likewise. By 1905 or 1906, there were fifty members of the Lambs' Club in the summer colony: William Courtney, Robert Hilliard, Harry Woodruff, DeWolf Hopper, Louise Closser Hale and her husband Walter—who was more of an artist than an actor—Alice Fisher Harcourt, Mary Mannering, Bertha Galland, Nanette Comstock, Brandon Hurst, Vincent Serrano, George Giddens, Edwin Stevens, Dewitt Jennings, Aubrey Boucicault, Frank Gillmore, now president of the Actors' Equity—the list could be prolonged to include, at one time or another, all the headliners of the stage between 1895 and the outbreak of the World War. Naturally, playwrights and producers came, too, such as Bronson Howard, Percy Mackaye, Morris Gest, and Daniel Frohman.

To see some interesting reminders of those stars and their days in Siasconset, go back stage in the Casino and examine the photographs on the wall. There is one delicious picture of Mrs. Gilbert just after a benefit performance in her honor. On this occasion she has been presented with a rocking chair, adorned with a huge satin bow, and a capacious silver tankard or loving cup. In the photograph she grips the back of the rocking chair with one hand and holds on to the tankard with the air of not having the faintest idea what to do with it.

In those days there was at least one benefit performance during the season for the Casino—which was chronically in debt—put on by the actors. Those were rare occasions, and the actors threw themselves into their parts with the greatest spirit and sense of camaraderie with the audience. Even when the benighted days of the movies came and only a few actors were still returning to the village, it was not unusual for the leading man of the picture to step up into the spotlight and make a few "well-chosen remarks." Vincent Serrano on such an occasion rode the local donkey into the auditorium and obligingly trotted up and down the aisles. Mr. Fawcett, while one of his early films was being shown at the Casino, was summoned to the stage for a speech; and there he solemnly assured the audience that they were fools to pay fifty cents to see him on the screen when, for nothing at all, they could see him any day working in his garden by just leaning over the fence. That, he assured them, *was* something to see!

Another place to find relics of the actor *régime* is the old golf club. This is now left as a resource for people who do not belong to the Sankaty Head Club, but there was a long time when it was the center of village life. Among other souvenirs there hangs on the wall a picture of a grand concourse of the colony, in front of the club house, photographed perhaps thirty years ago; and, alas, nobody on the premises now has any idea who they are.

This golf club sprang from the enthusiasm of Mr. Fawcett and Mr. John Grout, an old-time Siasconset cottager. Together they essayed to build a golf course, by hiring what was left of Bloomingdale, and sinking a matter of nine holes in some corrugated turf. The total cost came to $196, and it was well worth that tremendous outlay. Thereafter, small boys from the village made good money by their quite amateurish services as caddies. Terrific rivalries sprang up over individual prowess. Particularly in the first year of the Club, Digby Bell and Bill Thompson strove with might and main to "beat Fawcett," who was always just a shade too good for them. On one afternoon the rumor spread that Bell, who took his game very seriously, was about to break a hundred. Bulletins were issued and flying messengers were sent by his friends to his cottage. He did succeed, to the jubilation of all beholders. His friends managed to keep him at the club until dusk, and on his return home he found that his wife and neighbors had illuminated their little street in honor of the great achievement.

Those were the palmy days of Siasconset. Not only actors but writers and artists and musicians came to spend their summers here. But this period gradually came to an end, beginning with the ghastly year 1914. In the earlier days the actor enjoyed a security under his contract, and the theater business was good. Gradually, the bottom fell out. Nobody knew where he stood for another year. Road companies ceased to exist. The movies began their conquest. A common sight was the stranding of a well-known actor at Siasconset after the failure of a play for which he had long rehearsed, faced with the bleak prospect of no employment ahead for the fall and winter. These actors were kind to each other, for each knew that, in spite of present popularity and reputation, his own time might come. As a whole, they were as fine, interesting, and withal picturesque a group of good friends as one might hope to find the world over.

Although careful dressers on Broadway, many of these leading men went about the village happy in baggy trousers and flannel shirts. You would not have known the Broadway star from the fish man of Codfish Park except that the latter was probably more particular about his attire. Perhaps this was one of the chief reasons that endeared the place to the actors. For the summer months they could be off display and have a natural, human time.

On the other hand, there were those who always dressed the part. Twenty years and more ago, the visitor arriving at the steamboat wharf in Nantucket at the height of the season would probably have his gaze arrested by the spectacle of the handsome figure of a man with greying hair, arrayed in white flannels, wearing a half bushel of scarlet geraniums in his buttonhole and a tie to match, a white silk band on a rakish Panama hat, and leaning negligently on a cane. He always stood well down stage, approximately center. This was Robert Hilliard, famous in those days for his success in *A Fool There Was*.

In those halcyon years Hilliard had, next to his Siasconset house, a caravansary for guests, which he kept filled with his actor friends, and he always came to the wharf to welcome them. When you saw him there you looked about, as the passengers filed down the gangplank, to see whom you could recognize. And you would stand and stare unashamed as the theatrical stars climbed aboard the little train for Siasconset.

Among these guests one summer was "The Russell," Lillian, the blonde beauty of the eighties and nineties. She had hoped to slip into Siasconset unobserved, but her friend DeWolf Hopper got wind of the visit and arranged a triumphal welcome. The actors arrayed themselves in bizarre costume. He himself, preceded by a bugler, paraded to the station in a flamboyant bathrobe and enormous, flapping beach hat, trimmed with plumes. Others, with elegant gestures, strewed the road ahead of her with rambler roses. "A good time was had by all," except possibly Lillian herself.

Today there is hardly a trace of the actor colony. Mrs. Thompson (Isabel Irving) and Miss Agnes Everett are still honored citizens, and Mrs. Fawcett often drives over from town during the summer. But these are all who are left of that famous group. Representing the present generation, Miss Patricia Collinge has become a summer resident, with a new cottage on the far end of the South bluff, but there the list ends. The actors of Siasconset are one with the snows of yester year.

'Sconseters are proud of the fact that two Presidents thought it worth while to drive over from town to see the village. The first was Grant, in 1874. Imagine that taciturn figure with a cigar in his mouth, driving through the Siasconset lanes! The other was Woodrow Wilson. It was the war year, 1917, and he came to visit his daughter, Mrs. Sayre, who was then a summer resident.

Of President Wilson's visit there is an unpublished story. The afternoon that he was to arrive, Secret Service men communicated with the keeper of a small boarding establishment to have a supper ready for the entire Presidential party. The idea was to save Mrs. Sayre the necessity of feeding so many people.

The whole village buzzed with excitement, and what went on in the little boarding house can readily be imagined. The proprietor, a large and bulgy person, who had never been seen abroad or at home except in his suspenders, a buttonless shirt held together by a safety pin, and sleeves rolled to the elbow, effected a marvelous transformation into coat, collar, and neck-

tie. The one waitress hastily journeyed in the bus to Nantucket
for the purpose of having her hair waved and her nails mani-
cured. A grand lobster dinner was prepared. Many candles
illumined the specially decorated table. All was in readiness.
His Excellency and Mrs. Wilson appeared in the village at last,
jogging through the streets in a carriage surrounded by the
official guard. To everyone's consternation, he drove past the
scene of the banquet directly to his daughter's cottage!

Still the dinner waited. Anxious 'Sconseters gathered about
the lighted windows to see what would happen. The proprietor
was there with his lobster and his speech of welcome. Alas, no
President! The candles sputtered low and dripped mournful
tears of wax upon the snowy tablecloth. Finally, a messenger
was sent to Mrs. Sayre's house, and was indignantly informed
that the President had already supped on scraps from his
daughter's refrigerator, having waited in vain for the dinner
which was supposed to have been sent to the cottage. All that
lobster, all those candles, those flashing finger nails, that self
flagellation of coat, collar, and tie!

The conclusion of this story is that Mr. Wilson sent for the
unhappy host, shook hands with him, expressed his regret for
the misunderstanding, and offered to pay for the uneaten dinner. When the man declined to accept this, the President
thanked him, and on his return to Washington sent him a
photograph inscribed "To my friend," which was one of the
pleasantest things Woodrow Wilson ever did.

During the last quarter of the nineteenth century the social
life of the summer colony was centered on the beach. It was the
custom for each cottager to erect a sort of tent or awning, on
the posts of which he sometimes tacked his calling card. Here,

for the greater part of any fine day, was the place to look for a family, rather than at their cottage. Here the ladies brought their sewing and their books. Here they interchanged visits, and the children dug in the sand or splashed in the water all day.

Early in the twentieth century the social life shifted from the beach to the Casino, which was built in 1900, by a tremendous effort on the part of the citizens and a wide, overhanging mortgage. Thereafter, the rivalries between Siasconset and Nantucket were intense in whatever field of contest could be devised. In the rear of the Casino stage, among the photographs of actor celebrities, is one of a baseball team bearing on their uniformed chests in large letters, " 'Sconset," a team which existed for the sole purpose of beating a corresponding assortment of athletes from Nantucket. Later, as baseball faded out, it was tennis and golf, especially the former. And these contests still go on to a degree, but without one-tenth of the old-time excitement and crowds as when it was an all-day affair to make the journey to or from Nantucket. In those days, residents of Nantucket and Siasconset affected to be "going slumming" whenever the one visited the other. Now, when it is only a matter of a ten minutes' drive, the old partisanship has almost vanished and the rollicking fun that went with it.

On one occasion, in the old days, there was a testimonial or benefit performance given in the Siasconset Casino. The Nantucketers came over in full force, for the famous stars of the actor colony were all advertised to appear and shine. All went well, but during the intermission there was a subdued hum of "They won't go home till morning," from certain unregenerate 'Sconseters, the point of which was not then apparent. The

Nantucket delegation had chartered a special train for the event; and, when the show was over, the party boarded the train and settled into their seats for a jolly ride back to town. The locomotive tooted and started off bravely, but when it came to a slight upward grade, suddenly the wheels spun on the tracks without gaining an inch. An investigation was started with a feeble lantern. Out from the bushes came the same theme song, this time sung lustily, "They won't get home till morning." Finally the distracted engineer discovered that the rails had been thoroughly greased with bacon rind. Then, for some time, Nantucket gentlemen in their party clothes grubbed about with their bare hands in the dark to throw sand on the rails. At last, the train managed to get headway and the Nantucket party arrived back in town. But the musical prediction of the 'Sconseters had been fulfilled.

Now, alas, there is no little train, no galaxy of famous actors, and no such fun.

The horseless carriage was a rare apparition on the island before 1914, and in that *annus mirabilis* the city fathers passed an ordinance forbidding the contraptions entirely. There was, of course, the state highway on which Nantucket ordinances didn't count. Accordingly, the mail carrier would leave the limits of the town in his automobile and come to a stop at the limit of the state road at Siasconset. Thence, when he moved, he had to be dragged by a horse. There used to be a popular postcard, picturing the mail man sitting behind the wheel of his touring car but hitched to a horse. There was a strong feeling that automobiles did not belong on a little island like Nantucket any more than in Bermuda. Some objected that the lanes and streets were too narrow for motor cars, and others opined that they "might hurt the hosses."

But the pressure was too strong. Four years later the prohibition was repealed and the cars swarmed over the island like grasshoppers. Unfortunately, the raising of the embargo tended at first, during the boom years, to bring a class of "summer people" who threw money about, drove their red devils regardless and bragged about their "pre-war stuff." These newcomers did not fit in with the spirit of either Nantucket or Siasconset. On the other hand, many parts of the island have been opened up for summer residence which would have been impracticable without the motor car, such as Squam, Quidnet, Shimmo, and Monomoy. Unquestionably, the automobile is here to stay. It will soon be as indigenous as the old tip cart or box wagon. It is a familiar sight now to see a farmer bringing home his cow from pasture tethered to an ancient but honorable Ford.

There is a real danger, however, that the old-time simplicity of Siasconset may be lost. Fifty years ago the young people met in the railroad station for candy pulls and charades, or danced in the dining room of the little hotel. There was ice cream with lemonade and cookies, and the boys and girls went home about eleven o'clock. And there was great fun in picnics and clam bakes on the shore, frequently extemporized in a hurry and all the jollier for that. The elders, for their part, never thought of formal dinners or receptions or calling, in white gloves, with visiting cards. It will not do to let the Philistines conquer Siasconset; it must not be allowed to become just another summer resort; but happily there are signs that a reaction is setting back in favor of the ancient tradition. The old Siasconset was beloved for its magnificent surf bathing, its picturesque cottages, its moors with their winding roads, its scented breezes, its circling blue ring of ocean, and, above all, for the simple neighborliness of genuine, unpretentious people. That tradition is still strong, and may it never surrender!

The poet Bliss Carman once walked the lanes of Siasconset and roamed over the moors. He wrote:

Did you ever hear of 'Sconset where there's nothing much but moors,
And beach, and sea and silence and eternal out of doors—
Where the azure round of ocean meets the paler dome of day,
Where the sailing clouds of summer on the sea-line melt away,
And there's not an ounce of trouble
Anywhere?

Where the field larks in the morning will be crying at the door,
With the whisper of the moor wind and the surf along the shore;
Where the little, shingled houses down the little grassy street
Are grey with salt of sea winds, and the strong sea air is sweet
With the flowers in their dooryards;
Me for there!

CHAPTER XIII

THE ISLAND

AS long ago as 1882, a certain Mr. E. K. Godfrey, who managed The Philadelphia Candy Store and Tourists' General Registry Agency, on the corner of Orange and Main Streets, published a magnum opus on: *The Island of Nantucket; What It Was, and What It Is; Being a Complete Index and Guide to this Noted Resort, Containing Descriptions of Everything On or About the Island in Regard to Which the Visitor or Resident May Desire Information, Including Its History, People, Agriculture, Botany, Conchology, and Geology, with Maps of the Island.* As this title suggests, there is a prodigious amount of information packed into the little volume, and it is conveniently arranged by the letters of the alphabet so that the reader finds, for example, "Distinguished citizens" followed by "Drowning: methods of resuscitation."

Most of the ground covered in that guide book must be included somehow in this chapter. Having gone sight-seeing in Nantucket and Siasconset, at the two opposite sides of the island, we should now consider the whole. The reader, however, is hereby advised that if he wants any "agriculture," "conchology," or "geology," he will not find a trace of them in these pages; for that matter, there will be practically no exact information on "botany," or any of the other sciences. Whoever requires the Latin names of plant, bird, or beast on Nantucket, must turn to Mr. Godfrey or to any of the books written on special

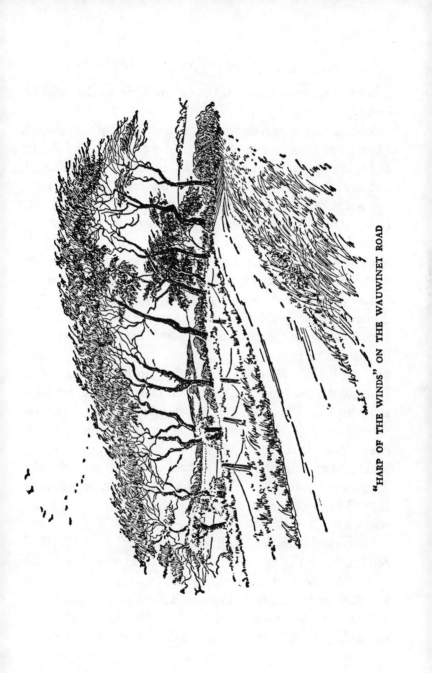

"HARP OF THE WINDS" ON THE WAUWINET ROAD

subjects, of which there are several, notably in the field of botany.

A glance at the map shows Nantucket to be an island, shaped like a lamb chop, lying south of the elbow of Cape Cod. Being a glacial dump of sand and gravel, its coast line has changed frequently, even in the memory of living men. One long sand spit reaches to the north, Great Point, where there is a lighthouse. Another, Coatue, makes the western boundary of the Great Harbor. The outlines of these are constantly being altered by the sea. At the Wauwinet end of this harbor is another stretch of sand between it and the ocean. This is known as the "haul-over," because at this point the fishermen drag their dories across to avoid the long journey around Great Point. Here is one of the conspicuous examples of the changes wrought by the sea. In 1875, a gale cut an open channel right through into the harbor. Then it was closed again by another storm. In 1896, the sea broke through once more and opened up a strait between a quarter and a half mile in width. This remained a navigable exit and entrance for the fishing fleet until twelve years later, when another freak storm filled it all up again and made it once more a "haul-over" as it is today. The shoals surrounding the island, also, are no sooner carefully charted by government survey than they shift in outline and position.

Nantucket's location, well out at sea and near the Gulf Stream, has given the island a climate of its own. It is like a ship anchored thirty miles out, a vessel fourteen miles in length and three and a half miles in beam. The winters, therefore, are milder and the summers cooler than the climate of a corresponding latitude on the mainland. The sea water is much less chilly for bathing than it is on the coast only a short distance to the north. Hence, it is not hard to understand why Nantucket developed the reputation of being a health resort.

Crèvecoeur observed that "In summer the climate is extremely pleasant; they are not exposed to the scorching sun of the continent, the heat being tempered by the sea breezes with which they are perpetually refreshed. In the winter, however, they pay severely for those advantages. . . . The north west wind, the tyrant of this country . . . blows with redoubled force and renders this island bleak and uncomfortable." Here he is describing February and March, months none too seductive anywhere north of Florida.

Although nowadays it is not considered good form by some to admit there are fogs in Nantucket, it was not ever thus. The old-timers took pride in the astonishing specific density of the real Nantucket fog. They boasted that a genuine one could make the inside of a custard pie look thin and transparent. There is an ancient tale of a whaling captain who left the harbor mouth in a fog so dense that he made a deep gash in it with his harpoon. When he returned from his cruise, three years later, he ran into the identical fog, but was able to steer into the harbor by recognizing the scar that he had left there with his harpoon!

The combination of strong sea winds and glacial soil has given the island its peculiar vegetation. A very thin surface deposit of vegetable matter over gravel and sand meant that the ground was promising for neither forest nor farm. Every visitor who came to Nantucket, up to a generation ago, remarked on the general aspect of a treeless barren. Crèvecoeur observed it in the eighteenth century and Thoreau made a similar comment nearly a hundred years later.

Here is what the former jotted down:

There are but few gardens and arable lands in the neighbor-hood of the town, for nothing can be more sterile and sandy than this part of the island. . . . There are very few farms . . . [the settlers] not being possessed of a single tree in the whole extent of their dominions. . . . It appears to be a sandy submarine mountain covered here and there with sorrel grass, a few cedar bushes and scrubby oaks.

Also, when Thoreau made his visit in 1852, he noted that the commons looked "like a prairie."

It isn't certain that Herman Melville ever came to Nantucket, but at least he knew it by reputation. Here is a paragraph from the fourteenth chapter of *Moby Dick:*

Nantucket! Take out your map and look at it. See what a real corner of the world it occupies; how it stands there, away off-shore, more lonely than the Eddystone lighthouse. Look at it— a mere hillock, and elbow of sand; all beach without a back-ground. There is more sand there than you could use in twenty years as a substitute for blotting paper. Some gamesome wights will tell you that they have to plant weeds there, they don't grow naturally; that they import Canada thistles; that they have to send beyond seas for a spile to stop a leak in an oil cask; that pieces of wood in Nantucket are carried about like bits of the true cross in Rome; that people there plant toadstools before their houses, to get under the shade in summertime; that one blade of grass makes an oasis, three blades in a day's walk a prairie; that they wear quicksand shoes, something like Lap-lander snowshoes; that they are so shut up, belted about, every way inclosed, surrounded, and made an utter island of by the ocean, that to their very chairs and tables small clams will be found adhering, as to the backs of sea turtles. . . .

It was the middle of the nineteenth century before it occurred to anybody to plant shade trees on the streets, while in all other Massachusetts towns elms and maples had been set out long before. This treelessness was a stock joke. Even as late as 1860 Porte Crayon, in illustrating his *Harper's* article on Nantucket, made a drawing of a mullein stalk and a bayberry bush together, which he entitled "A Grove." Whittier, having this lack of trees in his mind, refers to the "shrubless hills" of Nantucket in his poem "The Exiles." If there is one thing that the island has always had by the million, it is shrubs!

It used to be thought that when the settlers arrived the isle must have been thickly wooded, but a recent study by Mr. Bassett Jones settled conclusively that there never were any forests —never in the history of the white people, anyway. The soil is not friendly to deep roots, the winds are very powerful, sometimes carrying salt spray clear across the island and thus blasting leaves and pruning the branches with a ruthless hand. All the trees tend to lean toward the southwest, probably because of the high northeast gales, laden with salt. No doubt, too, in the days when the ten thousand sheep roamed the commons, left to themselves to fend for their own food, they gnawed away everything that lifted a shoot. To make matters worse, every now and then a fire would get started in the dead grass and sweep across country for miles before it was checked.

Just before the Coffin brothers set out their little elm saplings on Main Street, another philanthropist, Josiah Sturgis, tried

IN THE STATE FOREST

planting groves of pines out on the commons. When Thoreau visited Nantucket, he noted that Captain Gardner of Siasconset was at that time planting pine seedlings on the east slope of Bean Hill. Unluckily, Captain Gardner found out that he could buy pine seed cheaper in Europe than in Massachusetts, and sent across the water for a quantity. This seed was duly planted, but like many another bargain it brought little satisfaction, because with it came the pine tree moth, and it is said that Nantucket is the only spot in the United States where that pest is known to exist.

Unquestionably, there are far more trees on the island now than at any time in its history. The highways to Siasconset, to Surfside and to Cisco lead through pine woods, flourishing remarkably well under the protection of the state. The enemies of all trees are the high winds that lash to death the tender growth and the rot that starts early and works fast in the damp atmosphere. Most trees on Nantucket, therefore, are short-lived. And yet, if given protection, as in the settled districts, they will flourish as on the mainland. On the corner of Ray's Court and Main Street, for example, is a fine patriarchal sycamore, said to be the largest and oldest tree on the island.

Of the pines, an interesting experiment was made at Wauwinet in the grove of Japanese black pines planted by the father of Mr. Bassett Jones in 1895. These are the tallest pines on the island and they survive in their exposed location because their species is accustomed to similar conditions of sea winds and salt water on the coast of Japan.

There are other varieties. Scotch and white pine are the kinds planted by the state. Of these the Scotch seem to take to the local conditions better than the white pines. The commonest sort are the poor relations of the family, the scrub pine, and this is the species that suffers most from the "tip moth." Visitors in June wonder why these pines have such a dead, brown look where the fresh shoots grow. This is the work of the tip moth larva.

Of the hardwood trees the kind that seems to do best is the sycamore maple, of which there are some splendid specimens, both in town and in Siasconset. During the fall their leaves do not turn a glorious gold or scarlet like other maples. They wither off apologetically in a brown decay. But this is forgiven when it is realized that these same leathery leaves in early June were just tough enough to take the late northeasters and come through alive.

The more protection they get the more the trees will flourish. Interesting examples of this fact are the "hidden forests." One is on the Maglathlin farm. Another, better known and more accessible, lies within a half mile of the first, being on the property of Mr. David Gray, just off the road to Wauwinet. Mr. Gray purchased this grove to preserve it, and it is open at least once during the summer to the "Nantucket Neighbors."

This is a fascinating place. From the road no one would suspect the presence of any "forest" at all. The tops of the trees seem identical with the rest of the surrounding growth of scrub oak. But after entering the path through the stile, we realize that we are actually in a grove. And this realization increases as we walk on. Primarily, it is growth of beech trees, which are seen nowhere else on the island. On each side of the path there are tall specimens of holly, not a common tree in this latitude. Even the huckleberry and bayberry bushes grow to giant heights. The climax of the walk is reached in a little clearing

BEECHES IN THE HIDDEN FOREST

where two huge beech trees stand with sprawling, outstretched arms. The secret of this forest is that it lies in a hollow, snugly protected from the easterly gales, in particular, and to a considerable degree from the other winds, also. The top soil here must be much deeper, in order to feed the roots of such large trees, for it is a swampy, peaty ground, watered by a little brook. In spite of their large girth these trees do not lift their branches above the surrounding growth; instead, they snuggle down in the hollow and spread their limbs abroad rather than on high.

Before leaving the subject of trees it should be said that the brothers Charles and Henry Coffin, who planted the elms on Main Street, set out other trees in every direction to see how they would flourish. Probably most of these perished, but the growth of fine larches and Scotch pine near Miacomet Pond is a beautiful memorial to Henry Coffin who planted the seed so long ago.

All the unfenced land lying between the settlements and the individual farms used to be known as the "commons," because this land was dedicated to the common use of all. Here is where the sheep fended for themselves all the year to get a living. "Commons" this region still is to the Old Inhabitants, but the "summer people," especially 'Sconseters, have long since given it another name, the "moors." And, as the old inhabitants have a way of passing off the scene, "moors" it is likely to remain.

There is another objector to this term, the scientific man who is a stickler for accuracy. He will insist that this type of country is not moor but heath. A moor is low, boggy, and peaty. A heath is rolling, upland country. And the typical growth on a heath is what Nantucket has in greater profusion than any other spot in the country; namely, the bear berry or mealy plum. But who ever listened to the stickler for accuracy? "Heath" it may be to the man of science, but no one on the island would have any idea what you were talking about if you used that term. Hereafter, in these pages this open country will be called moors.

There are fine highways from one end of the island to the other and from one side to the other, but no one should imagine that he has really seen the moors by staying on these asphalt boulevards. To have real fun, one must follow the rutted roads and explore the intimate back country. The best way is to go on foot, if one is a hardy, old-fashioned pedestrian, spending the whole day on the moors. Another excellent way is to go on horseback. The third and the easiest method, and the one that covers the most ground in a given time, is by motor. For this purpose it will not do to bring to the island a shiny, stream-lined, low hung contraption such as fashion decrees. A car of this kind cannot navigate the deep-rutted roads, for it would soon have to slide and bump along on its belly, which is not wholly beneficial to the works. What the knowing ones do is to bring an ancient chariot of the Ford or Chevrolet persuasion, one that sits lofty and unashamed, high hung and high spirited, that can leap like an ibex from one gully to the next. Its sides should be so weatherbeaten that, when the scrub oak or pine boughs beat a tattoo on the paint work, the driver feels no concern because he knows it cannot be made to look worse. If you have that kind of car you are equipped to have a grand time on the moors. You can take any rutted road there is, or leave the road entirely and scrunch along over the mealy plum vine and huckleberry bushes, making your own road, as they

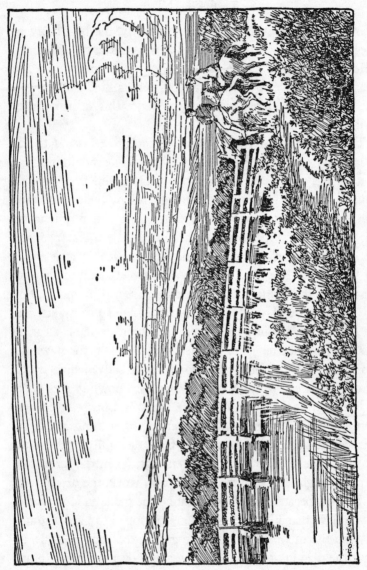

MASSASOIT BRIDGE, LONG POND

used to do in the day of the old tip cart. You can then go gaily "o'er moor and fen, o'er crag and torrent till" you end up in a scrub oak thicket or the Atlantic Ocean.

This is the way to see the ponds, the woods, the wild life—the deer in particular—and in general to know the island by heart. It is only by getting off the highways that you can discover the little pools that lie out of sight of the main road, fringed with blue flowers in early summer or with scarlet leaves in September, or explore those long ponds that stretch to the sea on the South Shore, deep in cat-tails and alive with herons. After rantum-scooting like this on the moors, driving on the state highway seems as dull by comparison as riding in the subway.

Apparently, the sheep made such a devastating job of feeding in the old days that they did not leave much to bloom. Crèvecoeur makes the sweeping comment that "The island furnishes the naturalist with few or no objects worthy of observation." But since the sheep have gone, the situation is very different. Nantucket is one of the most interesting spots on the eastern coast for the botanist. Professor Asa Gray used to declare that he was never surprised at anything being found on Nantucket. He said, too, that the island had a larger group of flora than any other locality in the United States.

In the first place, thanks to the Gulf Stream, the unique climate is responsible for the fact that the island is the northern limit for some southern plants, such as the cactus, and the southern limit for some northern ones. For example, botanists say that the creeping snowberry, which is a plant of cold, northern habitat, thrives in the warm bogs here in company with the pitcher plant and two varieties of cranberry. For some species, between their habitat in Nantucket and the nearest one on the mainland, there are gaps of hundreds of miles, and in one case as much as a thousand. Also, being cut off on an island, some varieties have developed differences from their general species.

To the layman, the most unusual of Nantucket plants is the Scotch heather. This exists on the island in two varieties, the white—which is very rare—and the pale purple. People who love it will not divulge where it grows for fear that it might be all pulled up by the roots and become extinct in a single summer. Suffice it to say that it does thrive, even to growing into the middle of a rutted road. Once a year the doubting and disbelieving have an opportunity to see the heather for themselves at the wild flower show in the Maria Mitchell house. A third variety, the bell heather, was discovered on the island long ago, growing near the present fair grounds, but it has since died out. The bell variety, it is said, has never been found in any other part of the United States.

There are various stories of how the heather came. Some say that this is the only spot in the country where the plant is native. Another explanation is that it was planted by an Irishman named O'Connell, who had a homestead by Hummock Pond and who set out both heather and gorse brought by him from the Emerald Isle. Still another is that the seed came in the roots of pines imported from Scotland.

The Scotch broom is on the island in large quantities and in June is glorious with its golden flowers. This had been started in 1860, but in the nineties a Nantucket visitor, Mrs. A. E. Powers, sent to friends in Scotland for a large amount of the seed, and, filling shoe boxes with it, she drove over the moors in a pony cart scattering it in all directions.

Gorse, also, was planted on Nantucket, but it has not been so fortunate as its Caledonian cousins, for in the severe winter of 1933 it was so badly damaged by the frost that most of it was killed.

For anyone interested in botany there is a wealth of material in both the Atheneum and the Maria Mitchell libraries on the flora of Nantucket, both of the uplands and, as one title has it, the "Boggy Solitudes." In these scientific works one may find the Latin names, *calapogon, pogonia, tephrosia, pipsissewa, sabatia gracilis,* and so on. As for that little pink sabatia, there is a legend that it was so named because the Pilgrim Fathers saw it for the first time on the Sabbath after they landed at Plymouth. Unfortunately, the botany book says that it was named after an Italian botanist named Sabati, who probably never heard of the Pilgrims. So there's another pretty story gone wrong. However, the sabatia has always been a favorite flower with Nantucketers. It is appalling, by the way, what official names some of these inoffensive little blossoms carry, such as *pycnathemum, gnaphalium,* and *xanthium,* but botanists seem to like them that way.

Of course, it may be that the reader is, like myself, no botanist at all; indeed, even the sort of person who finds it difficult to distinguish between "flora" and "fauna." In that case he will be patient if the following plants are mentioned simply because of their beauty, abundance or fragrance, and not because of their rarity. Commonest of all is the wild rose, which blooms in between the sweet fern and the bay for miles of pale pink. Its fragrance is something always associated with the moors to anyone who has tramped over them early in July. Barren heath, or Hudsonia, in bloom on Saul's Hills, is memorable also, although its golden beauty has a brief span of only two or three days in late May or early June. The common indigo plant, with its bright yellow blooms, is a gay little flame, too, blazing everywhere beside the rutted roads. And for a rich red there are the wood lilies, or "moor lilies" as they are called here. One of the handsomest wild flowers imaginable is the pink mallow, which is to be looked for in the marshes. There is a sister variety that is white, but the pink mallow is the favorite. This blooms in late summer and is not too easy to discover.

The most glorious of all the moor plants at the proper season is the plain old familiar huckleberry which grows everywhere. While the summer visitors are on the island it goes about its business of producing berries in plain, working garb, but in October, when the crowds are all gone, these bushes turn a rich wine red and the entire landscape becomes a blaze of color like an oriental rug.

Of bird life there is aplenty for the amateur Audubon. In fact, that great bird specialist visited the island back in the eighteen-forties, but apparently he did not take much interest in the ornithology of Nantucket. He was chiefly interested in getting subscriptions for his book of plates, but the thrifty whalemen's wives declined with thanks. Some, indeed, probably omitted the thanks! So he shook the dust of the town off his feet—or rather, the sand—and went away in an altitudinous dudgeon. But the birds are all here, even if Audubon did snub them. If any ornithologist asks whether such rare species can be found as the Yellow-Bellied Bulbul, the Ruby Crested Canary, the Swedish Nightingale, or the Crow Magnon, answer yes. Remember that Asa Gray learned not to be surprised at any specimen that was found on Nantucket.

In Godfrey's guide, referred to at the beginning of this chapter, there is an impressive list of birds compiled by the ornithologist Herbert Sweet. Even in this list all the little, ordinary birds were left out, as being of no particular interest, because they could be taken for granted. Apparently every creature that flaps a wing has been identified at one time or another on Nantucket, except possibly the ostrich and the dodo. Mr. Sweet's catalog includes such strange-sounding birds as the Auk, the Red Breasted Merganser, the Hooded Merganser, the Harlequin, the Puffin, the Barnacle Goose, and the Roseate Tern.

Without knowing anything about such extraordinary specimens as these, the layman takes delight in the great horned owls that flap about the moors at twilight, the herons that haunt the fringes of the ponds, the wild ducks and geese, and the pheasants that fly up from every turn of the road. In order to attract the hunter, attempts have been made to introduce partridges and wild turkeys, but these are still in the experimental stage. Probably the most familiar bird note that the visitor used to carry away as a memory, associated with the fragrance of the moors, is the song of the meadow lark. Unfortunately, this is becoming all too rare now. Together with all the other small song birds, it suffers from the pheasants, which destroy its eggs. For example, the bobolink, which used to be very common, has completely disappeared from Nantucket Island.

Snakes are not plentiful. Only rarely is one seen, and then it is usually a little garter snake. But the moors are by no means as snakeless as the land of the Shamrock. The workmen of the

Mosquito Control came upon reptiles four or five feet long in the marshes and ponds, and it is said that some of these were water moccasins.

But there is a good story about snakes left in Obed Macy's notes. Before he died, he assembled a collection of odds and ends of information which, he said, might be useful if his history of Nantucket went into a second edition. Among them is this anecdote about snakes. One Jethro Swain told Obed that when he was young snakes were numerous, especially toward the east end of the island. In fact, there is a spring still called Snake Spring, which is situated just to the west of the links of the Sankaty Head Golf Club.

"He said," writes Macy, "that at a certain time of the winter or spring the sun shined bright and warm, many snakes were discovered crawling about near Snake Spring. As soon as the people were informed of the circumstance they mustered a company and repaired to the premises and dug two holes, and with Hay Rakes raked as many of them into the holes as they could. The snakes were so benumbed with cold that few of them escaped. It was judged they raked in about two carts full. In order to destroy them they made great fires over them, as the heat caused them to attempt to escape they were driven back and killed until they were all subdued. . . . Among them were two rattlesnakes."

Then he goes on with his prize snake story: A certain youth, John Barnard, was out by Gibbs Pond duck hunting one day, and was crawling quietly through the bushes to get within shooting distance of some ducks on the pond. Suddenly he was paralyzed by the apparition of a huge snake that reared his head and part of his body in front of him. Though Barnard had a loaded gun, Obed explains that "being somewhat agitated he thought it safest to leave the premises altogether." It appears that "this story was somewhat doubted by some." But— "Sometime afterwards Grafton Gardner was passing the same swamp with a cart and oxen. The oxen stopped suddenly with their ears pricked forward and refused to budge. When Gardner walked forward to see what the matter was he saw a huge snake gliding across the road. He stood and looked at it until it had vanished in the bushes." He said that he "believed that it was eleven or twelve feet in length and as big around as a round rail." Macy adds, "Confidence was placed in the story as the beholder stood quietly and had a full sight of his Majesty. He never was seen afterwards."

There seem to be no sea serpent stories in the annals of Nantucket ship captains except for the sloop *Fame,* which was sent to sea in the year 1833 for the commendable purpose of hunting the sea serpent. Sad to relate, she returned to port without having sighted a single one.

There have been all sorts of four-legged creatures on the moors since the sheep went. One chronicler speaks of "an evil minded person" who introduced foxes. Perhaps he only had the ambition of enlivening the landscape with pink coated huntsmen and baying hounds. At any rate, they all died off. Thoreau speaks of seeing raccoons. These, too, have become extinct. Prairie dogs were introduced on the island and multiplied so fast that they had to be exterminated. Jack rabbits were a late importation (1925). Cottontails were here long before, and they have thrived and multiplied by the million. They are witless wights that run out on the road whenever they hear a car coming, and commit suicide by trying to scamper across at just the wrong time. The highways are marked by the pathetic remains of these creatures, but there are plenty left, hopping all over the moors.

The prize addition to the fauna of the island is the deer. Until 1922 they were unheard of here. In that year some fishermen discovered a buck swimming out in the middle of the Sound and on the point of exhaustion. They hauled him aboard and landed him on Nantucket. Four years later, Mr. Breckinridge Long, taking pity on the creature's solitary life, brought two does and turned them loose. From these have sprung a herd of astonishing numbers. They became so numerous that people who had farms and gardens and nurseries outside the town complained bitterly of their depredations. They ate not only the garden truck but gnawed off the bark of ornamental trees that had been carefully planted and nurtured, besides destroying bulbs and flowering shrubs. Finally permission was given for an open season of hunting the deer.

This was a matter of a few days in February, 1935, and the hunters went out in full force. Since the deer were so tame, the sport must have been almost as thrilling as shooting the cows in a pasture. At any rate, the killing was just as easy, and the slaughter reached such proportions that a great protest arose which stopped the hunting by Governor's decree. Thereafter, the deer were never so tame again, though it is still a pleasant game to drive over the moors about sunset and see how many deer can be sighted. While driving at night, also, one must keep a watch for the deer that may jump out suddenly from the trees at the sides of the highway. Mr. William Wallace has made his property, "Ram Pasture," a game preserve, and there the deer are still unafraid.

The fall season of deer hunting in 1935, one week, was closed suddenly by the killing of one hunter and the serious wounding of another in the first two days. With something like two hun-. dred amateur trigger-pullers blazing away at anything that moved on the moors, it was hardly safe to drive even on the highway.

It would seem as if there might be a better solution for the problem of the deer. Feeding, especially in winter, might save the farms and gardens from harm. Superfluous deer might be given away to other municipalities for their parks, and the whole business handled by the Game Warden.

There is another field of sport deservedly popular, and that is the fishing. This interest is centered chiefly on bluefishing. Many of the inhabitants do this by standing on the shore and throwing, with practiced hand, a gadget called a "drail." The off-islander, however, prefers to try his luck in a boat, and if the creatures are hungry he will have as lively a day's sport as he could wish.

The bluefish are very temperamental. Before the year 1763, the year of that mysterious plague that afflicted the Indians on Nantucket, there had always been a great quantity of bluefish to be caught anywhere around the island, from July first to the middle of October. Just as the epidemic passed off the following year, the bluefish vanished completely, to the superstitious wonder of the Indians, who associated the phenomenon in some way with their recent pestilence. Not a bluefish reappeared for a full generation. Since the beginning of the nineteenth century, however, the bluefish has made his annual visit to

Nantucket waters, and furnishes now the greatest attraction to the sport-loving visitor.

It is said that ten thousand people come to Nantucket during the summer season, and doubtless they go away thinking that they know the island intimately, especially if they belong to that numerous tribe who return year after year. But there are other aspects which the summer visitor does not know at all. The most beautiful month of the twelve on Nantucket is October. Here is the place of all places to experience the perfection of a New England Indian summer. Frost is long delayed, the sunshine stays warm, and the breezes soft. It is still good weather for sailing, and some still take their regular dip in the surf. There is an atmosphere of peace and relaxation, for the crowds are gone.

Out on the moors there is a gorgeous transformation from the grey greens of summer. Masses of ruby red and scarlet, with here and there flecks of gold, make a resplendent pattern over the wide stretches of open country as far as eye can see. Down along the shore the marsh grasses turn a pale yellow, orange, pink, or saffron, with the intense blue of the sea or the bay making a rich background. The wise ones who manage to visit Nantucket at this season, or who are fortunate enough to be able to stay so late, know it at the time of year when it is most beautiful.

The best way, in general, to get a sort of bird's-eye view of the whole island is to go out on the moors to the region known as Saul's Hills, the district that lies between the highway to Wauwinet and Siasconset. In the midst of these "hills," there is one higher than the rest. A signboard on the rutted road leading to it from the highway says, "To Altar Rock." As with "moors," here is another instance of the summer visitors putting their own name on a Nantucket landmark. For nearly two centuries this was called Macy's Hill, but the presence of boulders on the top suggested the more poetic name, which is now officially recognized. This is the highest spot on the island. From here the eye takes in a grand sweep of moor, forest, and town, with the blue rim of ocean on the horizon.

To have an experience that is not likely to be forgotten, drive to Altar Rock some fine October afternoon just about sundown, and look over the grey-green and scarlet moorland across the deep blue of the harbor to the pale violet silhouette of the town in the distance. If you are fortunate enough to have some fine cloud masses in the west, so that the sun, as the old skippers used to say, is busy "setting up shrouds and backstays," then you will know for the first time how perfect a sunset can be.

CHAPTER XIV

THE ISLANDERS

THE first lesson for any off-islander to learn is not to call the island people "natives." "Natives?" they will ask indignantly. "Do you mean the Portuguese?" In the old whaling days the word native always meant a Kanaka. No, they do not like to be referred to as if they were tattooed aborigines, for they have too much reason to be proud of their past. One might as well call the citizens of Back Bay, Boston, of Richmond, Virginia, or of Charleston, South Carolina "natives." When Lafayette was entertained in Boston and distinguished people were honored with invitations, it is said that more of these were dispatched to Nantucket than to any other community of her size. Natives indeed!

In the stories of the Old Boys and the Old Girls it was noted that the isolation of the people very naturally tended to develop personalities, "characters," and eccentrics. Individuals described in those chapters were, as a rule, known outside the island as well as in. But there were also some who were even more picturesque, though known only among their neighbors, such characters as could not possibly be developed in these days of frequent and easy communication with the mainland.

One of these, the earliest of this group, was Richard Macy. He was the grandfather of the Obed Macy who published, a hundred years ago, his entertaining and still valuable history of Nantucket. Richard Macy also was the man who built Nantucket's first wharf, the "Straight," in 1723. He was, therefore, a contemporary of Elihu Coleman and a rival carpenter. He, like Reuben and Deborah Chase, was famous for his gigantic strength. Contemporary description says that "he was thought to be stronger than a horse." On one occasion, while on the mainland, he came upon some soldiers trying in vain to budge a cannon off the ground. By a harness of rope over his shoulder he lifted it single-handed, a weight of 1800 pounds. He used to do all the work on his buildings with his own hands, even to burning shells for lime and hewing out the timbers. About the time he constructed the first wharf he was asked also to undertake the erection of the first windmill. He had never seen one in his life, and those were the days before pictures came to Nantucket. He pondered on the problem and finally, he said, the whole plan came to him in a dream! On the basis of that he went ahead with his mill, which worked perfectly. Like so many of his townsfolk he lived to an advanced age, dying, as his biographer says, "in peace with all mankind," at the age of ninety. His prowess and skill remained a legend on the island for generations.

Another "character" was the son-in-law of Elihu Coleman, named Micajah Coffin. Classical education in Nantucket was as rare as rubies during the whole of its history. One of its sons noted that no other town in Massachusetts of its wealth and size sent so few boys to college. But Micajah's father was a schoolmaster who had had the classics dinned into him in his day and saw to it that, whaling or no whaling, his son, too, should grow up with a thorough grounding in Latin. It was when Micajah had reached the advanced age of ninety-six that the Governor of Massachusetts came to Nantucket to pay a visit. To his amazement, that worthy had to stand and listen to an oration of welcome delivered in Latin by the old man. Of course, the Governor had no idea what was being said or whether it was being said correctly; no more did anybody else, but it created a sensation.

Micajah was the father of Zenas Coffin, the wealthiest of Nantucket whaling captains, and the grandfather of Charles and Henry Coffin, those public-spirited brothers who planted trees on Nantucket streets and elsewhere on the island and brought plants to try out in Nantucket gardens. Micajah lived to be nearly a hundred. In his latter years he used to stroll about the streets, and if he saw an unfamiliar face he would say, "My name is Micajah Coffin. What is thine?"

Contemporary with Micajah lived three sisters, who also have passed into legend, the "Newbegin Girls." Their story was put into the form of a little romance, entitled *An Island Plant,* by Mary Catherine Lee. It is just possible that the author invented the romantic and tragic love interest, but the narrative appeared in *The Atlantic Monthly* and was afterward published in book form, in 1896, under the auspices of the Nantucket "Goldenrod Literary and Debating Society," so what further verification could a reader ask? Here is the story in brief:

In the days when the settlers left their houses in Sherburne to set up new dwellings in Wesco, there lived alone in one of the abandoned cabins a girl named Phebe, an orphan. She was known to be "queer," was often heard talking to herself as if she were addressing spirits near her. She brooded over the mysteries of the Book of Revelation in the only volume she possessed, her Bible.

One November evening, as she was trudging the long way

home from town, she was astonished to see the most fiery red sunset, which seemed to her to bathe the earth and the heavens in blood. It was like one of those terrible visions in Revelations, and she thought it had been sent as a divine warning. Then, as the colors faded, there sprang up a cold wind that buffeted her, and made her feel suddenly alone and helpless. She dropped on her knees. What sin had she committed? Yes, she had refused all offers of marriage; that must be it. She had been comely, but the only boy she had been interested in had been lost at sea. Perhaps she had angered God by refusing to take a husband. She vowed, therefore, to accept the first offer that came to her and trusted God to send the right man.

As she rose from her knees there came along the rutted roadway a cart with a sail attached. It was the half-wit, James Newbegin, driving back to his home. He offered her a lift which she gladly accepted. Alas, it was only a few minutes before James was offering his hand in marriage, despite Phebe's frantic efforts to stop him. So that was what God sent her! But it was like Jephthah's vow, that promise of hers—unbreakable. Accordingly, Phebe and James Newbegin "stood up in meeting" together.

Of that marriage three daughters were born, the eldest named Phebe after her mother. One day the three girls went to shearing in order to share in the festival and also to gather the stray fluffs of wool that the poor were allowed to glean from the ground. It happened that a young whaling captain named Dudley came there, too, for a holiday. He was handsome and dressed elegantly in the mode. The three Newbegin girls, who lingered on the outskirts of the crowd because of their poverty, fell under his eye, one after the other. And, being a quick worker, after the fashion of seafaring men, he kissed each in turn, Phebe the last. The first two were just blowsy, stupid country girls, but Phebe had the refined, spiritual beauty of her mother. Dudley was so impressed with her looks that he not only kissed her but pinned on her kerchief the silver ship scarf-pin from his own ruffle. He told her that some day he would come back for her, and then was off to join his ship.

Forty years passed. Also, in the fashion of seafaring men, the easy kiss was forgotten by Dudley. He returned but rarely to Nantucket, and then only for the briefest stay. Finally, he brought his ship into the harbor, determined to retire and live his remaining days in Nantucket along with his old acquaintances. He then remembered that day of the shearing, and thought that he would find out something about his Phebe of long ago. Accordingly, he made a pilgrimage out to the wretched hovel where the three eccentric sisters lived. One, Anne, had sense enough to make trips to town to sell the eggs which were their only source of income. But when she walked she tacked back and forth across the road, for some curious superstition of her own, also turning three times round every post on the route. Dudley witnessed this performance without knowing who she was. But what was his horror when he reached the house to find the other two sisters waiting, with vacant minds, one by the fire and the other looking out of the window. There they had sat and waited for forty years for the youth who had kissed them to come back. Dudley, on turning to the woman at the window, saw on her withered bosom his little silver ship—it was Phebe.

Anne whispered to him confidentially that her sisters think that the Captain is coming back for them, whereas she knows that *she* is the girl he really loved. Dudley, overwhelmed with horror, returned to his ship and left Nantucket forever.

Such is the story. There is no question but that the Newbegins in real life were very eccentric women who lived together in one squalid room on their father's old place for many years. This was the lot that lay next to the Elihu Coleman homestead on the east. They were proud. They would not leave their dirty room, in which the hens laid eggs in the bureau drawers and roosted on the beds. They associated with no one. They pulled thorns from the hawthorn trees to use as needles for sewing. To keep potatoes from freezing in winter, they spread them between the double mattresses on which they slept. Outside the house stood a boulder around which the three weird sisters would march many times in a kind of rude ritual of their own.

The Overseers of the Quaker congregation saw to it in a tactful way that the old women always had the necessities of life without having to take charity. Once, in their latter years, they were brought into town to be taken care of in the Friends' Boarding House for Aged People at 111 Upper Main Street; but they escaped one night and trudged all the long route back to the old house, from which they refused to be moved again, though later, as they became feeble, they had to return to the Home. In spite of their unhygienic way of living, they all survived to a ripe old age; Anne dying in 1853 at eighty-one, Phebe in 1860 at ninety-four, and Mary in 1863 at ninety-three. Being orthodox Wilburites, they were buried without any headstones in the Quaker graveyard. Their house was torn down about seventy years ago, and nothing remains of the "Newbegin Girls" but their legend.

Among those gnarled and twisted thorn trees near their old farm, which, it will be remembered, hold the tormented spirits of the spinsters of Nantucket, there are three by the road easily recognized as the most peculiarly distorted of them all. These are the Newbegin Girls.

In the chapter on Siasconset, reference was made to Captain Baxter, the man who drove the stage to Siasconset and operated a post office in the little cottage opposite the town pump. Baxter may serve as a type of the nineteenth century "character," for he became quite a famous personage.

He fancied himself as a humorist and left behind a whole body of legends. The following is one of his advertisements in the Nantucket *Inquirer and Mirror:* *

Back-stir

Ancient Mariner, by sea and land, has forsaken the former and confines his efforts no more to trackless wastes. His side wheel craft, Swiftsure, will be launched Monday, May 11, 1891, for the season. She has been newly rigged, and is supplied with hard cushions for invalids and soft seats for sweethearts. Deaf ear turned to cooing and billing, all confidences strictly confidential, and no gossip repeated. Rates reduced to all parts of the island.

As the advertisement suggests, whenever he recognized a pair of lovers or a honeymoon couple, he pretended to be very deaf, understanding not a word unless it were shouted. Also, it was his delight to do and say things to mystify the off-islanders. For example, during a foggy journey over the moors, he would pause solemnly, thump the handle of his whip in the sand, taste what it brought up, and then "giddap" with an air

* *The Nantucket Scrap Basket,* Macy & Hussey, p. 63.

of relief. He would explain that he knew by soundings all the soils of Nantucket and could always find his way in a fog by this method.

On one occasion some busybody reported that Baxter flaunted the sign "Post Office" on his door without the official permission of the government. An investigator was sent to look into this heinous matter. Naturally, on getting off the boat and seeking the stage to Siasconset, he met Captain Baxter. Naturally, too, he inquired of the stage driver if he had ever seen the offending sign on a house in Siasconset. Baxter replied that he had lived there many years and hadn't seen it yet, but that he would be glad to take the investigator around to every house so that he might see for himself. Whereupon he drove to Polpis instead of Siasconset. There the two men solemnly examined every farmhouse, the inspector returned to the boat satisfied, and all was well.

Fortunately, a likeness has been preserved of this amusing old character. On the wall of Captain Grant's little office in the whaling museum hangs an enlarged photograph which reveals a gnarled old face with a crooked and quizzical twist to the mouth.

So much for individual characters who, of course, could be added to almost indefinitely. From these and their kind may be drawn certain characteristics of the island people of the old days. Being without much formal education, they made their way by native wit, industry, and courage. Consequently, they developed a sturdy independence of mind. They didn't care what anyone else thought, except in matters of religion, and even there the Nantucketer jumped the Quaker traces in the early nineteenth century.

It must be admitted that they did not cultivate a sense of the beautiful. The fine arts had no chance in a place where the inhabitants lived in the odor of sanctity mingled with that of whale oil. Where art was starved out, sentiment was on slender rations too. The story is told of a returning whale captain who

met his wife for the first time, after a three-year cruise, as she was going to the pump with a bucket. "Here, thee take this and fill it," she said, "and then come on in to dinner." There is another anecdote of a captain on his way to his ship remarking suddenly that he had forgotten to say good-by to his wife. "Oh, well," he added, continuing his way to the wharf, "it doesn't matter because it's only a year's cruise."

The thrift for which the islander was famous is illustrated by the story told in the memoirs of Daniel Webster. A Quaker called on the famous statesman in his office in Boston and asked him how much he would charge to take a case in the Nantucket court.

"I will attend to your case," Webster replied, "for a thousand dollars."

This sounded appalling to the Quaker, but after a bit of thinking he agreed to the fee if Webster would promise to attend to any other matters that his client might present during the sitting of court. Webster consented.

When the time came the famous jurist won the leading case, and then found another put into his hands. He won that, too. Another and still another came along for Webster to argue, all of which he won. Finally, the distinguished counsel got impatient and protested.

"I hired thee," explained his client placidly, "to attend to all the business of the court and thou hast done it handsomely; so here is thy money, one thousand dollars." He had won enough in these other cases to give him Webster's service on the main suit free.

The simplicity of the early islander is illustrated by a thousand anecdotes. When the town crier, Billy Clark, enlisted in the Union army, he surprised his fellow townsmen by reappearing in their midst shortly afterward arrayed again as a civilian. On being asked the reason for the shortness of his military career, he explained that the doctors had rejected him as "being non compous, or something like that." Even if he had known the meaning of *non compos mentis,* he probably would not have changed his story. What of it? Who cares what the army doctors said or thought anyway?

Then there is the more recent tale of an old lady who was taken for the first time to the Cottage Hospital. As the nurse was peeling off one petticoat after another to get her into bed, the old lady suddenly piped up in delight, "Oh, land sakes, there's that petticut I've lost for the longest time; I couldn't think what become of it!"

Finally, there is that classic advertisement in the paper

put there by Benny Cleveland announcing that he offered "to sleep at the homes of timid ladies; one night for fifteen cents, two for twenty-five." There is a poem extant on that unique advertisement, reprints of which were made by the *Inquirer and Mirror*, the journal in which that notice first appeared.

Nor would it be proper to leave the island story without a profound salaam in the direction of this paper. The Chicago *Tribune*, with the modesty characteristic of the Windy City, carries under its heading on the front page, "The World's Greatest Newspaper." If acreage were the standard of measure, that title should go to the *Inquirer and Mirror*, for it is the last journal in the United States still using the large, flat press, and is almost as wide as the old-fashioned single topsail.

There have been several rival papers in the history of Nantucket journalism. Since the combining of the *Inquirer* and the *Mirror* there has been no one else in the field. Like so many other features of the town, the paper has an individual flavor that appeals to visitors even more than to the readers at home. The subscription list carries addresses from all over the world. May it never change!

Of the independence of thought and action characteristic of the Nantucketer of other days, there are many examples. His dismissal of all the outside world in a single category, "off-islanders," is enough in itself. People who live in that outside area really do not count for much. Many years ago a schooner was wrecked on the island. The account of the disaster, appearing in the Nantucket paper, is said to have been to the effect that there were "two souls lost, and three New Bedforders."

This hard-shell indifference to what outsiders thought was shared also by the local business man. There was a well-known dry-goods storekeeper who used to sit in his shop all day with his feet on the counter and his nose in a newspaper. If anyone came in and asked for goods, he would grunt, "Look and see and help yourself," not stirring from his chair or lifting his eyes from his paper. Of course, methods are different today, but the psychology of salesmanship was never heard of in ancient Nantucket.

Finally, though the ghosts of the Coffins and Husseys and Folgers may rise to smite me, these old-timers seem to have been unduly conservative. To them the old way was always the best way. At every step of progress, whether it was to introduce inoculation, or public education, or street lighting, or paving, or installing a water system, a dead weight of opposition had to be overcome. And when the whaling business collapsed, there seemed to be a paralysis of the imagination. In this crisis it was the women who took the lead in finding a way to make a living. In *My House and I,* Miss Starbuck remarks that during the dark days when whaling was ended and the soldiers and sailors

trooped home from the Civil War to find their old occupations gone, Nantucket's chief industry was raising schoolmarms. At one time there were sixty-eight Nantucket teachers in the district of Boston alone. "So," adds Miss Starbuck dryly, "of course, it is not to be wondered at that Boston has kept for so long her intellectual prestige."

But school-teaching did not develop any resource on which to base prosperity for the island town. There was still a good market for fish, especially the cod. Yet Gloucester was permitted to make for herself a monopoly of the cod fishery on the Banks. At this day, when the economic future of the town presents a serious problem, on account of the conditions in the local fisheries, it is interesting to note how many of the businesses on Main, Centre, and Federal Streets are in the hands of off-islanders who came in and saw an opportunity to turn a pretty penny where the islanders saw nothing. And much of this money leaves for the mainland when the summer season is over.

The mixture of races observable in Nantucket streets is not due to any recent importations. The ancestors of these negroes and mulattoes of "Guinea," the pure bred Portuguese, and the mixed breed "Bravas" from the Cape Verde Islands, shipped on whalers long ago and were stranded here when the whale

business died out. And here they brought their families. Some of them took their employers' names. A few clung to their own. To the poetical question "Who is Sylvia?" the answer in Nantucket is, "the Portuguese." Perhaps that was the one Portuguese name that the islanders could pronounce; at any rate, that is the name practically all the Portuguese families answer to. In fact, there soon came to be so many Manuel Sylvias, and Antone Sylvias that they had to be distinguished by their work or their habitat, such as "Manuel Golf Links" or "Antone Gas House."

There seems to be no problem in the presence of these diverse racial elements, for the children all go to school together, and some of these swarthy citizens make a good living where the descendants of the First Families fail. In fact, the whole cast of the island population is changing rapidly. In the dark days of the period following the Civil War, many left to make homes elsewhere, and at the same time there has been a steady infiltration of new blood from the mainland.

One outstanding characteristic of the Nantucketers from the beginning is their amazing longevity. There must be something about the air that keeps the old cardiac pump going longer than it does on the mainland. "Three score years and ten" never meant anything more than callow youth in Nantucket. Crèvecoeur speaks of the remarkable number of "green old men" whom he saw. As one reads the life stories of various people born here, it is astonishing how many lived to be over ninety. And this is true of those who were born in Nantucket but moved away in their youth. Both men and women were unusual for the way they clung to life. Indeed, it is only recently that an old lady of Nantucket finally decided to call it a day and turn in at the age of one hundred and two. Not only did these ancients live long, but they kept their vigor. Men in their eighties used to take their dories out deep-sea fishing and think nothing of the hard, physical labor. Benjamin Hussey, for example, was over eighty when he was killed, while standing at the wheel of his ship, by falling ice from an iceberg in Greenland waters.

Of the living Nantucketers who hark back to the old days here are two whom it is an honor to present. The first is Mr. James Wood, known to every child in town as "Grandpa Wood." He is a splendid example of that "green old age" which Crèvecoeur admired. Mr. Wood is well into his nineties now and he is no longer to be seen sitting in his surrey drawn up at

"GRANDPA WOOD"

the curb waiting for fares. Many a generation of horses has passed on to crop grass in Elysian fields, and Mr. Wood lets younger hands take the reins now.

One day I approached Mr. Wood as he sat on the driver's seat and asked him his rates of transportation. "Two dollars an hour," he replied. That seemed a considerable sum when you can get a forty-mile trip on a sightseeing bus with one of the rival Folgers (Admiral and Captain), for one dollar and a half. But I noticed his G.A.R. badge, and decided to make the financial plunge. That investment proved worth while. Mr. Wood can remember more about Nantucket than any other living man, and he has had an adventurous life of his own. You must sit alongside of his starboard ear because he is hard of hearing on his port side.

In his childhood Mr. Wood attended a cent school and he is probably the last surviving alumnus. At the age of fourteen he sailed off on his first whaling voyage on the schooner *Rainbow*. It was only a "plum pudding" voyage, for it lasted just seven months. His "lay," naturally, was very small. The schooner *Rainbow,* despite its promising name, brought in only twenty-five barrels of sperm. When James's mother went down to the wharf to collect her boy's profit on the voyage, it turned out to be exactly sixty-five cents. "Jim," said the mother in a burst of maternal generosity, "I'll give you a big half." Whereupon she passed out to the young whaling man thirty-five cents and kept thirty.

Jim went to sea again, this time on a ship. But he didn't like it aboard that vessel at all, and when the ship put in at Barbados he ran away and hid. After the hated sail had disappeared over the horizon, Jim came out of hiding and presented himself to the American consul. This official arranged for him to go on an English ship, which promptly burned up that night. (Jim, be it explained, had nothing to do with that.) And then the consul sent him to an American ship which was flying the English flag and bound for Philadelphia. On this he was kindly treated and gained not only his passage to America but also twenty-five dollars in wages.

That was the year 1862, which explains the British colors on the American ship. Confederate commerce-destroyers were making a massacre of American shipping in those days. Having landed in Philadelphia, the youngster enlisted in the Union cavalry, and galloped off to war.

In the fighting about Winchester, in the Shenandoah Valley, he was wounded in the leg. When he recovered, he transferred to the navy and was a seaman on the steam frigate *Minnesota*. He was soon promoted to "level man" on the huge forward smooth-bore pivot gun, firing a ball weighing 300 pounds. It was during the bombardment of Fort Fisher that the terrific detonation of that gun damaged the drum of his left ear. He chuckles now as he tells how the ear specialist in Boston told him that if he had only kept his mouth open during the bombardment his ear would have been all right.

"I couldn't do that, Doctor," he explained, "it would have been fatal to my heart."

"Why?"

"Because all the time my heart was in my mouth, and it would have dropped out!"

After the bombardment Jim went ashore in the famous naval charge across the sands up to the earthworks of Fort Fisher. This was a diversion to permit the army to attack with success on the other side of the fort, but it was a massacre of the sailors and their officers, who had to approach over an unprotected plain. In this charge the well-known Admiral "Bob" Evans, at that time a midshipman, fell with a bad wound, and not far from him Jimmy Wood received another flesh wound in the same thigh that had been hurt at Winchester. He was able, however, to hobble back to the boats.

When he recovered, he was again in action on the wooden river boat *Sassacus* in its attack against the Confederate iron-clad *Albemarle.* If Jim's heart was in his mouth at Fort Fisher, where did he wear it on this occasion? The *Sassacus,* an un-protected boat, rammed the iron-clad and received first a shell that tore through the boilers and then another that ripped off her upper works. The disabled vessel then drifted down stream, and was just saved from blowing up by the heroism of a volunteer crew that went into the steam-filled engine room and drew the fires. The *Albemarle* was sunk later by the intrepid *Cushing* in one of the most daring acts of the war.

Finally, when the great conflict was over, Jim happened to be sent to duty in Richmond just after Appomattox. And once —here is the greatest memory of all—President Lincoln came out of the door where the lad was standing sentry and laid his hand on the boy's shoulder.

"Well, my boy," said Lincoln gravely, "it's all over. Now you can go back to your mother." Mr. Wood once told that little story in Milton, Massachusetts, before an audience of six thou-sand people gathered for a Lincoln celebration. And it was the hit of the day.

For years Mr. Wood has been in charge of the Memorial Day ceremonies around the Monument at the bend of Main Street. He has never missed a ceremony on that day for sixty-seven years. There is only one other G.A.R. veteran in Nan-tucket and he is confined to his home. Two dollars is a small price for a ride back into the battles of the Civil War on land and sea, to say nothing of the ancient days in Nantucket when whaling was still the career for every boy as it had been for his ancestors before him.

Mr. Wood has his own convictions. He thinks little of liquor and automobiles and still less of them when they mix. In fact, he believes that they have done the island great harm. It is pleasant to observe how he drives along in the middle of the street, and never swerves an inch to let one of these "machines" go by. In the course of our drive we passed a gleaming Packard which had to crawl humbly along the curb to get past the surrey. And it was clear that the horse shared his master's sentiments, for when the car came along, the animal bent outward a most contemptuous shoulder as if he wanted to bump the motor into the telegraph pole, and turned away his head with scorn and loathing.

Before we take our leave of Mr. Wood it should be said that he is also the last of the great race of dory fishermen, and there was none better. He still holds the title of "high hook"; that is, the greatest single catch of codfish ever recorded on the island.

The other Nantucketer to be introduced is the gentleman mentioned already in the discussion of the whaling museum, Captain George Grant, the custodian of that shrine of the whaling era. And right appropriate it is that he should be the presiding genius there, for he is the last survivor of the race of American whalemen; at least, his record of whaling voyages antedates that of anyone else. Although a decade younger than Mr. Wood, he began his career on a whaler long before; to be exact, in the year 1856, when his mother carried him, wrapped in banana leaves, aboard her husband's ship *Mohawk* at the island of Upolo in the Samoan group, where the babe had been born. This initiation in the whaling business took place when George was three weeks old, which may stand as a record.

His father, Captain Charles Grant, has already been mentioned as the "luckiest" of whaling captains, and his wife also as that intrepid woman who upset the Nantucket tradition by going with her husband to sea and living there with him for thirty-two years, having her babies here and there among the islands of the South Seas. If someone objects that George Grant does not qualify as a born Nantucketer because his birthplace was a lump of coral in the Pacific Ocean, let him remember that in those days the Pacific Ocean was simply Nantucket's pasture lot.

Of the young sailor's career on the sea, it reads like something out of another age. By the time he was two years old he had circumnavigated the globe. It was nine months after the Civil War began before his father, Captain Grant, got wind of it, but his luck stood him in good stead. Despite the activity of Confederate cruisers he never fell in with any and carried on his whaling straight through the war.

The year that George was born, his mother attempted to remain in Nantucket with her baby, but it was pretty dull there after the life at sea and she couldn't stand it, so she picked up her infant, closed the house and went back to her husband and his ship. She took passage to Melbourne, Australia, from New York. Thence she shipped in a schooner to the Bay of Islands, New Zealand, where she knew her husband would be coming at that season of the year. She did not have to wait long before the familiar masts of the *Mohawk* were seen in the harbor, and to the astonishment of Captain Grant, his wife and babe, whom he had supposed to be safe in Nantucket, came aboard. Thereafter, until her husband retired, Mrs. Grant never tried to stay ashore during a cruise.

THE ISLANDERS

The deck of a ship was the scene of the young whaleman's boyhood. At twelve he had begun to take his oar in the whaleboat with the men, and at sixteen he harpooned his first whale. At twenty-two he married, and then the very next day went off on a three-year cruise! In mid-Pacific he was able to visit his father's ship and astonish his parents not only with his sudden appearance but also with the news that his sister was married and he likewise.

Meanwhile, the rapid decline, not only of whaling but of the entire American merchant marine, made it impossible for him to make a fortune on the Seven Seas as his father had done. In 1890, his ocean-going career came to an end, and he made his home thereafter in Nantucket. Of course, there are other whalemen both in Nantucket and on the mainland who can remember the day when they harpooned their first sperm, but none of them carry their memories back to the days in which Captain Grant began. He literally was born and bred a whaleman. It is, therefore, most appropriate that he is the appointed curator of the Whaling Museum. He is very patient with visitors, but you had better measure your words if you approach him. He likes to tell of one woman to whom, in answering a question, he mentioned the fact that he had been born on one of the islands of the Samoan group.

"Oh, Captain Grant," she gushed, "and was your mother there at the time?"

Questions like that have given him a patient look of resignation. I think he is rather glad when the summer is over, the Museum closed, and he can spend the afternoons with his friends at the Pacific Club.

OLD SOUTH WHARF

The great problem that faces the islanders today as never before since the great decline after the Civil War is what is the future for the younger generation. There are several hundred children in the schools. How are they going to make a living?

The problem is acute because of the condition of the fisheries. It is a strange situation. The prosperous fishing days of fifteen to twenty years ago, when it began to look as if the town had discovered a substitute for the whale fishery of the previous generation, are vanished. The same thing that happened to the whale business has happened here. The fish were killed off in such wholesale quantities that they have become much more costly to get. For example, dredges have destroyed the weed on which the fish used to feed and the voyages have to be made much farther out. And yet the paradox is that as the fish have become scarcer the price has gone down to a point where it hardly pays to let down a net. Two or three years ago many a fisherman owed so much on his outfit that in trying to settle matters after a season he had to give up his boat. Things are a bit brighter now, but not much. The introduction of gasoline and Diesel engines has made the "overhead" still more expensive than in the days when one merely hoisted sail.

One elderly Portuguese fisherman told me his story. He has a family of seven in New Bedford. Said he, in broken English, "I have no money to give them shoes. Last June I owed the grocer for bread $165, and was only able to pay up $115 on the bill. We never eat meat." At that, it is more profitable to fish from New Bedford, they say, than from Nantucket, because the ice is cheaper there.

Apparently, then, the only dependable source of revenue is the summer visitor, and for that reason it is essential for the townspeople to do everything possible to preserve just those qualities that make Nantucket attractive—the antiquity, beauty, peace, and friendliness of this island town. This is their treasure. There are tens of thousands of summer resorts, but there is only one Nantucket.

CHAPTER XV

THE OFF-ISLANDERS

IN the graveyard of St. Michael's in Charleston there is said to be an epitaph telling that a man lived sixty-nine years in that city, "almost long enough to be a real Charlestonian." So it is in Nantucket. A stranger, or off-islander, may live here sixty-nine years, and he would be qualified only to become "almost an Nantucketer." Yet the summer visitors are not made too conscious of their lowly status, for the same people come year after year, decade after decade, their children and their children's children; so it must be that they feel at home.

Among the visitors to Nantucket there have been a host of celebrities. Whether you consider Presidents of any particular consequence or not, there have been six of them at Nantucket: Grant, in 1874; Arthur, in 1882; Harrison, in 1890; Cleveland, in 1897; Wilson, in 1917; and F. D. Roosevelt, in 1933. However, the last named Chief Executive remained on his boat in the harbor.

In addition, there is a long list of other people distinguished in the arts, letters, and sciences, who have come to Nantucket to stay for one summer or many. The earliest of the artists was Eastman Johnson, the painter of portraits and genre scenes, whose work is coming more and more to be prized. In the eighteen-seventies visitors always remarked his cottage with its adjoining studio on the Cliff Road. Since Johnson's time there

DOORWAY, "WALLACE HALL"

have been numerous artists, some, like Walter Crane, from the other side of the Atlantic. They come because the waterfront, the town, and the moors appeal to the painter's eye. But, happily, so far Nantucket has escaped the typical Bohemian "artists' colony."

There have been famous writers also who have haunted Nan-

MARTIN'S LANE, RAINY EVENING

tucket, and their name is legion. Many a successful book and play has been written under the low ceiling of a former whaling captain's house, for what better place for working in peace can be imagined? Nor is it the strictly literary alone who have found delight in writing here. Only recently, a surgeon, who is famous the world over, slipped into the town under an assumed name, to finish his *magnum opus*. Hobbyists come here too. A well-known novelist, who is secretly addicted to painting in oil, runs away to Nantucket, where nobody will tell on him, and has a happy spree, "trying to learn color," as he explains apologetically to anyone looking over his shoulder. Also, there is an architect, who is an authority on New England architecture, but who seems to find infinite delight in exploring the moors for Indian arrow-heads. And so it goes. The isle is a happy hunting ground for the man with a hobby.

Then there are others who have found in the peace and unpretentiousness of Nantucket life the kind of living and the kind of friends they like to know. Among these are a number of Southerners who cherish certain old-fashioned values, in spite of the machine age, and find them still treasured among people who love Nantucket.

Indeed, the visitors come from a wide area. A careful watch is kept of the license plates on the cars, and by mid-July the *Inquirer and Mirror* triumphantly announces that automobiles are present from every state in the Union, Porto Rico and the Canal Zone, besides various provinces of Canada. Until recently, nobody seemed to want to come to Nantucket in a car bearing the license plate of Oregon. At last, in the summer of 1935 such a car, bound for Nantucket, was spotted on the wharf at Woods Hole. Great was the rejoicing, and the Westerner was given precedence for car space on the very next steamboat. The roster of forty-eight states was thus made complete.

In general, the off-islanders have not failed to show their appreciation of Nantucket. No worthy appeal is ever made without a generous response, and many have distinguished themselves by special acts of kindness that have benefited the community. For example, Mrs. Henry Lang, of Montclair, N. J., gave the Easy Street Gallery for the benefit of artists and art-lovers. (Incidentally, no one should miss the sign in the lobby of that gallery, "Out of respect to the ladies, gentlemen are requested not to smoke in this room," which came from the cabin of some steamer, needless to say, of long ago.) Another of Mrs. Lang's benefactions was the gift of a building for the headquarters of the local post of the American Legion. Still another was the organization of the Island Service Company, which brought types of service to the town which it had not enjoyed before.

A very important gift to the community was the Cottage Hospital. Before this came into being, anyone suddenly in need of an operation either made the crossing to Woods Hole or New Bedford, to be transferred thence to a hospital, or else took a one-way passage over the river Styx. In 1911, a group of interested people met and incorporated a hospital association. Two years later a building on West Chester Street was bought, and the following August (1914) it was opened. In fact, the opening was hastened in order to take care of a serious emergency operation, which saved a life. In later years other units have been added by generous benefactors in order to enlarge the scope of the work.

Of course, the hospital would not be normal if it were not chronically in need of money. To keep it going, also, is chiefly an off-islander responsibility. The earlier method of raising money was by means of the Main Street Fair, a custom inaugurated in 1931. For this occasion heirlooms were displayed in Main Street mansions, a tip cart rattled back and forth over the cobbles, everybody dressed in ancient costume, a town crier rang his bell, and pretty girls sold flowers.

All this was very picturesque, but it meant enormous labor in preparation. It was discovered that Nantucket people would give just as readily if a solicitor came to the door. So the Fair has been abandoned in favor of a Hospital Drive. There is a smaller affair, however, that takes place on the old North Wharf, and this has come to take on much of the same character. It is a fete

for the benefit of the Nantucket Neighbors, under the auspices of the Civic League, and is known as the Water Front Carnival. This is always popular. Catch-penny devices range from pony rides to fifteen-minute portraits by Tony Sarg. The Goddess of Chance is worshiped by grab bags and bets on a turtle race. Each year some novelty is introduced and everybody has a good time.

But the old Main Street Fair, with its picturesque costumes, its cent school, its tip cart and all the rest, was great fun. It had all the charm of a historical pageant. Perhaps it will be revived one of these days.

The Nantucket Neighbors, mentioned above, also is an institution. Some years ago, a retired clergyman, Reverend Herbert A. Jump, decided that too many strangers came alone to visit

MAIN STREET FAIR

Nantucket and remained alone all the time of their stay, not knowing where to go or what to see, and making no friends. Acting on this thought, he inaugurated the "Nantucket Neighbors." This is an informal organization of summer visitors for the purpose of getting acquainted and making excursions to different parts of the island. They have also the opportunity of listening to interesting talks by those who know Nantucket by heart. The founder has since died, but his idea marches on most successfully. All the stranger needs to do is to watch the columns of the *Inquirer and Mirror* for the program of the week, and then show up at the place and the time indicated. This remarkable organization has no constitution, no by-laws, and no dues!

The off-islander has also brought drama to Nantucket. As in so many other New England towns at the present time, there is sure to be a theatrical program during the summer, given by professional actors, headed by some well-known star. These plays are produced on the stage of the Yacht Club. In addition there has been created a Little Theater, chiefly for plays of Nantucket legend and history. This is housed on what was once an old storehouse on Straight Wharf, hence "The Straight Wharf Theater." The company is headed by Mr. and Mrs. Robert Wilson, who write, direct, and act in the plays. As Mrs. Wilson is the daughter of the late George Fawcett, the company calls itself the "Fawcett Players." These plays have been very popular.

For the populace generally, however, the Dreamland moving-picture house satisfies the craving for drama. This looks like any other moving-picture house in a small town, but the building has had as much of a past as many of the screen darlings seen therein. This structure started out in life as a Hicksite Quaker meeting house. Then it became a straw factory, in the days when people were trying to think of something that Nantucket could manufacture. Next, on the collapse of that business, it was used as a town hall. Following that, it became a wood-working shop, then a roller-skating rink. Still later, it was moved to Brant Point to serve as part of the "Hotel Nantucket," and finally it returned to town to its present site, where it seems content to rest.

While we are on the subject of islanders and off-islanders, something should be said of two famous clubs in which both types of Nantucket people come together. One is the Pacific Club, which occupies the ground floor of the famous Rotch Market. Like the old Union League Club on Fifth Avenue, New York, the windows open directly on the sidewalk so that the passer-by can look in and see the members taking their ease. As a matter of fact, the club is not old in comparison with other Nantucket institutions, for it dates only from 1860. In that year a number of whaling captains chartered the steamer *Island Home* to make the trip to New York to inspect the steamship *Great Eastern,* at that time one of the wonders of the world. The captains had such a jolly time together on this junket that they decided to form a club, and took over for that purpose the first floor of the Rotch Building. The club still exists, and it is a great honor for an off-islander to be admitted to membership; but, as may be imagined, the original requirement that to be eligible one must be a sea captain is no longer in force.

The other club is not so easily identified by the stranger. Out on the North Wharf there is a small shed with red painted shingles. Over the door is a modest sign, "Perry & Coffin." This is the headquarters of the Wharf Rats Club. The visitor, however, need not hesitate to step in, for it is also a fisherman's store. Here, under expert advice, he may buy anything for a fishing trip, from a long-visored cap such as the fishermen use in these parts, to flannel shirts and thick boots. At the same time, this one-room building is the club house for the Wharf Rats. A curious placque on the wall represents a rat, argent, rampant on a ground azure. (The rat is smoking a churchwarden pipe and leaning on a cane.) This coat of arms is the sign and symbol of the organization, one of the most exclusive clubs in the United States.

Near this piece of heraldry just described—in the proper terms, I trust—is the club motto, "No Reserved Seats for the Mighty." That is the colloquial translation of the official motto, which is, *Deposuit potentes de sede et exaltavit humiles.* The club interpretation of this formal version is that it was an epigram of the ancient Chief Nickanoose of Nantucket as expressed in his own Indian tongue.

The President and absolute autocrat of this club is the "Commodore," Herbert Coffin, who is also the proprietor of the store. He can spin more interesting yarns of old Nantucket than could be packed into a five-foot shelf. During the summer, club members and privileged guests sit on the wharf side of the building overlooking the harbor. In cold weather they gather inside, round a potent stove that stands in the middle of the room, one of those heaters with a wide rail, convenient for the feet. When the north wind is howling and the waves are smacking on the piles of the wharf, this is a snug place to listen to the Commodore spin yarns about Nantucket storms and shipwrecks.

It is said also that the Wharf Rats have a secret board of directors, but what they have to "direct" must likewise remain a mystery. The important fact is that one has to be just the right kind of man, a genuine, true-blue sort of person to make the grade. The point of the club motto is that money, or the social register, or fame, does not amount to anything in itself for membership. If the Commodore decides that a candidate does not measure up to the standard, that settles it. They say that there are hundreds on the waiting list. To be privileged to fly the Wharf Rat pennant aboard your own boat or hoist it in your quarters at home, is a real patent of nobility. The old Nantucket tradition of democracy, every man on his own merits, flourishes still among the Wharf Rats.

As to off-islanders in general, it may be said that while they are, on the whole, desirable, indeed quite necessary for the financial well-being of the island, there are some that might be spared, the sort who have a noisy and unpleasant idea of what constitutes a "good time." It is the very essence of Nantucket history that it has been the "land far away at sea." Happily it has not had to suffer like Long Island by its ready access from New York, or Cape Cod by its nearness to Boston. The motorist has only to travel now along routes six and twenty-eight to see what these highways have done to the beauty and charm of the Cape. In these days of easy travel the danger that will have to be watched is that Nantucket may be a land not far enough at sea.

In a little verse by Maria Mitchell entitled "An Old Story," there are these lines referring to the Indian legend about the origin of the island:

> Ill judging Sachem, would that you
> Had never shaken here that shoe;
> Or, having done so, would again,
>   And join Nantucket to the Main.

Probably there were times when Maria wished that she were nearer Boston and Cambridge, especially in the dead of winter. But happily her wish can never be brought to pass. Nothing would so completely ruin Nantucket as to be "joined to the

OFF-ISLAND COSTUMES

Main," within reach of hordes of Sunday excursionists with their banana skins, comic supplements, pop bottles, and vandal habits. Indeed, many who love the island, whether born there or not, would like to see it moved another fifty miles farther out to sea.

This sentiment has recently surged up in the breasts of a number of citizens who have proposed, with a possible twinkle of the eye, that Nantucket be given her independence like other islands, notably Ireland and the Philippines, or allowed a sort of dominion status like Bermuda. It happens that Nantucket is

Republican, while the Massachusetts state machine is Democratic. Thus, what goes on under the gilded dome on Beacon Hill is viewed with a jaundiced eye in a Nantucket town meeting.

It stimulates the imagination to think what Nantucket might be as a principality like Monaco in the prosperous times, able to pay dividends to its citizens instead of levying taxes, but the chances at present seem remote. The island will probably have to make the best of it and continue to struggle along as a part of Massachusetts and of the United States.

Being "the far-away island" has now more to do with its atmosphere than with its actual geography. What endears it to off-islanders is the sense of being far away from the jangle that makes up modern life on the mainland. If anyone is tired of trying to be a "go-getter," of beating down "sales resistance," of keeping up with the Joneses, then Nantucket is paradise enow.

There is one aspect of the town that few off-islanders know, a Nantucket Christmas. Frequently the winters are so mild that violets and snowdrops are blooming in the gardens right through December and January. A white Christmas is said to be rare, but it does come sometimes, dressing the old town in new beauty. The snow—and it stays white here—lends an unexpected charm to the old houses, trees, and narrow lanes. One has the sensation of living inside a Christmas card. This feeling is heightened in the evenings during the holiday season because of the local custom of decorating the windows with electric candles and trees, resplendent with colored lights. With the shades up in these houses, the gay splendor streams out on the street, making splashes of warm color on the snow. Along the Square the shops are illuminated, too. Strings of electric lights criss-cross from one side to the other. A large fir tree in front of the Bank glitters with many hues, and there the carols are sung on Christmas Eve.

All through the holidays there is much neighborly visiting and exchange of Christmas cheer, such as Charles Dickens would have applauded. In fact, it would not be at all surprising to see Messrs. Tupper and Snodgrass of the Pickwick Club, in company with Scrooge's nephew, come dashing around the corner to buy holly wreaths, or Bob Cratchit sliding belly-bumper down Orange Street with a crowd of school children. There are off-islanders who go a long way for the sake of spending Christmas in Nantucket.

"There are few places of equal magnitude the annals of which would afford matters for a more valuable volume." This measured observation by Obed Macy was quoted at the beginning of this book, and should serve even better to mark the end. An insignificant island, its barren soil drove the inhabitants to wrest their living from the ocean. Beginning with the fishery around its shores, her sons scattered to all the Seven Seas. Men of Nantucket held their "gams," as if in their own back yards, among the Fiji Islands, off the coast of Japan, or in Baffin's Bay. To these people, rounding the Horn in a two-hundred-ton vessel was a mere routine, as commonplace as going down Main Street to the post office. Yet what adventures they had in far waters! Pirate and cannibal and mutineer, scurvy and shipwreck and slow starvation—not half the story has been told in these pages. Much remains stowed away in the locker of old logs, letters, and memoirs.

Then the characters. Some of them have been introduced, and

what a varied group they have made! Crèvecoeur, the elegant French noble, all aglow with enthusiasm for liberty, fraternity, and equality; Reuben Chase, that gigantic Long Tom Coffin, at home only on the sea; Walter Folger, placidly doing everything better than anyone else could do—artisan, mathematician, astronomer, physician, jurist, and statesman; Ratliff, the British bluejacket, spinning his yarns about that cruise to St. Helena

with the great Emperor "Buonaparty"; Billy Clark, the town crier, tooting his horn and ringing his bell; Sir Isaac Coffin, brave in gold lace and cocked hat, coming to an island he had never seen in order to found a school for his kinsfolk—there's an assortment of types.

And what women the island bred! Wonoma, the Indian heroine; Mary Starbuck, called the "Great Woman" by her contemporaries, a queen born to rule by intellect and character; Keziah Coffin, the ruthless profiteer; Deborah Chase, tossing luckless males upon a roof or into an oil vat; Maria Mitchell, the astronomer; Lucretia Mott, the crusader; the three New-begin girls, tramping round and round their boulder and shooing the hens off the bed when they went to sleep—here are characters no less varied than the men.

Among both the men and women of Nantucket those who have been elected for mention have had to be chosen from many. If someone raises a challenging finger to demand: "Why did you not include Zaccheus Macy, the famous 'bone-setter' of the eighteenth century, who performed 2000 surgical operations and without pay? Why no mention of General Joseph Smith, the first graduate of West Point, chief military engineer of the army at the age of twenty-eight, and one of the most distinguished railroad engineers of the nineteenth century? Or why leave out Phebe Hanaford, preacher, editor, and lecturer, who fought in the front ranks of reform, together with Susan B. Anthony and the rest of that militant band?" For that matter, why not a dozen others? There is no satisfactory answer except that from so rich a store of personalities only a limited number could be chosen.

In the Introduction it was said that the purpose of this book was to "catch as far as possible the particular charm of this little island town; with its rich history, its traditions, its streets and wharves and houses, and its surrounding moors." In retrospect that purpose seems to have been over-ambitious. Charm, such as a historic town possesses, has proved to be an elusive thing to catch and transfer to paper; and perhaps all that can be hoped for is that these pages have succeeded in suggesting the qualities that endear Nantucket to those who have fallen under its spell.

Although it is natural to emphasize history and tradition,

ALONG THE WHARVES

there are other things to enjoy that never grow old: the salty tang of the wharves, and the fragrance of the wind over the moors, the fighting tug of a bluefish on the end of a line, the pull of the tiller in a stiff breeze, the heave of a great comber breaking over the swimmer's head, the lope of a horse through the pines and over the rutted roads. Indeed, the Little Grey Lady offers much with her hospitality. As the Orientals say, "May her shadow never grow less," and may the advancing years find her increasingly serene and beautiful!

THE END

INDEX

INDEX